A Godly Heritage

Historical View of the Laestadian Revival and the Development of the Apostolic Lutheran Church in America

Edited by:

Aila Foltz
Rodger Foltz
Jouko Talonen
Elmer Yliniemi
Miriam Yliniemi

Papaver Laestadianum

Illustrated by Nora Bergman

Self-published by the Editors

Except where otherwise indicated, all Scripture quotations in this book are taken from the King James Version of the Bible.

This book contains a collection of articles translated from the Finnish language or written by the editiors. Articles used by permission of authors or their heirs.

A GODLY HERITAGE
Edited by Aila Foltz and Miriam Yliniemi
with Rodger Foltz, Jouko Talonen and Elmer Yliniemi
Illustrated by Nora Bergman
Cover design by Eno Yliniemi

© 2005 by the Editors.
ISBN 0-9769423-0-5
Self-published by the Editors
19505 County Highway 39
Frazee, MN 56544

Website: www.sprucegrovechurch.org
Printed in the United States of America.

TABLE OF CONTENTS

Foreword v

Acknowledgments vii

1. Background.. 1

2. What is Laestadianism? 9

3. Lars Levi Laestadius.. 17

4. Lars Levi Laestadius as Scientist 37

5. Lars Levi Laestadius as Family Man............................ 43

6. Mary of Lapland (Lapin Maria) 53

7. Lars Levi Laestadius as Revival Preacher 59

8. The Main Features of the Proclamation of Lars Levi Laestadius 67

9. True Christianity 73

10. Parables by Laestadius.. 81

11. Juhani Raattamaa... 87

12. Erkki Antti Juhonpieti (1814-1900) 101

13. Aatu Laitinen 113

14. Absolution Introduced "In Jesus' Name and Blood" 125

15. The Power of the Keys 135

16. The Impact of Immigration History on Apostolic Lutheranism......155

17. Laestadianism in North America Until 1885 183

18. Laestadianism/Apostolic Lutheranism in North America Today....195

19. Apostolic Lutheranism (Laestadianism) From an International Perspective..211

20. What Can We Learn from History?.............................217

21. Farewell Sermon of Laestadius..................................221

Bibliography...223

About the Authors and Editors 229

Foreword

In recent years there has been renewed interest in the "roots" of the Apostolic Lutheran Church. There have been numerous questions and requests for information on its history and background. To fill this need, the editors many years ago began compiling information for the American reader and recently have put forth a major effort to complete the project.

Many people in the Apostolic Lutheran Churches, especially the younger generation, have little or no knowledge of their spiritual heritage, which traces back to Lars Levi Laestadius, the great revival leader in northern Scandinavia in the mid 1800s. Laestadianism or Apostolic Lutheranism has been a significant influence in the Finnish-American community since the late 1800s. When the other Finnish church bodies (Suomi Synod and the National Church) assimilated into larger American churches in the 1960s the Apostolic Lutheran churches remained independent. Today people of many nationalities are included in the membership rolls of the Laestadian/Apostolic Lutheran churches as mission efforts have made it an international movement.

There is a vast amount of historical material written in Finnish that has not been available in the English language. This book is a collection of writings carefully selected and translated from works by noted scholars on Laestadian history to give a significant amount of basic information about the beginnings of the revival movement in Lapland, its spread to America, and the situation today. In addition the editors have written some chapters to fill in the gaps. The book is not intended to be a scientific study or an exhaustive presentation but an information packet for the general reader interested in the background of the Apostolic Lutheran Church. It is neither a study of doctrinal positions nor an explanation of disputes but a historical sketch that will clarify the Apostolic Lutheran scene to today's members and descendants of this heritage.

Since this is a collection of articles by various authors, there is some repetition, but getting different perspectives can offer new insights.

In-text footnotes are used only when referencing direct quotes. The bibliography is a compilation of general references used throughout the book and serves as a guide to additional resources regarding American Laestadianism.

Some may have an interest in this book because the Laestadian revival movement is part of their heritage or the heritage of someone they know. Others may be seeking answers following painful experiences due to schisms in the movement. Many may be seeking more information about the movement in which they have found a spiritual home—where they have experienced the forgiveness of sins and encountered the living Lord.

We hope to provide a glimpse into the history of a movement of God that has brought thousands to glory over the past 160 years despite difficult circumstances and frailties in the people God has used.

The Editors

Acknowledgments

We are thankful to the many people who have encouraged us and helped us get this book published. We are grateful for the vast amount of research on Laestadianism done by the late Dr. Uuras Saarnivaara (1908-1998) and the late Dr. Pekka Raittila (1923-1990). Without their pioneering research, it would be very difficult to continue with the study of Laestadian/Apostolic Lutheran history today. The editors are grateful to have been able to work with them and are pleased to make their work available through this book.

We thank Erkki Raittila, who has given us permission to translate and use the writings of his late father, Pekka Raittila. Dr. Raittila was a meticulous scholar who was a pleasure to know.

Dr. Saarnivaara was a diligent scholar and a prolific writer who taught in Finland and America. He did the first major studies on Apostolic Lutheranism in America, which are published in both English and Finnish.

Thank you to Seppo Leivo for giving us permission to use his research articles and to Dr. Arnold Alanen who graciously gave permission to use his migration map on the "Norwegian Connection."

The time and talents of our illustrator Nora (Tumberg) Bergman are greatly appreciated. The pictures add so much to the book.

Without the able assistance of Eno Yliniemi, we would have had difficulty getting this into a printable format. Her computer skills saved us much time and money in getting this to the printers. She also designed the cover, which is a colorful addition to the book. Our thanks also go to Mia (Yliniemi) Reynolds for the time-consuming job of proofreading the manuscript for errors.

Our sincere thanks to everyone who has assisted in one way or another, including the many people who have given information, interviews, encouragement, made helpful suggestions and corrections in the manuscript.

"For what thanks can we render to God again for you, for all the joy wherewith we joy for your sakes before our God" (I Th. 3:9).

1

Background

Aila Foltz

In order to understand any phenomenon, it is helpful to know about the environmental and social conditions in which it was born. This is true also of revival movements. Laestadianism took root and flourished in Lapland, from where it spread primarily to Finland and the United States.

LAPLAND AND ITS PEOPLE

The Laestadian movement was born in the second half of the nineteenth century in Lapland, which is comprised of the northern regions of Norway, Sweden, Finland and the Kola Peninsula of Russia lying largely within the Arctic Circle. It is a land of mountains, hills, swampland, meadows, forests, lakes and rivers. In the northernmost part, the sun disappears November 22, and does not reappear until January 25—that makes two months of perpetual blue twilight created by the moon and stars shining on the snow and colorful displays of northern lights. Spring brings a torrent of melting ice and snow. The summers, though short, are intense with the sun circling the horizon for seventy days. The earth brings forth Arctic poppies and berries; birds return to their Arctic nesting places. The summer season ends in a blaze of color.

Lapland Scene

The indigenous people of Lapland, who call themselves Sami, have lived in the Scandinavian peninsula since prehistoric times and were pushed northward by encroaching Finns, Swedes and Norwegians. Their language is remotely related to Finnish. Until recent times many lived a semi-nomadic life, traveling with their reindeer. In the winter they lived in the lowland forests where the reindeer ate the lichen, and as spring approached they moved to the Arctic Ocean to fish or to the mountains where their reindeer could feed on grass. Fishing, hunting and handicrafts supplemented their incomes.

A Sami tent

Their dwellings were huts made of bark or sod in which they lived on a permanent basis or seasonally. During their wanderings, the Sami lived in tents like the tepees of the Native Americans of the Great Plains. Reindeer were essential for the Sami. They provided them with furs, milk, cheese and the meat that constituted the greatest part of their diet. Reindeer provided them with transportation, pulling sleighs called *ahkios or pulkas*, which look somewhat like canoes that have been cut in half.

The Sami lived in superstitious fear of the spirits inhabiting lakes, forests, and mountains. They chose unique outcroppings of stone or man-shaped stumps in scenic high places as homes for their gods, to whom they made offerings in return for success in hunting, fishing and reindeer herding. For really difficult problems, they turned to their shamans (medicine men) who used drums for sending themselves into a trance or soliciting answers to questions by rolling pawns on their drums. They feared angering the underground spirit-people who were like them but were unbaptized. If a child disappeared, it was believed that it had been snatched by underground spirits, and young men and women were warned about spirits who might charm them and carry them away to their homes underground.

A Sami man riding in his ahkio

Finnish settlers moved into Swedish Lapland before 1809 while Finland was still a part of the kingdom of Sweden. The Swedish government encouraged permanent settlers by offering them homesteads with special tax incentives. Interestingly enough, for the most part, only Finns took advantage of the offer, and even today the traveler in Swedish Lapland finds people of Finnish background everywhere.

The settlers made their living by hunting and fishing, keeping reindeer and a few cows and sheep for family needs, and some boiled reindeer horns for glue. The settlers managed to grow some barley and hay. As for garden crops, only turnips, radishes and onions grew there. Potatoes were introduced later. The layer of topsoil is thin, the permafrost is very close to the surface, and the growing season is short; the last of the ice melts in early June, and the first snow falls at the end of September. In his book about agriculture in Lapland, Laestadius observed that for those fortunate enough to own land in the valleys there was fertile soil, which supported the growing of numerous root crops, and the swamps and woods provided cloudberries and lingonberries. Nevertheless, many settlers appeared to prefer hunting and fishing to farming.

The mining industry provided work for some of the settlers, and Sami were conscripted to haul ore with their reindeer.

Life was difficult in the wilderness of Lapland. The Sami had made their adjustment over the centuries. With little education and living at the mercy of the forces of nature, they were easy victims for the sellers of liquor. Market fairs, held in church villages several times a year in connection with church holy days, provided an opportunity to carry on trade, pay taxes, participate in circuit court sessions, attend church—and buy liquor. For the Finnish pioneer settlers, life in Lapland proved even more difficult. The long, dark winters, the harsh environment and the loneliness took their toll, particularly on the women. As the Sami woman Maarit observes in Erkki Kokko's book about Lapland, *Neljän tuulen tie* [*The Way of the Four Winds*], "She either becomes a Christian or goes crazy."

These are the people Lars Levi Laestadius spent his life serving.

When Laestadius went to Karesuando in 1826, this parish close to the Finnish border, covering about 3500 square miles, was very sparsely populated. Its population of 809 consisted mostly of Sami people who were elsewhere most of the year. The remaining 220 inhabitants were Finnish pioneer settlers. Sami from Finland and Norway also showed up in church on their migrations. The lifestyle of the Sami made it difficult for the church to minister to them and educate them; even when they were within the borders of the parish, they lived far from the church. Literary pursuits were next to impossible in their dwellings which were crowded, smoky and dark. In addition, they had their own language with its many distinct dialects, whereas sermons were preached and teaching was done in Finnish. Laestadius was exceptional in that he preached also in Sami and conversed with the Sami people in their own language. Working with the pioneer settlers was not much easier. Whenever their farm work permitted, the men spent weeks on end fishing in remote lakes, sometimes as far as Ruija (Norway). Thus, during the three months after haymaking, there might not be a single soul in church on Sunday.

Drunkenness was a serious problem in Lapland. The Sami men did most of their drinking at the market fairs. When it was time for worship services, they were in no shape to attend or showed up drunk and caused a disturbance. Often they returned from these journeys drunk with only some gaudy trinkets, having been cheated out of the goods they had gone to barter for necessities, and their reindeer herds, left untended, were ravaged by wolves. When the government prohibited the sale of liquor in Lapland, smuggling from outside Lapland and across the border from neighboring countries became a lucrative industry. Pioneer settlers also saw an opportunity to make money by distilling liquor and traveling to the mountains to sell it to the Sami at their grazing grounds.

Thus the Sami women also had access to liquor, and even nursing mothers indulged giving some to their children. Laestadius writes: "When mothers lay all day or half a day in a drunken stupor, the little children were left to bawl until they developed an umbilical hernia…How many of those little ones must have cried themselves to death seeing that the angel of murder or the unclean spirit of liquor has raged among the people for hundreds of years?" As a result infant mortality was high; in fact, in some parishes the population decreased. The pioneer settlers were not a whole lot better. Their drinking took

A Sami cradle

place in large part in connection with church holidays and market days, leading to disturbances. Among them, too, women drank hard liquor and gave some to their children.

Laestadius saw the hold alcohol had on the people of Lapland and the resulting poverty. He saw that the law prohibiting the sale of liquor in Lapland and its importation did not reduce the consumption of alcohol; in fact, it increased. Nevertheless, he welcomed the law as giving him support in declaring drunkenness and the sale of liquor a sin. Initially his revival efforts were largely focused on temperance. Laestadian lifestyle continues to emphasize abstinence from alcoholic beverages.

As is to be expected, drinking led to fighting and domestic disputes, to which the settlers were actually more inclined than the Sami. People perjured themselves in connection with court cases resulting from smuggling and liquor sales.

Reindeer rustling was also prevalent, practiced by both the Sami and settlers. They did not, in fact, view it as a serious crime. Since it was practically impossible to apprehend rustlers in the wilderness, the only way reindeer owners had of making up for their losses was to help themselves to somebody else's reindeer. The theft of inanimate property, however, was considered a grave sin by the Sami, while the settlers were more prone to it.

As an arm of the government of Sweden, the church was able to require that all citizens attend church and communion a certain number of times a year. People who lived near the church were to attend services every Sunday, whereas those who lived in distant parts of the parish were expected to attend every second and third Sunday which were designated as holy days (as well as on the high holy days and annual days of prayer). On the Sundays when they did not attend church, these people were told to hold a service at home or to get together with their neighbors to read a sermon on the text for the day without comments or additions. Ordinary people rarely owned Bibles. The church was also authorized to mete out punishments to those who did not conform to its regulations, such as sitting in the stocks at the church entrance or on a special bench reserved for wrongdoers, banishment from communion, or incarceration on bread and water. The government had begun to promote church activity among the Sami towards the mid eighteenth century, but the effect was very superficial. Pagan beliefs and customs were still deeply ingrained in the Sami people as well as the pioneer settlers at the inception of the Laestadian revival movement.

The pastors were charged with ensuring that the people living in their geographical areas learned to read and recite the catechism as well as acquire knowledge of Bible history. The pioneer settlers were responsible for the basic education of their own children. Due to the Sami people's lifestyle and living conditions, the church had to take special measures to achieve even modest results in educating them. Catechists and missionaries were assigned to travel from one Sami dwelling to another. There were schools in four parishes, and Sami children were boarded with local settlers so they could attend. The results were unsatisfactory, and by 1846 these efforts were discontinued. However, the six schools operated by the Mission

Society were achieving results, and Laestadius as a superintendent had the opportunity to hire teachers who were not only competent but also had a missionary zeal. During his time the level of literacy and knowledge of Christian doctrine improved greatly.

These schools became centers for the Laestadian revival, as adults attended devotional meetings there. Home services were held in remote villages, and preachers trained by Laestadius traveled from one place to another, often in twos or threes. After calling up a strong singer from among those present to choose the hymns and lead the singing, the preachers would sit behind a table as they read Scripture and preached or read one of Laestadius's sermons. The preacher followed the text verse by verse, elaborating and commenting on each, his voice often rising to a shrill, emotional pitch, and his hearers were frequently overwhelmed by feelings of sorrow over sin or rejoicing over their salvation. These expressions of emotion ("rejoicings") were called *liikutuksia* in Finnish and *rörelser* in Swedish.

It was customary for the early Laestadians to greet one another with *Jumalan terve* in Finnish or *Gud's frid* in Swedish. Americans of all the Laestadian groups greet one another with "God's peace." The greeting has come to identify the greeter as a Laestadian Christian. Furthermore, many Laestadians will not use this greeting when addressing people not belonging to their own group of Laestadianism.

Map of Scandinavia

**This map shows the major places related to early
Laestadian history**

2

What is Laestadianism?

Pekka Raittila (1981)

Laestadianism is one of the great revival movements within the Evangelical Lutheran Church of Finland along with the Awakened and Evangelical movements. It differs from the others as to origin and distribution. Having begun in northern Sweden, it rapidly spread beyond national boundaries wherever the Finnish language is spoken.

THE HERITAGE OF THE EARLY DAYS OF THE REVIVAL

Great revival movements broke out in all of the Scandinavian countries during the early part of the 19th century. These in turn gave birth to the first vigorous national movements in the Nordic countries. Laestadianism was one of the movements that flowed into the stream of these revivals and movements. Its special quality was shaped chiefly by Lars Levi Laestadius's unique personality and the conditions of the Arctic region of Scandinavia.

The visible beginning of the awakening was in the preaching and pastoral care activity of Laestadius (1800-1861). In 1846 when the movement began, Laestadius was senior pastor in Karesuando [Sweden]; soon afterwards he moved further south, to the Finnish-speaking parish of Pajala, a parish covering a large territory. He also had the responsibility, as visitation pastor of the parishes in northern Lapland, of overseeing their spiritual care.

The cutting edge of Laestadius's proclamation was his preaching of repentance, in which he relentlessly attacked the traditional lifestyle of his parishioners. "Sober drunks," "virtuous whores," "honest thieves," and "gracious whiskey merchants" got a piece of his mind Sunday after Sunday. He appears to have been impelled to carry through a program of social reform directed radically against the decline of Western civilization—even though he rejected the revolutionary political trends of his day just as emphatically.

The second powerful purpose in his sermons was to awaken his hearers and lead them to faith through the colorful portrayal of the Passion of Jesus, "the thorn-crowned King of Zion." As the revival began to solidify into a movement, this evangelical feature became more noticeable. At the same time, it crystallized into the proclamation of the forgiveness of sins "in the name and blood of Jesus."

The objective of Laestadius's preaching and soul care was to bring people to a definite crisis leading to a change in their entire being: the Holy Spirit became the ruler even though sinfulness continued to be a reality. Thus the early days of the Laestadian revival were characterized by strictness. The boundary between "Christians" and others became distinct. A community of believers took shape, which cared for its own members and carried on missionary work among those outside the fellowship.

The community of believers is characteristic of all revival movements. In Laestadianism it received special significance when Laestadius strongly emphasized the experience of a spiritual crisis and when, on the other hand, laymen in the extensive but sparsely populated northern parishes were, due to the prevailing circumstances, obliged to take responsibility for religious work. At the founder's death, his pupil and assistant Juhani Raattamaa (1811-1899) became the leader of the movement. The spiritual priesthood of all believers became a reality in the Laestadian community even in its leadership.

The spiritual priesthood has received its most important expression in the use of the Keys of the Kingdom. The Keys of the Kingdom and confession are teachings of the Lutheran Church. Laestadianism is credited with the revival of these teachings. However, the Keys and the spiritual authority connected with them were transferred from the pastors to the Laestadian community of believers which was a radical departure from the traditional teachings of the church.

The public confession emphasized by Laestadius soon lost some of its original stringency. The Laestadian confessional usage has, however, remained the distinctive mark of the movement. A requirement for joining the Laestadian community was the confession of sins and absolution from the fellowship or its representatives. Also sins committed against others were to be confessed to them and restitution made as far as possible. The Keys are used regularly in mutual soul care. Personal absolution as a "staff for the journey" has created a sense of security and fellowship.

One feature of Laestadian meetings—more frequent in earlier days—was the "rejoicings." Due to their powerful emotional outbursts, Laestadians were derisively nicknamed "hihhulit" [the nearest American equivalent is "Holy Rollers"]. These rejoicings were held in esteem within the movement itself because they were viewed as special evidence that the Holy Spirit was working in an individual.

Since the beginning, the most important strength of the movement has been the community of believers which developed. The use of confession gave it depth in soul care. The "rejoicings" were one manifestation of the spontaneity characteristic of the fellowship. All of this increased the sense of uniqueness and independence felt by the Laestadian community. In spite of this, great conflicts with the national Lutheran churches did not develop in the Arctic region of Scandinavia. Lay activity was accepted as natural, and there were no other religious movements of any significance in the region.

DISTRIBUTION AND SCHISM

Karesuando is situated at the remote meeting point of three countries [Finland, Sweden, Norway] and four cultures [Finnish, Swedish, Norwegian, Sami (Lapp)]. By means of natural contacts and also through planned mission work, Laestadianism spread far and wide from that area into the entire Arctic region of Scandinavia during Laestadius's lifetime. The most vigorous expansion began soon after his death. The northern parts of Sweden, Finland and Norway became the main area of the movement. The wide region around Oulu [Finland], was included as a whole. Vital Laestadian centers were born as far as southern Finland and St. Petersburg [Russia]. The religious organization of Finns in America began in Laestadian congregations. Practically speaking, Laestadianism has spread wherever the Finnish language is spoken. The movement, as a whole, gained only a slight foothold among the Swedish and Norwegian speaking populations.

Expansion into areas completely different from each other posed a threat to the unity of Laestadianism. When the most prominent early preachers died at the beginning of this century, the transfer of the tradition to the next generation set in motion a powerful crisis in a movement which had originally emphasized the experience of conversion. The ideal of the tightly knit fellowship of believers also promoted fragmentation. Even within the movement's tradition, references have been made to differences of opinion regarding the teachings of Christianity.

The process of disintegration began in the 1890s and led to an eventual split during the first decade of the twentieth century. This resulted in three main groups which, after initial confusion and attempts at unity, organized and developed independently of each other. The names of the groups reflect their attempt to preserve the Laestadian tradition. The "Vanhoilliset" [Conservative Laestadians of that time included both the present Apostolic Lutheran Church of America and the Laestadian Lutheran Church or SRK] defended the more evangelical tradition of the movement and stood, in a way, between the other groups which were smaller. The "Uusiheräys" [New Awakenism] was critical of the tendency in some circles to emphasize the community of believers at the expense of inner experiences, and this group required a new awakening and a return to Laestadius's teachings. The "Esikoislestadiolaiset" [Firstborn Laestadians or Old Apostolic Lutherans in America], believed they adhered to the Laestadian tradition most consistently. They maintained that the authority of the community of the Firstborn (comprised of individuals whose sins are forgiven and have received the Holy Spirit) led by Raattamaa had been passed on to the Laestadian leaders of the Jukkasjärvi-Gällivare region [in Sweden]. In addition, this group was characterized by asceticism in daily living that was stricter than the others.

From the beginning, the Conservative Laestadians formed the largest group. It has continued to expand even after World War II. In the 1930s a significant split took place in Conservative Laestadianism. The Rauhan Sana group, whose counterpart in the United States is the Apostolic Lutheran Church of America, was separated from the mainstream, referred to as SRK for Suomen Rauhanyhdistysten Keskusyhdistys. This split meant an even greater concentration of the SRK Conservative group within the boundaries of Finland, most notably in the northern province of Oulu.

The adherents of New Awakenism also reside mainly in Finland. However, the Firstborn and Rauhan Sana groups have a considerable following in Sweden, Norway and North America.

SECT OR REVIVAL MOVEMENT?

The relationship of Laestadianism to the state church has been ambivalent from the beginning. The founder of the movement was a pastor in the Evangelical Lutheran Church of Sweden, who by example and in his writings rejected separation from the Church of Sweden. Membership and participation in the sacraments within the state church, as well as respect for the office of the church as a representative of government, has become established tradition which is not likely to be broken easily. On the other hand, Laestadius himself provided the theological basis for emphasizing the fellowship of believers and the merciless criticism of pastors and bishops. In the northern latitude, Laestadianism rapidly developed into a movement that was quite self-sufficient and independent of the church in its soul care and other activity. This, in turn, explains why Laestadianism has commonly been considered a sect. However, at different times and in different countries, the relationship between the movement and the church has been viewed in different ways. In Finland during the twentieth century, Laestadianism has become a respected revival movement within the church. Its self-sufficiency has nevertheless led to conflicts. Lately these have increased due to demands in state church circles for ecumenism on the one hand and confessionalism on the other.

Their loyalty to the Church of Finland and their general willingness to participate in social endeavors is reflected in the activity of Laestadians in the governing bodies of their local congregations and in the church convention. In this connection, Laestadians have generally defended traditional ways of working, criticized symptoms of secularization in the church, and taken an uncompromising stand against the ordination of women. In various instances, the Laestadians have emphasized to the leadership of the Church of Finland and to others the importance of adherence to Lutheran doctrine. On the other hand, some of them have an understanding of baptism, in particular, which has justifiably been charged with being un-Lutheran. Undoubtedly this is not due solely to inconsistency. Luther is an esteemed authority in Laestadianism. The teaching regarding the Keys of the Kingdom and justification by faith obtain support from Luther himself. To be sure, the confessional books have not been given a very firm position in Laestadian tradition. In any case, all of the Laestadian groups consider themselves to be—and want to remain—genuine Lutherans. The influence of the movement's own living tradition can thus lead to difficulties, particularly in those groups that include trained clergy.

Of the Laestadian groups, the New Awakened are the most assimilated into the church. This characteristic has been reinforced by an interest in missions which has led it into close cooperation with the Finnish Evangelical Lutheran Mission. In practice, the most closed group is probably the SRK. After World War II, a large number of pastors joined this large group. The tension between this element and the lay tradition led to a crisis in 1960, at which time most of the pastors withdrew. Even though the SRK rapidly replenished its clergy, the lay leadership has maintained its position of authority.

Relations with other religious groups vary in the same manner as assimilation into the Church of Finland. In some instances, Laestadians are able to work together with other revival movements within the church. They relate to other denominations more negatively, however. Thus loyalty to the Church of Finland also influences their attitude towards other movements.

THE ROLE OF LAESTADIANISM IN SOCIETY

The agricultural population formed the original backbone of Laestadianism. Farmers formed the most important group among the lay preachers. City dwellers and skilled workers became significant as the movement spread to the city of Oulu and further south. The center of activity began to shift early on from the countryside to the cities. Along with the country people, lower and middle class city dwellers formed the bulk of those with Laestadian convictions. The upper classes and civil servants were very sparsely represented for a long time. A significant change took place after World War II. As the educational level of the general population rose, the negative attitude towards education within Laestadianism was overcome. More and more children from Laestadian homes have acquired a college education. Thus Laestadianism has maintained its contact with an increasingly diverse society and taken greater responsibility for its functioning.

In evaluating the social significance of Laestadianism, we must first and foremost keep in mind the change that the movement has effected in the lives of its adherents. Laestadius's revivalistic sermons produced a transformation in the life of certain parishes in the Arctic region of the Scandinavian countries. This change affected only a very limited area, however, and its influence soon ceased. On the other hand, as the movement spread, it was characterized by temperance, honesty, industriousness, sense of familial responsibility, and respect for authority. For this reason, Laestadians have generally been looked upon as reliable employees.

The self-sufficiency and isolationism of Laestadianism has partially limited its participation in society. Laestadians have nevertheless participated extensively in local government and common endeavors which promote material progress.

After the political parties organized at the turn of the century, Laestadians appear to have participated cautiously. The rise of socialism and communism became an important stimulus. There was a desire to join in opposing an atheistic world view and at the same time in safeguarding law and order. A rejection of the Left has—in spite of the development which has taken place in the left-wing political parties—remained one of the fundamental elements in the political attitude of all of the Laestadian groups. Nowadays, this position has taken on more of a political than an ideological content and significance.

Of the political parties, the conservative Coalition Party and the Agrarian-Centre Parties have received the most consistent and extensive support from the Laestadians. Over the decades, particularly among the Conservative Laestadians, support has become more concentrated in the Centre Party. Since the beginning of Finnish independence, most of the Laestadian members of Parliament have represented that party; some of them have also served in the Cabinet. Since the 1960s the contribution of Laestadiansim in government leadership has decreased noticeably. In any case, the movement continues to have political influence in the Oulu province.

LAESTADIANISM TODAY

The various Laestadian groups have existed for a couple of generations largely unaware of each other. In spite of that, certain features of their common tradition are to be seen in all of them, albeit with differing emphases. This has promoted the communication which has started to occur among the members of the smaller Laestadian groups.

The fellowship of believers, personal absolution, and the opportunity for confession continue to be the most important of the positive characteristics that appeal also to young people. On the other hand, the religious meetings as well as the organizational structure of the groups are becoming more formal and follow a set format; this has to do with the age of the movement and the general evolution of society. Thus the "rejoicings" have decreased.

The ascetic attitude toward life and the preaching of repentance connected with it, as well as the set of norms binding the membership, are still characteristic of Laestadianism, particularly of the Firstborn and SRK groups. This attitude has aroused new problems as the urban environment and the rise in the standard of living as well as the high educational level of various professions previously unknown cultural and technological options from which to choose. Their disapproval of television has received a disproportionate amount of publicity. This can be looked upon as an example of how a minority culture of northern Finland strives, even at risk of becoming isolated, to defend itself against national policies aimed at creating a homogeneous population. Particularly in SRK Laestadianism, the prohibition against television serves to promote unity in the group and discipline within the community of believers.

The most important factors behind the development that has taken place in Laestadianism and the problems which have become critical in recent times may be twofold. The movement, which in the beginning was strong on conversion and inner experiences, has shifted its emphasis more and more from revival Christianity to Christian upbringing. The growth of the Laestadian groups has mainly taken place through Christian education within the family. Another factor is the change in the society surrounding them. The transition which accelerated after World War II has particularly affected the northern Laestadian areas.

Published as "Lestadiolaisuus" in *Mitä Missä Milloin 1981*, Helsinki: Otava, 1980. Translated by Aila Foltz.

3
Lars Levi Laestadius
(1800-1861)

Uuras Saarnivaara

"THE PROPHET OF LAPLAND"

The northernmost regions of Finland, Sweden and Norway were to experience a revival at about the same time as the Rosenius revival spread in Sweden and when other revival movements generated new life elsewhere in Finland. This revival was to change the moral climate of Swedish Lapland, spreading into Norway and Finland, as well as eventually making inroads into other parts of the world. The man chosen by God to awaken the people of the far northern regions of Scandinavia was Lars Levi Laestadius, sometimes called the "The Prophet of Lapland."

CHILDHOOD AND YOUTH

Laestadius was born in 1800 in Swedish Lapland on a pioneer farm in a place called Jäckvik in Arjeplog parish, where his father was the manager of a silver mine. After the mine was closed, he became a pioneer farmer. He was descended from a long line of pastors whose name was derived from the village of Lästad in central Sweden. His mother, who was also related to the Laestadius family, had been deeply affected by the Läsare (Readers), a pietistic revival movement influenced by Moravianism which had spread to central and northern Sweden. It was so named because they diligently read the Bible and Luther's and Arndt's sermons. The humble, quiet godliness of their mother and her patience in the sufferings and trials of her life of poverty with a husband who was abusive when drunk made an indelible impression on Lars Levi and his younger brother Petrus. Later when he was away from home, Lars Levi recalled his mother's tears whenever he was tempted to do something wrong. This memory was a restraining power keeping him from sinful ways or at least causing him to have a bad conscience when he strayed.

Lars Levi had a brother, Karl Erik Laestadius, from his father's earlier marriage. When Lars Levi was eight years old, he and Petrus, along with their parents, went to live with Karl Erik, who was serving as senior pastor in Kvikkjokk. Karl Erik had been an exceptionally gifted student at the University of Uppsala, and he was encouraged to pursue a university career. He nevertheless chose to be a pastor in Lapland in order to help his poor relatives. The tutoring he provided for the boys made it possible for them to enter the college preparatory school in Härnösand.

After graduation Lars Levi enrolled at the University of Uppsala. Like his brother Karl Erik, he was interested in botany and harbored ambitions of gaining fame in this field. For economic reasons, however, he had to give up a promising scientific career and enter into ministry in the northernmost part of the country.

FIRST YEARS IN THE PARISH

After about a year of service as superintendent of the elementary schools of Lapland, Laestadius was appointed senior pastor of Karesuando in 1826. This was the northernmost parish in Swedish Lapland, and the church was on the Muonio River, which forms the border between Sweden and Finland. The population of this remote Arctic parish was made up of some two hundred Finnish pioneer settlers and about six hundred semi-nomadic Sami (Lapps). There was not a single true believer in the entire parish nor was there any spiritual concern among them. These words of the Bible literally describe the situation: "There is none righteous,...none that seeketh after God.... Whose mouth is full of cursing and bitterness.... Destruction and misery are in their ways, and the way of peace have they not known" (Romans 3:10-17). Their pastor, however, did not see anything particularly alarming in this situation, for he himself did not yet know the way to peace with God. In the early years of his ministry, he was more interested in flowers than in the salvation of souls.

Nevertheless, Laestadius was diligent in promoting Christian education. In the winter he traveled among his parishioners for five or six weeks examining them on their literacy and knowledge of Christian doctrine. In the beginning he held confirmation classes for three or four weeks at a time and later for as long as five weeks. When people signed up for communion, he examined them and would not allow those to commune whose Christian knowledge and reading skills were deficient. If this did not bring results, he required that such people attend confirmation again. Consequently, Karesuando became one of the foremost congregations of Swedish Lapland in literacy and the knowledge of Christian doctrine. To be sure, such knowledge was "dead head knowledge," as Laestadius said later. But even then it undoubtedly laid a foundation for the revival to come in which this knowledge became a living faith and bore fruit.

Although Laestadius himself lacked a personal saving knowledge of Christ, in his sermons and his educational work he taught an order of salvation in compliance with the Catechism and the "orthodox" Lutheran textbooks. Martti E. Miettinen describes Laestadius's proclamation from that period:

> From the beginning his sermons did not reinforce in their false peace those whose "faith" was dead.... He pointed out in his proclamation that the person who was not born again and in whom the natural man still reigned is condemned, that awakening is necessary, sorrow for sin and heartfelt contrition is essential, and also on the other hand, it is necessary to taste and experience the power of living faith. In his preaching he mercilessly exposed the self-deception of those who practice a superficial, external form of godliness, he spoke of sin straightforwardly and in detail, proclaimed God's righteous judgments and emphasized the necessity for change in their lives. But for a long time his proclamation lacked what is most important, the vitality and power which come from a personal experience of Christianity and which make it effective in awakening and breaking the heart of a person on the one hand and in igniting the flame of faith on the other (Agricolasta Pakkalaan, pp. 332ff).

The besetting sins of the people living in Lapland were drunkenness, adultery and dishonesty. Their dishonesty mainly took the form of reindeer rustling and smuggling across the border. Laestadius rebuked the people of his parish for these sins, but the people did not change their ways.

In 1832, at 32 years of age, Laestadius fell seriously ill, and he feared that he would die. He did not, however, experience any true awakening of conscience or concern for his salvation. After his recovery he carried out his ministry as before. He was diligent in teaching children and adults as well as collecting and studying plants. Not a soul in his congregation turned from darkness to the light. The death of his beloved son Levi in 1839 diminished his attachment to the things of this world but did not lead to any further development in his spiritual life.

CONVERSION

Laestadius became seriously ill again in 1842. It was as if he heard in his heart a voice saying, "Set thine house in order: for thou shalt die and not live," as did Hezekiah long ago (Isaiah 38:1). He himself wrote, "I saw the eternal consequences of my ungodly life; for my entire life had been more ungodly than godly even though the world had considered me a paragon of virtue. All the sins of my youth were revealed to me."

Laestadius now became aware that not only was he himself a lost sinner on the way to hell but that his "flock" was on the same path. Even after he recovered from his illness, his soul continued to be troubled. The one burning question in his life became how to receive forgiveness for his sins and new birth as a child of God. In his distress he used to walk around a certain hill so often that he wore down a path. "He's looking for a way to heaven," the Sami people said, and started calling him "Walking Lassi." Laestadius felt that a higher power was pursuing him, and he could not escape. God had laid His hand on him and was drawing him to His Son.

Concern for the salvation of his own soul awakened in Laestadius a concern also for the souls of his parishioners. His proclamation took on a new note of seriousness as he earnestly warned people that their souls were in danger. Nevertheless, he himself still lacked the power of God's Spirit that was needed to awaken people.

Near the end of 1843, Laestadius went before the Cathedral Chapter of the Härnösand diocese to take the pastoral examination, a requirement for pastors seeking permanent calls. His pastoral thesis, entitled *Crapula Mundi* [*The World's Hangover*], was an outspoken description of the spiritual and moral condition of a sin-loving and indifferent world as well as a call to repentance. The sermon which he preached in the city aroused considerable attention. In this sermon he severely criticized sinful living and issued a call to repentance. He rebuked the clergy for turning a blind eye to their parishioners' sins instead of calling them to repentance.

On his return journey, Laestadius was assigned to make an inspection tour of the parishes in Lapland. On this journey he experienced the fundamental change for which his soul had been fervently longing during the last couple of years. He himself describes the event as follows in his periodical *Ens ropandes röst i* öknen *[The Voice of One Crying in the Wilderness]*:

> In the winter of 1844 while on an inspection tour, I went to the Åsele region of Lapland. I met a few Readers of the more moderate type there. Among them was a Sami girl named Maria who, after hearing my sermon from the altar, opened up her heart entirely to me. The experiences of God's grace that this simple girl had encountered were something I had never heard of before. After traveling far and wide seeking light for her darkness, Maria had come to Pastor Brandell in Nora and opened up her heart to him. Through him Maria had been released from her doubts and had come to a living faith. The thought came to me: Here is another Mary sitting at the feet of Jesus. For the first time I could see the way that leads to life. It had been hidden from me before. Her simple account of her pilgrimage and experiences touched my heart deeply, and the light dawned on me as well. That evening spent with Maria I experienced a foretaste of the joy of heaven.... As long as I live I shall remember that poor Maria, and I hope to meet her in the glorious world beyond the grave....

Juhani Raattamaa, a disciple and friend of Laestadius, reports that Maria encouraged Laestadius to believe in grace and forgiveness in Christ just as he was. God ignited this faith in Laestadius's heart through the Holy Spirit, and consequently he, too, was born a child of God. He received power from on high not only to believe in the forgiveness of his own sins but also to lead lost sheep to the Shepherd of their souls.

THE VOICE OF ONE CRYING IN THE WILDERNESS

Upon his return to Karesuando, his parishioners soon noticed that Laestadius was a changed man. He preached repentance as before, but his words had a new penetrating and infectious power and he spoke in a new way about Christ, the Friend of sinners, as well as atonement and forgiveness in His blood. The faith that he preached about was no longer merely doctrine and a moral life, it was new life in Christ through the indwelling Holy Spirit.

Laestadius wanted to be "a voice of one crying in the wilderness" like John the Baptist. In his sermons he described in graphic terms the souls and lives of people living in sin as well as the resulting wrath and judgment of God. His hearers recognized themselves in his portrayal. A feeling of doom and the fear of damnation began to burn the consciences of one hearer after another. Soon after his conversion, Laestadius spoke the following words to the parents of his confirmands in April of 1844:

> Do you think that your children will support you in your old age when you yourselves live empty lives, show your children a bad example, and make them children of hell, worse than you yourselves? Do you think that they don't have ears to hear your curses, your idle talk and your insults? Do you think that they don't have eyes to see your drunkenness and the quality of your godless life? Do not deceive yourselves! Of course children learn from their parents when they observe cursing, drunkenness, stealing, fighting, and a vain and empty life every day at home.

Laestadius's proclamation was severe and uncompromising, but it came from a heart that loved souls. A loving concern for the salvation of the flock entrusted to his care constrained Laestadius to reveal their self deception in order that the people would be led to the true way of life. In his sermons he made plentiful use of parables and illustrations taken from the Bible and the everyday lives of the people of Lapland. Thus, they left a strong impression on his parishioners.

The first effect of this new preaching under the influence of the Holy Spirit was that people were frightened and offended. The liquor vendors predicted that he would soon empty the church by his preaching. In the beginning this prediction seemed to come true. People were unable to stand the stinging brine of his sermons, and they stayed home. But soon the salt made them thirsty, and before long they came to church in greater numbers than before.

In the winter of 1845, about a year after the conversion of Laestadius, many people began to be bothered by the restlessness and hardness of their hearts. A few of them came to the parsonage for counsel and help. Not a single person had ever done this before. At first Laestadius felt that he was inexperienced in spiritual counseling. The theological seminary in Uppsala had not provided any instruction on how to proceed when people asked what they should do to be saved. Laestadius tried to help people by showing them Bible passages which seemed to apply to their condition, trusting that the Lord would bring to conclusion the work that He had started in them. At the same time he counseled them to search their hearts and lives in the light of God's Word and pray that the Lord would have mercy on them and help them. In his sermons he explained the "order of grace" as he understood it at the time and tried to console those who were under conviction of sin. In a sermon that he once preached to people whose consciences were awakened he said:

> ...self-righteousness often brings thoughts like this to the awakened person's mind: "I, who am so unclean, dare not come to Jesus. There is so much sin in me that it horrifies me. How can I become a child of God when I am full of uncleanness and immorality, anger and other horrifying sins." ...It is not sins that prevent you from becoming a child of God, it is self-righteousness that has bolted shut the door of your heart so that not a drop of grace can flow into it. You want to earn grace by improving your life, but you have chosen a way that is totally wrong. If you do not become a child of God through grace, you will certainly never become a child of God by improving your life. — Open your mouth, baby sparrow, your Parent is bringing you food! Open up your heart, sorrowful soul, and receive from the Savior the drop of grace that He pours into it! This is for those who are hungry; it is for the nestling sparrows who can't yet fly. But it is not for the wolf cubs who eat carcasses. Let them lap up the sleeping potion concocted by the father of lies in his cauldron.... If the lamb that has been wounded by a wolf does not quickly take refuge in the shepherd, it will become a meal for the wild beasts. If the awakened person does not quickly take refuge in the Savior's grace, the enemy will come and shoot his fiery arrows into that person's heart....

On Christmas Day 1847, people were congregating in the church in large numbers. Laestadius saw them as he approached the church and stopped, bewildered, asking himself, "How can I, great sinner that I am, lead these blind people out of darkness?" As he looked toward the church, he saw a bright light rising from the roof into the sky and then sinking to the south. He received this as a sign from God: It was not he who was leading these people, it was the Lord of heaven and earth, He who had created them and redeemed them through His Son. He had

The Karesuando Church where Laestadius served as pastor 1826-1848.

come to ignite the fires of heaven by His Word and Spirit in the hearts of the people here in the far northern region of Lapland.

Laestadius taught convicted sinners to take complete responsibility for their sins and without blaming others frankly admit their guilt. After that they could believe that God had cast all their sins upon Christ, and they could therefore believe them forgiven for the sake of His sacrifice on the cross. Saving faith takes refuge in and rests on the substitutionary sacrifice and victory of Christ in His resurrection. But this faith is always accompanied by "signs of grace," the inner testimony of the Holy Spirit and the accompanying peace and joy, which is often expressed in shouts of praise to the Lord. The kingdom of God is righteousness, peace and joy in the Holy Spirit. There are not always external signs, and when they do appear, they vary in intensity. However, true saving faith can never exist without some experience and "tasting" of God's grace as the Bible teaches. After conversion it is important for the Christian to strive to keep his faith and a pure conscience in order to maintain a good relationship with God and with other people.

Laestadius described unbelief and the accompanying love of sin as an "infernal passion" that the devil has put into a person's soul. "Because the carnal mind is enmity against God: for it is not subject to the law of God, neither indeed can be," as St. Paul says in Romans 8:7. Living faith he called a "heavenly passion," which enters the heart through the Holy Spirit and drives out the "infernal passion." Constrained by "the love of God [which] is shed abroad in our hearts by the Holy Ghost" (Romans 5:5), the person then begins to love God above all things and his neighbor as himself. This "heavenly passion" drives Christians to bear testimony to their Savior and labor to win others to repentance and faith.

In much the same way as Zinzendorf and Viklund, Laestadius made a distinction between repentance induced by the law and repentance brought about through the Gospel. The former includes a knowledge of sinful deeds and the judgment of God which follows. The latter includes, in addition, an awareness that unbelief is the source of all sins and that these sins make him guilty of Christ's suffering and death. "...thou hast made me to serve with thy sins,[1] thou hast wearied me with thine iniquities" (Isaiah 43:24). Only in this "evangelical repentance" does one become truly broken in heart. The "legalistic repentance" tends to lead one to attempt to mend his life and even to build up self-righteousness. It may also, however, lead to contrition and the confession of sins as well as a quest for the grace promised in the Gospel, and so it should. Evangelical repentance takes place "at the foot of the cross," where the person's heart is truly broken in accordance with God's will. When the Holy Spirit reveals to such a person Christ's redemptive grace and forgiveness in His blood by means of the Gospel, he comes to a true knowledge of Christ and through new birth becomes a Christian who bears good fruit.

THE GREAT REVIVAL

The awakening among the people of Karesuando began in 1845, but it was not until the fifth of December that the first person was actually converted. That was when Pekka Piltto's wife experienced release from her burden of sin and received a "sign of grace," an inner witness by the Holy Spirit that she was a child of God. She heard a

---

[1] According to the RSV this reads: "But you have burdened me with your sins...."

voice that said, "Your sins are forgiven you," and her heart was so filled with joy that she started to jump about and praise God aloud. At the same moment an earthquake was felt in the area. Laestadius felt that even nature trembled with joy when the first sinner experienced grace and thus new life burst forth. From that day forward, the revival spread rapidly from Karesuando to neighboring parishes as well as to Finland and Norway.

Even before coming to faith, Laestadius had preached and taken action against drunkenness, but at that time he had only called for moderation, not total abstinence. After coming to faith he became convinced through experience that a drunkard who had been converted could easily have a relapse if he so much as tasted alcohol. For that reason he started to teach total abstinence. Believers were not to use alcoholic beverages even as medicine. One of his associates said, "If alcohol becomes medicine, the devil will be sure to make a lot of people sick."

The Conventicle Act issued by the Diet of Sweden-Finland in 1726 banned private devotional meetings outside the church. This ban was primarily due to a fear that nonconformist and sectarian "radical Pietism" would spread, but it was also applied to revival movements that operated within the church and were faithful to it. In order to avoid colliding with this Act, Laestadius founded a temperance society. For five years, beginning in December 1847, he sent nearly thirty Christian men into the congregations of Swedish, Finnish and Norwegian Lapland with letters of recommendation from the temperance society "to promote temperance." He provided them with handwritten copies of his sermons as well as a temperance speech written by him in the Sami language. In temperance meetings they read these documents and discussed their contents. This "temperance work" was in reality evangelism, where the purpose was not simply to lead people to give up drinking but also to repent of sin and turn away from the world. Laestadius knew that only genuine conversion, coming to faith, freed people from the shackles of alcoholism.

Within approximately eight years, the revival had an amazing effect on the Torne (Tornio) river valley and its surroundings. By 1853 there were only three people left who were known to use alcohol. In the Jukkasjärvi parish the last liquor dealer poured out his "devil's brew" on the ground in 1850. About five years earlier it was estimated that six to eight thousand measures of alcohol had been consumed in the parish. This parish was not even part of Laestadius's responsibility.

The "infernal passion" of drunkenness did not stay in hearts set aflame by the "divine passion" of faith.

The government of Sweden established so-called mission schools for the purpose of educating children in the northernmost parts of the country and appointed Laestadius chief superintendent of these schools. In this capacity he had an opportunity to place Christian men in these schools as teachers. In the years 1848-59 the schools had about twenty teachers who had come to faith, some of whom also became prominent lay preachers. Attending the schools were some adults who, after coming to faith, wanted to learn to read so they could study the Bible. Numerous children and adults repented and came to faith in these schools and the meetings held there. The evening devotions at the schools became gatherings for the entire village providing an opportunity for holding devotional meetings within a format allowed by the Conventicle Act.

About three years after the revival began, Laestadius applied for the position of senior pastor of Pajala, a parish further south, and he was chosen. He assumed his duties in the spring of 1849. In his first sermon in Pajala, he spoke about how God's Word can break even hearts that are hardened by sin and self-righteousness, just as the stone from David's sling crushed Goliath's forehead. "Just you wait, Goliath," Laestadius said. "You may have an iron

The altar and Chasuble (the outer, sleeveless robe worn by the pastor celebrating mass) in use at the Pajala church when Laestdius was pastor

breastplate, but there must certainly be a bare spot where a slingstone can strike you." Some of his hearers thought, "Aren't you the proud one! Your boasting will be in vain!"

The hope Laestadius had was not in vain. Also in Pajala the Word of God penetrated many consciences. The fires of revival spread not only in Pajala but in ever larger areas. One reason for its rapid spread was the fact that Laestadius did not attempt to labor alone. He urged every convert to preach repentance to his neighbors and friends. Also a growing group of lay preachers from within the movement spread the revival to ever wider areas.

Laestadius wrote out his sermons and gave the manuscripts to men whom he had trained for the work so they could read and discuss them with their audiences. Soon these men started to preach on their own without the manuscripts. Laestadius's written sermons continued to be read even after preaching without them became prevalent. Even today it is customary in the group called the Firstborn [Old Apostolic Lutheran] to read one of Laestadius's sermons first, and after that the preachers speak. Laestadius's sermons have been collected and published as "postils," and they have also been translated into English in the United States.

As the revival spread and the number of believers increased, so did the number of people who were offended by Laestadius's straightforward preaching of repentance. The emotional outbursts that took place during Sunday worship and in home services were another cause of offense. These took the form of loud weeping, wailing, and praising the Lord, sometimes accompanied by the clapping of upraised hands and prancing about. The people who were offended sent complaints from Pajala to Bishop Israel Bergman in Härnösand who investigated the matter on his visitation in Pajala. He could find no actual fault in Laestadius. In order to calm the situation, the bishop made a Solomon-like judgment: Laestadius was required to hold two services every Sunday, one for the unawakened, who could not stand the weeping of the repentant and the rejoicing of the believers and another for the awakened and the believers. After some time this arrangement was discontinued because the church was empty during the services for the unawakened.

Subsequently, the opponents of the revival sent complaints about Laestadius to the Cathedral Chapter of the diocese as well as the civil courts. Each time Laestadius was found to have been carrying out his pastoral duties satisfactorily. Nevertheless, all of this caused him a great deal of grief and trouble. He was slandered and insulted also in the newspapers. But that is exactly what Jesus told His disciples would happen: People would speak all manner of evil against them.

REPENTANCE, CONFESSION AND ABSOLUTION

The Bible says, "If we confess our sins, he is faithful and just to forgive us our sins, and to cleanse us from all unrighteousness" (1 John 1:9). Laestadius understood these words to mean that sins should be confessed not only to God but to other people as well. In the early phase of the awakening, he taught that sins were to be confessed publicly before the congregation. A person was not truly contrite if he wanted to continue hiding his sins. "Thief of grace," Laestadius said, "have you truly repented of your sins when you continue to cover up and conceal your sins?" In one sermon he proclaimed, "The virtuous whores and honest thieves of our day do not want to confess their sin to anybody because they would rather go to hell with their honor than go to heaven without honor or as a whore and a thief." The confession of sins was to take place in detail and publicly "before the congregation, that is to Christians" and not just all lumped together in a general way.

It soon became evident that this kind of public confession of sins had some undesirable aspects. The unawakened sometimes ridiculed believers because of the sins that they had heard confessed publicly. And it was not good for children especially to hear about the sins of adults. For these reasons the public confession of individual sins was discontinued except for those sins that had been committed publicly and were more or less commonly known. People were exhorted to confess other sins in private according to the instructions given in the Small Catechism.

Laestadius taught that true contrition and repentance always implies a desire to become reconciled with those whom one has offended or wronged and to make restitution when possible. Many lawsuits came to an end when both parties settled their differences by asking and giving each other forgiveness. Stolen goods were restored to their rightful owners or restitution was made. In 1850 eighty-eight men from Pajala wrote to the Swedish government and confessed that they were guilty of smuggling. They offered to pay the government the money they owed in duties. The officials in Stockholm notified them that they could make payment to the parish fund for the relief of the poor. After this it became customary that if restitution could not be made to the individual wronged, payment would be made to a fund of this sort.

In the beginning Laestadius and his fellow workers consoled repentant people who had come to seek the grace of God with suitable

words from the Bible. They showed these people how Christ had paid
their debt of sin by His sacrifice on the cross and encouraged them to
take hold of the salvation which had thus been prepared for them.
Many souls were released in this way and experienced joy in the Lord.
Of course they were aware of what the Catechism taught concerning
confession and absolution as well as the words of Jesus quoted there:

> Whatsover ye shall bind on earth shall be bound in heaven: and
> whatsoever ye shall loose on earth shall be loosed in heaven.
> (Matt. 18:18)

> Whose soever sins ye remit, they are remitted unto them; and
> whose soever sins ye retain, they are retained. (John 20:23)

They did not, however, understand these teachings properly or
know how to put them into practice.

Juhani Raattamaa, the teacher in charge of the Lannavaara school
and Laestadius's most important associate, observed that many people
could not find peace with God when they were comforted and
exhorted with words of Scripture alone. On the basis of the teachings
regarding confession in the Small Catechism and the explanation in
Luther's Church Postil, Raattamaa in 1853 laid his hands on a woman
who was under conviction of sin and declared to her direct and
unconditional absolution, that is, forgiveness of sins. The woman
instantly experienced release and began to praise God. Encouraged by
this experience, Raattamaa started to proclaim absolution to other
repentant sinners as well, and other preachers began to do the same.
They experienced time and again that the good news of forgiveness
when declared in this manner was God's power for igniting faith in
repentant hearts. Raattamaa brought this before Laestadius, who
carefully studied the Bible, Luther's Catechism, and the Lutheran
Confessions. He came to the conclusion that the proclamation of direct
and unconditional absolution to the penitent was in conformity with
the Bible and Lutheran doctrine. He himself began to use it and taught
it in his sermons. He and the entire "Laestadian" movement
understood that the power to forgive sins has been given to the
Church, all believers. Laestadius explained this in one of his sermons:

> Christians receive the keys of the kingdom of heaven from the
> hand of the Savior. They open the door to the kingdom of heaven
> and let the repentant and doubting soul in through the grace which
> Jesus has merited for repentant sinners through His blood.

Luther believes that God's grace belongs only to penitent and broken hearts. But now Luther's faith has disappeared from people's hearts almost completely.... All those who profess dead faith argue that nobody knows who is penitent and who is impenitent and that a pastor...should turn them [the keys] this way and that...in this manner: "If your confession of sins is honest, your contrition is true and your faith sincere," etc...

When the keys of the kingdom are turned in this way so that both doors are opened at the same time, both...to the abyss of hell and to the kingdom of heaven, penitent souls fear that they will not gain entrance into the kingdom of glory....

Luther's teaching regarding true contrition and repentance is this: the church ought to impart absolution to penitent sinners. True repentance is manifested in genuine contrition and terror smiting the conscience... (Augsburg Confession, article XII). The person whose heart is grieved and whose conscience is filled with terror is not able to lay aside that grief and abandon it until God gives him power to believe. It is the duty of the Church of God to show to such a penitent soul that God is merciful to him, a sinner, and it is for this purpose that the keys of the kingdom of heaven are given her. She must open the door to penitent souls; but she must shut it to the indifferent.... Such is the faith of Luther.... The forgiveness that is declared to an impenitent sinner effects nothing and no joy follows it. When the impenitent believes his sins forgiven, he has only a dead faith.

Laestadian Christians soon adopted the view that confession and absolution are a normal part of every Christian's life just like the hearing of God's Word and participation in the sacraments, as Luther says in his Large Catechism:

Whoever is a Christian, or would like to be one, has here the faithful advice to go and obtain this precious treasure.... If anybody does not go to confession willingly and for the sake of absolution, let him just forget about it.... However, if you despise it and proudly stay away from confession, then we must come to the conclusion that you are no Christian.... And this is a sure sign that you also despise the Gospel.... If you are a Christian, you should be glad to run more than a hundred miles for confession, not under compulsion but rather coming and compelling us to offer it (From *A Brief Exhortation to Confession*).

Coming to faith can certainly take place also while hearing a sermon, occasionally while reading the Bible or some Christian book, and not just through personal absolution. But if a person does not need personal confession or absolution when coming to faith, he will need it later. Sin still dwells even in the Christian, in his flesh. No believer succeeds in his Christian walk in such a way that he never falls into sin or fault. For this reason believers need mutual confession and absolution, just as they need to ask each other for forgiveness and to forgive each other when they transgress against one another. Confession and absolution are important gifts of God for the purpose of helping the believer to keep faith with a pure conscience. Laestadius says, "Living faith quickly turns into dead faith if the conscience is not watchful." The light which dawns on the righteous is not mere emotionalism; it also includes the light of the conscience, watchfulness, prayer, the study and proper understanding of God's Word so that the believer's life is not fruitless.

Laestadius tells about a sick man who confessed his sins to him. The man also reconciled with those people against whom he had transgressed and whom he had wronged, and he begged for forgiveness from Christians whom he had opposed and ridiculed. In addition, he begged forgiveness from unbelievers whom he had reinforced in their unbelief and hypocrisy or to whom he had been a stumbling block and by his example led them to sin or who had given up their intention to repent because of him. This type of thorough repentance was common when the fires of revival were burning.

SCIENTIFIC AND LITERARY WORKS

In the field of botany, Laestadius was internationally known as an expert on the flora of Lapland. After his conversion his main interest turned to the salvation of souls. He started to write a large theological treatise to which he gave the title *Dårhushjonet: En blick i nådens ordning [Inmate of a Mental Institution: A glance into the order of grace]*. He labored on this book for more than a dozen years. The unusual title is based on the Biblical

Plant drawing by Laestadius-Lychnis alpina (Reillustrated)

words that the teaching of the cross is foolishness to them that perish, and Christians are often viewed as being insane, out of their minds.

In this book Laestadius demonstrates from both psychology and Scripture that the principal fault of man is the ungodliness of his heart which is his inborn fleshly enmity toward God, and the resulting unwillingness or inability to submit to God's will. In his innermost being is the "infernal passion" kindled by the devil. His reason, intellect and will are subject to this passion or sinful tendency and desire. Enlightenment of the intellect and exertions of the will cannot change his evil heart. It is when God changes a person's heart by His Word and Spirit that his heart as well as his intellect and will are transformed.

Laestadius shows that the "objective" reconciliation of mankind which took place once for all on the cross of Christ was essential because of God's holiness and love as well as the fallen and condemned condition of mankind. On the basis of the substitutionary redemption on the cross, the "subjective," that is personal and experiential, redemption or reconciliation with God takes place by means of the Word through repentance and faith brought about by the Holy Spirit.

The book was written in opposition to the rationalistic, moralistic and liberalistic tendencies of Laestadius's time. It was his purpose to defend and explain the fundamental principles and nature of living Biblical Christianity. It was one of the most remarkable theological works of the century, written with unusual intellectual acumen and logic, and it was inspired by the "heavenly passion" of faith influenced by the Holy Spirit.

Laestadius could not find a publisher for his book. The church leaders and theologians of his day, who represented rationalism and dead orthodoxy, did not understand him. It was finally published in Finland nearly a hundred years after the writer's death.[2]

HIS FINAL YEARS

As the "father" of the Laestadian movement grew older, the work was increasingly taken over by his "disciples." Laestadius's wisdom is evident from the fact that practically from the beginning he trained and sent out suitable Christian men to preach the Word

---

[2] Laestadius, L.L. *Hulluinhuonelainen.* Finnish translation by Lauri Mustakallio. Joensuu, 1968. Published in English as *The Bedlamite.*

and care for souls. In this way he gradually made himself unnecessary, particularly since a large number of his sermons were available for use in the movement. When the time came for him to enter the eternal mansions, there was a considerable number of lay preachers and even a few trained pastors. The movement continued to live and operate without interruption after he passed on from the Church Militant to the Church Triumphant.

In 1860 Laestadius was stricken with a severe stomach ailment, possibly cancer. The nearest doctor was over sixty-five miles away, and it was practically impossible for a sick man to travel such a distance in a reindeer or horse-drawn sled. Actually, it is unlikely that medical science at that time had the capability of treating him.

When Raattamaa heard that his beloved pastor and father in faith was ill, he hastened to visit him one more time and receive his last instructions. Laestadius said to him:

> I have been trying to examine myself and my teachings in the light of God's Word in order to find out whether they will stand at the judgment of God. I have not discovered in my teachings anything that is contrary to Scripture, and I can't change it. But I feel that I am a great sinner even though I am in faith.

He thanked God for having given him a happy marriage and for all the blessings in his life. He asked Raattamaa to bless him once more with the forgiveness of sins in the name and blood of Jesus. After saying a Christian farewell to his beloved spiritual father and teacher, Raattamaa left. From the vestibule he heard the dying servant of the Lord loudly

Tombstone of Laestadius at the Pajala cemetery

praising God for His grace.

When speaking of Laestadius, Raattamaa used to say, "the late Pastor, the first and best laborer in this Christianity."

Laestadius suffered excruciating pain in his final days, but he tried to endure it patiently. At times he asked his wife to forgive him for expressions of impatience during his illness. As he neared the end he said, "The Savior is coming with open arms to take me. Heavenly visitors are coming to fetch me." His eyes shone with a glorified joy as he spoke these words. After having said farewell to those around him, he passed on to his eternal reward with a happy smile on his face. This took place on the 21st of February, 1861.

From Uuras Saarnivaara. *He elivät Jumalan voimassa [They Lived in the Power of God]*. Suolahti, Finland: Ev. lut. Herätysseura, 1975. Translated by Rodger and Aila Foltz.

4

Lars Levi Laestadius
as Scientist

Jouko Talonen

The year 2000 was especially significant in the northern areas of Scandinavia. Two hundred years had elapsed since the birth of Lars Levi Laestadius (1800-1861) who was a revival leader, promoter of temperance, expert on Arctic plants and independent theologian. Laestadius, who served as a pastor in Swedish Lapland, was gifted in many ways as a preacher, scholar and thinker, and he continues to arouse discussion. Laestadius's significance is evident also from the fact that his sermons continue to be published and read. They have been published not only in Finnish, Lappish and Swedish but also in Norwegian, English, German, Russian, Estonian and Latvian.

HE BECAME INTERESTED IN BOTANY DURING HIS STUDENT YEARS

Lars Levi Laestadius was born on January 10, 1800, in Swedish Lapland in the village of Jäckvik in Arjeplog parish. His father, Karl Laestadius, was descended from a prominent family of clergymen whose name derived from the village of Lästad in Ytterlännäs parish located in central Sweden. His father had been employed at the Nasafjäll mine. Later he supported his family as a pioneer farmer in Arjeplog. Lars Levi Laestadius's mother was the daughter of a poor pioneer farmer and was a distant relative of her husband.

Laestadius has described his birthplace as a thoroughly desolate land inhabited only by "wolves, wolverines, hares and ptarmigans." Although the family moved closer to the Arjeplog church village in 1802, Lars Levi and his younger brother Petrus, who was born in 1802, spent most of their childhood in the wilderness of Swedish Lapland. Undoubtedly, he was affected in his childhood by the poverty of the home, his father's alcoholism, and his mother's pietistic ideals. Their half brother Karl Erik Laestadius, who was serving as assistant pastor in Kvikkjokk, took his little brothers under his wing in 1808. There in the scenic, mountainous area of Kvikkjokk Lars Levi's love of nature and interest in studying plants was aroused under the tutelage of Karl Erik who was interested in hunting and plants as well as recording meteorological phenomena.

The improved social conditions and the tutoring provided by Karl Erik Laestadius made it possible for the boys to continue their education. In 1816 Lars Levi and Petrus went to the Härnösand secondary school. After graduation in 1819, Lars Levi commenced his studies at the University of Uppsala. Although it was his intention to study theology, he took special interest in botany, attending lectures by the famous professor Göran Wahlenberg (1780-1851). He was admitted to the theological seminary in 1821, studying homiletics under Samuel Ödman. Showing maturity and keen intelligence even at this early phase of his education, he participated in botanical expeditions into Lapland and wrote his first book on the basis of his observations in the Luleå region of Lapland in 1821. His first monograph, *Om möjligheten och fördelen af allmänna uppodlingar i Lappmarken* [*Concerning the possibilities for and advantages of general agriculture in Lapland*], was first published in 1824.

In spite of his many talents and wide-ranging interests, Laestadius chose to become a pastor. After a brief assignment in his home parish of Arjeplog, Laestadius became senior pastor of Sweden's northernmost congregation, Karesuando, in 1826. A spiritual revival began as a result of his preaching in 1845-1846. In 1849 he transferred to Pajala and died there on February 21, 1861.

EXPERT ON THE FLORA AND FAUNA OF THE ARCTIC REGION

Laestadius's interest in the plant kingdom which developed during

**Viscaria
alpina**

his school years led him on expeditions to study plants of the Arctic region. As early as 1819 he took an extensive journey as far as Jämtland and Tromssa [Norway]. These journeys continued in 1820-1822 and 1824. Of particular significance was his journey to Skåne, Småland and the island of Öland with Professor Wahlenberg in 1822. During his years in Karesuando (1826-1849), Laestadius had less time for his scientific avocation, but he continued to keep up contacts with prominent Swedish botanists, not only Wahlenberg but also Professor Elias Fries. He continuously made new discoveries. There are a total of 6,700 plants collected by Laestadius. *Svensk Botanik* [*Swedish Botany*], a series of volumes containing pictures and information on plants of Sweden (published in 1826), contains over a hundred of his drawings of plants.

There are plants that have been named after Laestadius, such as Carex Laestadiana [Arctic sedge] and Papaver Laestadianum [Arctic poppy]. He was known as one of the first scholars in Europe to study willows. The noted German botanist Fr. Wimmer in his book *Salices europae* [*European Willows*] (1866) expressed admiration for Laestadius's expertise on willows. Laestadius's most significant botanical treatise was "Loca parallela plantarum" [Parallel habitats of plants], which was included in the series

Papaver Laestadianum (Arctic Poppy) named after Laestadius

Nova Acta regiae Societatis Scientarium Upsaliensis published by the Uppsala Academy of Science. As a botanist Laestadius was primarily an ecologist, taxonomist and collector. More than thirty plants bear names assigned to them by him. Laestadius also served as guide to a French scientific expedition which visited the northern area of Scandinavia in 1838. During the years 1835-1840, the government of France sponsored a large scientific expedition to study the Arctic region. The expedition was led by the naval doctor Joseph Paul Gaimard and included the famous scholar and writer Xavier Marmier. The journey was made by ship, a corvette called La Recherche owned by the French government. The explorations made in 1838-1840 included Lapland, Spitzbergen

Astragalus alpinus

and the Faeroe islands. Laestadius was one of the foreign members of the expedition but joined it for only part of the time when he led them from Alattio, Norway, to Sweden by way of Kautokeino. Thus, Laestadius established contacts with French scientific circles. For instance, he supplied Gaimard with an extensive collection of plants. In spite of original plans, his study of Sami mythology was not included in the series of reports detailing the findings of the expedition, but Laestadius is mentioned in several places in the large 29-volume report on the French expedition's findings, for example as an editor of the part on meteorology.

For his efforts on behalf of the La Recherche expedition he was honored with membership in the French Legion of Honor. In 1836 he was made a member of the Edinburgh Botanical Society having also assisted British scientists.

His interest in hunting and contacts with the hunting organization Svenska Jägareförbundet [Swedish Hunting Association] were further manifestations of his fascination with nature and the natural sciences. His zoological pursuits led him to write articles for this organization's publications. For example, in 1832 he wrote an account of the fish of Lapland which was the most detailed that had been published up to that time. In addition, Laestadius sent the organization animal specimens and information on birds, squirrels, the migratory patterns of lemmings, and wild deer. His interest in zoology led to a correspondence with Professor Sven Nilsson (1787-1883). It is also interesting to note that Laestadius, in accordance with contemporary practice, was known to have participated in "grave robbing." Skulls and bones of Sami people excavated from graves were used as material for study. The French expedition described above dug up a couple of sackfuls of such "material" in 1838.

While in Karesuando, Pastor Laestadius also diligently made geological observations and studied climatic changes in Karesuando. He recorded the maximum and minimum temperatures in Karesuando for 2922 days. Laestadius's small meteorological study entitled "Observations meteorologiques a Karesuando" was included in the series published by the La Recherche expedition.

THEOLOGIAN AND LAPPOLOGIST

Laestadius's contributions to the empirical biological sciences were a result not only of the experiences of his youth but also his lack of regard for philosophy. He was, of course, familiar with the philosophical as well as the psychological trends of his day, but he did not give much credence to "half-baked" philosophers. This attitude was due to his dislike of theological rationalism. Laestadius directed his intellectual and scientific energies towards sciences that were grounded on the concrete and visible.

Laestadius's main religious philosophical work, *Dårhushjonet* [*Inmate of a Mental Institution*], was published in 1949, nearly ninety years after his death. The book was an argument in defense of his pietism and the Laestadian revival that was under way. Laestadius knew the theological trends of his day and did not mince words in criticizing rationalism (neology) and the state church of Sweden. Laestadius rested his arguments on Luther and even more strongly on Philipp Jacob Spener, the father of Pietism. Theologically Laestadius clearly represents the pietistic tradition of Spener. Nevertheless, his basic attitude towards the fundamental premises of orthodox Lutheran theology was positive. The keynote of his religious worldview was clearly the pietistic ideal of the Reader movement which had been influential in northern Sweden, colored in addition by a Moravian tradition. The basic question was of the difference between "living" and "dead" faith. An adult could not be converted without being aware of this: the believer remembered the moment of his conversion. A "living faith" entailed a new life ethic.

Laestadius had distant Sami roots. As a child he learned the Sami dialect of Luleå, and the dialect of the northern mountains was not unfamiliar to him either. It was on the basis of the Luleå Sami that he created a literary (written) language for the Sami. As a Lappologist Laestadius was in the forefront of the experts of his time in his knowledge of the living conditions, culture, beliefs and religion of the Sami people. In this regard Laestadius can also be considered a student of comparative religions and a cultural anthropologist. His most significant study in this area, *Fragmenter i Lappska Mythologin*, was lost for over a hundred years, seeing print in Sweden for the first time in 1960. It has recently been published in English.[3] Laestadius was also skillful in using the traditional beliefs of the Sami in his sermons when attempting to communicate the classic message of Christianity to the people of Lapland.

Translated by Rodger and Aila Foltz

---

[3] Laestadius, Lars Levi. *Fragments of Lappish Mythology*. Translated by Börje Vahamaki. Beaverton, Ontario: Aspasia Books, 2002.

5

Lars Levi Laestadius
as Family Man

Aila Foltz

LAESTADIUS'S VIEWS OF MARRIAGE

By the age of seventeen, it was already clear to Lars Levi
Laestadius that he would not choose a wife from among the so-called
cream of society because these women were full of vanity and
worldliness and had only contempt for religion. His mother's godly,
devoutly Christian personality had a strong influence on him, and she
was her son's ideal. She was, he wrote in the autobiography published
in his periodical *Ens ropandes röst i öknen [The Voice of One Crying
in the Wilderness]*, "a truly gentle, submissive and blessed woman. My
mother's extreme patience, her quiet submission to God's will, her
stifled sighs and tears when she was abused, and her silent prayers in
bed at night had left an indelible impression on her son's heart." "An
unfortunate marriage—a hell on earth—can be the result of an overly
hasty choice," he said, and continued:

My future wife should not come from the upper class because her
expectations would be too great; she should not be rich because
wealth can make a man dependent on his wife; she should not be
educated, because education might draw her away from
housekeeping; she should not be fashionable or refined, because
such a person might demand to be served; she should not be a
whiner, because she would be altogether intolerable. She should be
poor so that she would consider herself fortunate to have a
husband who is assured of daily bread and have a secure future;
she should be uneducated so that she could be molded to suit her
husband; she should be a Christian...such unheard-of
requirements! She should be a bit passionate.

He viewed love within the bonds of marriage as sacred and
mystical. In his theological work *Dårhushjonet [Inmate of a Mental
Institution]*, he describes love as a neutral passion, neither good nor
bad of itself. Genuine love in a legal marriage, he says, is not a sin. In

fact, "...if love is wed to piety, it is pure and beyond reproach." He states further that marriage can fulfill its moral purpose insofar as the spirit of love is able to prepare the heart to receive the Holy Spirit by making it tender and inclined to more noble feelings *(The Voice of One Crying in the Wilderness)*.

HE MARRIES BRITA CATHARINA ALSTADIUS

The woman Laestadius perceived as most closely matching his ideal was his childhood friend Brita Catharina (Kajsa) Alstadius. She was five years his junior, and the daughter of a settler in the Peuraure area of Kvikkjokk. She came from an impoverished home where the diet consisted of milk, fried meat and fish, and hardly ever any bread. Her mother, the daughter of a shopkeeper in Luleå, died when Brita was small, and her father was incapable of maintaining the household and farm as before.

Early in 1827 Laestadius traveled to Jokkmokk to fetch his bride, and they were married in the Enontekiö church dressed in Sami fur coats. At that time Lars Levi was 27 years old and Brita 22. They spoke the Swedish and Sami languages but would learn Finnish in order to serve the largely Finnish population in northern Sweden.

PARSONAGE LIFE

The Karesuando parsonage to which Laestadius took his young bride was originally a farm which the congregation had bought from a pioneer settler in 1812. It was old and dilapidated, but some new living quarters had been added on. There were the usual farm buildings for horses, cows, and sheep as well as storage facilities.

Without the additional income from plants that Laestadius collected and pressed and sent to botanists in Sweden and other countries, his family would have been in dire straits. In his biography,

Laestadius: Pohjolan pasuuna [Laestadius: Trumpet of the North], Aapeli Saarisalo writes about his financial situation:

> Laestadius's income was very small and also uncertain, because he could not demand that those poor people pay the tithes required by law for the pastor or the small fees which at that time were imposed for performing ministerial acts such as baptisms, marriages, and burials. Only by exercising great frugality and self-denial could Laestadius make provision for himself and his rapidly growing family.

The rigorous conditions of the wilderness overwhelmed many a pioneer settler's wife, but Brita Kajsa, accustomed to the life of a poor pioneer settler, evidently adjusted well to her life as the wife of a wilderness pastor. Laestadius has written that, undeserving though he was, he was given the best possible spouse and enjoyed a truly happy and stable marriage. With her godliness and servant spirit, she made it possible for him to carry out the ministry God had given him. She did not complain when her husband went off on long journeys in the mountain wilderness. In the tradition of the other Catherine, Katherina Luther, she was very hospitable when their home became a gathering place for brothers and sisters in the faith. To her guests she would serve coffee and homemade reindeer cheese which was a real delicacy in Lapland. On church holidays there were such large numbers of overnight guests that even the floor was covered with bedding. After the revival began, people came from long distances, even from as far away as Ruija, Norway. Johan Petter Niilimaa recorded his recollection from the Laestadiuses' last years in Karesuando:

> Those were lively times! Everybody loved the pastor and his wife. She served everybody, even beggars. When the house was full of people, the pastor often had to withdraw to the neighbor's, where he could stay "behind locked doors," reading and writing into the night.

There being no commercial lodgings available, the Laestadius parsonage received visitors even from the continent. A couple of scientific expeditions came through. A German poet related that he was permitted to sleep among Laestadius's plants and books on a bed of straw, and he left with a lunch packed by his hostess. There was even the arrogant Frenchwoman Leonia d'Aunet, with her entourage of four people, who was the ungrateful recipient of their hospitality.

As mistress of the parsonage, Mrs. Laestadius was demanding but kind; and because she treated them well, she was liked by the workers in the house and farm whom she hired and directed. After the others went to bed, Brita Kajsa liked to make coffee for herself, and it is reported that she would often take some to her guests and hired girls in their beds.

She assisted her husband in keeping meteorological records for the Swedish Academy, a duty which was commonly assigned to wilderness pastors. She even trapped and skinned moles for Professor Carl J. Sundevall. People would frequently come to her asking for some of the wine left over from communion, believing it to be particularly beneficial for the sick. During the years of crop failure in the middle of the nineteenth century there was not enough grain for bread, and she went about in the villages teaching people how to bake bread from lichen and straw. It is even reported that farmers asked her to castrate their rams with her teeth in the Sami manner, because they themselves did not like to do it.

The cabin Laestadius had built in 1828 for living quarters as well as home services and meetings. Today it is a cultural museum on the grounds of the present Karesuando parsonage

According to information collected from some of their contemporaries by their great-grandson, Edvin Mäkitalo, Laestadius and his wife were compatible in their personalities and their way of thinking. Brita Kajsa was very impetuous and could at times make cutting and sarcastic remarks, much like her husband, but she was also quick to make amends. She was reserved by nature and not as emotional and melancholy as her quick-tempered husband. She was industrious and was on the go from early morning till late at night. She knitted and sewed clothes and stitched quilts not only for the family but also as gifts for friends and acquaintances. "The pastor's wife was like quicksilver, even in her old age," Mäkitalo reported.

THEIR CHILDREN

Lars Levi and Brita Kajsa were blessed with fifteen children between the years 1827 and 1851, all born in Karesuando except the last one, who was born in Pajala. One was stillborn and three died in childhood. Eleven were living at the time of their father's death. They were: Eleonora, Carl Johan, Sophia Wilhelmina, Emma Christina, Elisabet, Lorens Wilhelm, Fredrica Johanna, Hedvig Charlotta,[4] Lea Selma, Gustaf Leonard, and Daniel.

Elisabet's twin, Levi, died at nearly three years of age. His death struck his father

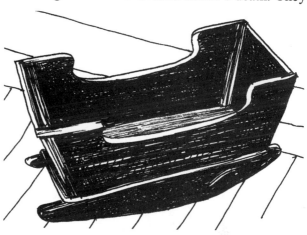

The baby cradle in the Karesuando parsonage Used by Laestadius's children

especially hard, but his mother did not display her grief as overtly as he did. Presumably she had to be the strong one at such times for the sake of the family, and she comforted him and upheld him in his despair. In a letter dated May 11, 1839, Laestadius wrote to a friend:

> My child was sick with the measles, and the grim visitor snatched away from this life one of the most beautiful seedlings that I owned. The little boy who was 2 years and 8 months old, and this

---

[4] In 1881 Hedvig Charlotta (known as Lotta) emigrated to the United States with her husband, Mikko Jokela, who was Pastor Andrew Mickelsen's paternal uncle, and lived out her days in Franklin, Minnesota. She was a leader in the fellowship there. Her gravestone can still be seen in the Finnish cemetery in Franklin.

loss has made me more weary than ever of this world and its plants.

My wife was sick in bed when little Levi died. However, the news of his death did not appear to touch her heart as deeply, for she considered herself fortunate to have been deemed worthy of bearing fruit for the kingdom of heaven.

On my heart, however, this death had a deep and long-lasting effect. Little Levi and his twin sister Elisabet would often come running to meet their father when he returned home from the woods. If there was a pretty bird in his hunting bag, the children were allowed to carry it inside to their mother. But now there was no Levi any more to carry in the pretty bird. Nevertheless, the sweetest thought of all was that little Levi would be the first to come and meet his father and mother on the beautiful shore of eternity.

Reflecting on this experience, Laestadius later said, "A person truly needs some reminders of his mortality; otherwise he completely forgets the purpose of life here on earth. Levi's death was such a reminder."

The fate of his family weighed on Laestadius's mind during a long period of illness. He was concerned that his wife and children should have a place to live after his death, not wanting to leave them homeless. Consequently he bought the northernmost pioneer farm in Lapland in a place called Kummavuopio. He eventually recovered from his illness and, as it turned out, his family never needed to move there.

THE MOVE TO PAJALA

There being no public school in Karesuando apart from the circuit schools that taught reading, Bible history and the Catechism, the education of children was the responsibility of their parents. Laestadius did his best to teach his children, as his half brother Erik had taught him, but it became overwhelming. When he heard that the position of senior pastor was open in Pajala, a larger community further south which had a school, he saw that as a solution to his problem. He told his friends:

I would not have applied to Pajala had I not had so many children whom I don't have time to teach personally due to all the parish work and so little income that I can't afford to hire [a tutor] for my children and don't have time to educate them myself.

After the family moved to Pajala in 1849, the Laestadius parsonage was the site of numerous village devotional meetings. Especially on Sundays, visitors from their own parish and different parts of Lapland gathered there, and the number of overnight guests was not diminished from their Karesuando days. Twice a week, on Tuesdays and Fridays, a big pot of soup was prepared, and it was served to everybody who came to the house. On those days, the pastor's wife liked to sit at the window sewing, peering down the village road. If she saw people walking by, she would knock on the window, invite them in, and serve soup. The farmers' wives who visited the parsonage were so happy to see Mrs. Laestadius that they threw their arms around her and wept for joy.

Towards the end of Laestadius's life, the church was moved from Köngäs and rebuilt on a new site in the present village of Pajala a couple of miles up the Torne [Tornio] River. A room was rented in the Pajala village for a church office until such time as the new parsonage would be finished. As it turned out, neither the church nor the parsonage was finished during his lifetime. In Pajala the Laestadius family was obliged to live for years in primitive conditions in an old building behind the parsonage. This building contained only two rooms and a pantry. The door to the left of the entrance hall led to the family room/kitchen, in the middle was the milk pantry, and to the right Laestadius's study. Even after the move, he often stayed on Sundays in the old parsonage in Köngäs, where his daughter kept house. Presumably part of the family continued to live there to relieve the overcrowding in their Pajala house.

THE LAST TEN YEARS OF HIS LIFE

Lars Levi's deep affection for his wife is evident from this passage in *The Voice of One Crying in the Wilderness*:

And the woman who most closely corresponded to this ideal has sweetened his [Lars Levi's] earthly pilgrimage so that in this regard there is nothing more to be desired. The twenty-five years of this happy marriage now seem like the only reality in the dream of life. All other joys of life have dissipated; only a dim memory of the past is left.

He wrote to her in September of 1858 from Stockholm where he had traveled to see a doctor about his eyes:

My dearly beloved wife

As I have loved you in life, so I will love you until I die. Perhaps this is the time for me to write you my last farewell. I have come down with a disease similar to cholera. If I don't meet you again in this time of grace, I nevertheless hope that we will meet on Mount Zion with the thorn-crowned King, and that we may look upon Him together and rejoice in the New Jerusalem. Tears of joy have been dropping on this paper. I can't give you any advice other than this: THE LORD WILL PROVIDE HIMSELF AN OFFERING. May the Lord be with you, beloved friend, and He will console you and refresh your heart and help you to bear the cross.

— Good-bye, and greet all the Christians from their dying pastor, good-bye.

Evidently this letter did not get mailed, for later in the same month he was able to add that it was not God's will to take him yet.

On his deathbed nearly two and a half years later, Laestadius reached for his wife's hand with the hand that was not paralyzed, interlocked his fingers with hers, and with his waning strength raised their hands in praise to God. Sofia Wilhelmina Niva described her father's final days in a letter dated August 31, 1861 (excerpts):

A few days before his death, he begged Mama for forgiveness, confessing that he had been impatient with her at times. Before his death one day while he was still able to speak, he first said good-bye to Mama and praised God who had given him happiness in this world and blessed his marriage with mutual affection and joy.

I also said my last good-byes to him. He couldn't say anything to me, because he became very emotional during our farewells. During his illness he was often moved to rejoicing and wanted somebody to read him sermons that he had preached to Christians who were ill. He frequently read the Bible and sang the Hymns of Zion, especially those which told of the reward for those who had fought the good fight and won the victory. I can't really describe to you the expression of joy and peace on his face. Whenever I had the opportunity, I enjoyed sitting at his bedside and observing how a believer leaves this world.

The passing of the faithful shepherd left a sincere longing and sorrow not only among the Christians and awakened but also among the unbelievers. With great heartfelt grief, we, his children, also miss him grieving deeply in our hearts.

Laestadius died on February 21, 1861. Per Lorens Stenborg, his son-in-law and successor, preached at his funeral. His body lay in state in the parlor of the new parsonage that he and his family never got to enjoy, as it was completed six months after his death.

6

Mary of Lapland (Lapin Maria)

Aila Foltz

LAESTADIUS MEETS MARIA

In his periodical Ens ropandes röst i öknen *[The Voice of One Crying in the Wilderness]*, Lars Levi Laestadius wrote:

> In the winter of 1844 I came to the Åsele region of Lapland in the capacity of inspector. I met a few Readers of the more moderate type there. Among them was a Sami (Lapp) girl named Maria who, after hearing my sermon from the altar, opened her whole heart to me. This simple girl had experienced the order of salvation in a way that was totally new to me. She had traveled far and wide, seeking light for her darkness. In her journeys she had at last encountered Pastor Brandell in Nora, and after she opened up her heart to him, Brandell released Maria from her doubts. Through him, Maria came to a living faith. And I thought to myself, "Here is a Mary who sits at the feet of

Wood sculpture which adorns the altar of the Karesuando church depicts Lapp Mary, Laestadius and Raattamaa at the foot of the cross of Christ. Sculptor was Professor Bror Hjort

> Jesus. For the first time now," I thought, "I can see the way that leads to life; it was hidden from me until I had the privilege of speaking with Maria." Her simple account of her pilgrimage and

experiences made such a deep impression on my heart that I, too, saw the light; that evening spent with Maria, I experienced a foretaste of the joy of heaven. But the pastors of Åsele did not understand Maria's heart, and even Maria recognized that they were not of this sheepfold. I shall remember the poor Maria as long as I live, and I hope to meet her in the brighter world beyond the grave.

About this event Laestadius's friend and fellow worker Juhani Raattamaa wrote in *Sanomia Siionista* 1890: 94.

Then he [Laestadius] started to seek salvation. But he did not understand it until the Sami girl, Maria, told him that he should believe his sins forgiven just as he was. That was when he experienced peace through faith in Jesus and started to preach empowered by the Spirit.

It is clear that Maria's story resonated in Laestadius's heart and that this young Sami woman, whom Lars Levi Laestadius called "a Mary who sits at the feet of Jesus," played a central role in his spiritual development.

MARIA'S LIFE STORY

The question of Maria's identity has intrigued individual Christians and scholars alike. Gunnar Wikmark researched the subject and came to the conclusion that there is strong evidence that she was Milla Clementsdotter, whose life story was first published in the Nov. 4, 1840, issue of the Swedish magazine *Nordisk Kyrkotidning*. Although the writer of the article was anonymous, it is believed that he was the Pastor Berglund mentioned in the story. This is not only a story of one woman's spiritual odyssey, it also provides insight into life in Lapland at the time.

Milla (a common variant of the name Maria) was born in northern Sweden on November 1, 1813, the eldest of three daughters of Clements Andersson and his wife Anna who were Mountain Sami. Due to her father's drinking, the family slid into poverty. During one of his drinking bouts, Clements was assaulted and became bedridden, eventually dying of his injuries. Milla's mother subsequently married Torkel Johnsson, who was seven years her junior, and the family joined their nomadic tribe on its annual winter migrations to Jämtland and Ångermanland.

On one of these migrations her parents left six-year-old Milla with a farm family living in Nässjö in Ramsele Parish who consented to take her on as a goatherd and teach her to read. As she was saying good-bye, Anna warned her daughter against taking food without permission. Milla understood, for at home Anna had poured burning coals onto the hands of Milla and her sisters asking, "Does that feel good? This," she said, "is how the fires of hell burn those people who do forbidden things."

Milla, unwilling to be left behind, wept as she watched her family ride away with the tribe in their reindeer sleighs. The farm family hid her clothes to prevent the girl from following. She often crouched in her sleeping place behind the large baking oven crying in her misery and loneliness, especially on Sunday evenings when dances were regularly held in the farm kitchen. One night in late winter while everybody was sleeping Milla, overcome by longing for her family, crept from behind the oven and set off in the direction of her parents' departure dressed only in her underwear and socks. Upon discovering the girl's disappearance in the morning, the farmer left in pursuit taking her clothes with him. Twelve miles away he caught up with her and took her back home.

The family tried to keep their promise to Milla's mother by making some effort at teaching her to read. She had previously learned the alphabet, but learning to read proved difficult, especially under harsh treatment. When she heard the other children reading the catechism, she tried to memorize it but could not retain it for long. Half a year later, Milla was placed in another home in the village of Fly where she was gently taught to read with gifts as an inducement. During the two years she was there, Milla received a catechism from the kindly assistant pastor of Ramsele, Paul Norberg.

After leaving Fly Milla traveled during the winter, as was the custom of the Sami people. She would go from farm to farm singing songs and hymns, and farm families would give her food and other necessities. Sometimes the people were kind enough to let her stay a few days and would give her instruction in reading the Bible and the catechism. Summers were spent herding livestock. Her future seemed brighter when she was taken into foster care by Police Chief Johan Gröndahl and his wife who helped her to memorize the catechism. This happy time in her life was short-lived, however, for her foster parents died, and Milla was forced to resume wandering.

On New Year's Day in 1826 when Milla was thirteen years old, her parents found her in Ström. When her stepfather demanded that she be confirmed, she objected at first because she did not feel that she had sufficient knowledge but then consented to go with him to the senior pastor of Föllinge, Carl Axel Rothoff. The pastor, who was obviously drunk, asked her only three questions, which she answered correctly. He also had her read some passages from the New Testament. She was then presented with the New Testament and given permission to receive Holy Communion.

Back in the region where she was born, a childless maternal uncle promised Milla that he would make her his heir if she would live with him and his wife. Milla stayed with them five years during which her uncle and aunt drank, fought, and gave away their food. Consequently she rarely had enough to eat, often having to resort to grinding reindeer antlers into meal, which she cooked for herself. Day and night Milla herded their reindeer all by herself getting little sleep. At night she would spin yarn for people to get a little income but had to give it up when her uncle discovered what she was doing and whipped her. Through this experience, she came to view drunkenness as a sin.

Milla did not fare much better when it came to nourishment for her soul. Her foster parents hid her books, but she managed to secretly read Peter Jonsson Topp's *En ropande Röst I öknen* [*A Voice Crying in the Wilderness*] which reduced her to tears. Once a year she had an opportunity to travel to church with some other Sami people and receive Holy Communion.

During one visit to the church, her parents demanded that she marry a Sami man who was much older; in fact he was her godfather. She refused, knowing that the man was a drunkard and lacking in Christian virtues. In town she met two Sami boys Lars Larsson and Lars Andersson who shared with her their spiritual quest and the good news of the Gospel they had heard from the lips of Pastor Pehr Brandell in Nora. On their next visit to the church a year later, Milla's parents plotted to get her married off to the Sami man to whom they had promised her. When she would not comply, they pinched her, pulled her hair, and were dragging her forcibly to the pastor to be married when the local teacher, Olaf Wassdahl, came to her assistance. She escaped several times from attempts to lure her into her suitor's arms. Encouraged by Lars Larsson, she decided to travel to Nora and Sollefteå to hear Brandell even though it meant losing the sizable inheritance she had been promised by her uncle.

For two years Milla lived with her parents and some other relatives who had settled in one area to engage in fishing. A younger suitor who was also a drinker and more violent than the last pursued her, and she had to fend him off forcibly. During this period she suffered from a troubled conscience to such an extent that people thought she was out of her mind. To restore Milla's sanity, her family subjected her to various superstitious procedures that were believed to be effective. She spoke to some others about spiritual things and tried to persuade her parents to give up their drinking and to stop working on Sundays. She did succeed in getting them to refrain from Sunday fishing, and her brothers and sisters began to be concerned about the salvation of their souls.

Milla's younger sister suggested that they take turns leaving home to earn money for the family while the other one stayed home. Milla was so overjoyed at the prospect of going to a place where God's Word was proclaimed that she left immediately even though it was nearly evening. Passing through a wilderness area, she arrived in Bergsvattnet where she fell ill suffering high fevers which caused hallucinations. She was afraid she might die and begged for help in finding the way to salvation but turned down offers to get the pastor. She even urged her host family to repent.

After five weeks in which she could not get out of bed, she thought she heard her hosts tell her to leave. She managed to get up and walk a mile and a half to Nybäcken, an effort that took seven hours. There a kind farmer paid someone to give her a ride for another twelve miles, after which she walked three more miles to Hoting. A poor family who felt called upon by God took her into their home to do so. Although it had been agreed that Milla should stay with the family for eight days, she was so anxious to get to Nora that she soon hitched a ride with a group of young people who were going to a dance. The group callously left her on the roadside in a deep forest on a winter night.

Weary and ill, Milla plodded along the road until she collapsed in the snow. Falling snowflakes covered her as she lay unconscious on the road. It was Christmas time, and nobody was abroad at that hour in this sparsely settled region. A short distance from where Milla lay was an isolated farm. The farmer's son had gone visiting with the intention of returning the following day, but he was so overcome with anxiety about his family that he hitched up his sleigh and left for home the same evening. After traveling some distance, the horse shied and stopped abruptly. When the young man alighted to investigate, he found the Sami girl lying in the road covered with snow. He picked her up, laid her in his sleigh and took her home. In the warm house, she recovered enough to continue her journey the next day.

There was again a period of five weeks when Milla was bedridden. This time her parents showed up and took her with them to Sollefteå. When she heard that Pastor Johan Berglund was holding his annual parish catechetical meetings there, Milla was eager to attend. Her parents would not let her go, however, so she left them to find Berglund who had a spiritual kinship with Pehr Brandell. Berlund had experienced living faith in Jesus Christ and emphasized the importance of personal soul care. When Milla expressed her fervent desire for more opportunities to hear the Word of God, Berglund encouraged her to stay and find work tending livestock. From that time on, she returned every summer to work and attend religious meetings.

Still eager to speak with Brandell, Milla set off again for Nora. When her parents learned about her departure, they pursued her and took away her better clothes. In Härnösand she managed to slip away and talk to Baron Hampus Mörner, the governor who is known to have been a Moravian, as well as Major J. W. Wahlstedt. She asked them, "Is it wrong to run away from my parents in order to hear the Word of God?" Receiving money to buy a pair of shoes, she was able to flee from her parents. Along the way she met another woman who was on the same mission, and together they traveled to Nora.

The article does not tell about Milla's visit with Pehr Brandell, but she must have told Laestadius about it because he states in his periodical that "Brandell had released her from her doubts and the girl was led by him to a living faith." A description of Brandell's influence as a well-known revival preacher of the Reader movement in northern Sweden is reflected in the report that the Nora church, which seated over 2,000, was filled to overflowing by people, many of whom traveled long distances to hear his preaching. In a time when preaching in general was superficial, Brandell's message of sin, grace and redemption drew large numbers of troubled souls who desired to hear his proclamation and personally receive soul care from him.

Not much is known about Milla Clementsdotter since that time. According to church records, she married Thomas Pålsson, a Sami farmhand from Frostviken, a few years before she met Laestadius, and she gave birth to a daughter a few years later. The communion record states that the couple would attend communion. The last notation indicates that the family probably moved to Norway.

7

Lars Levi Laestadius as Revival Preacher

Jouko Talonen, Ph.D.

Based on a presentation given at the Midsummer Services in
Muonio, Finland, June 2000.

INTRODUCTION

Lars Levi Laestadius was "man of the year" 2000 in the whole
Arctic region of the Scandinavian countries. The calendar for the
Laestadius project in the Tornio Valley lists over sixty events and
exhibits featuring Laestadius. The revival leader of northern
Scandinavia was of current interest, and he finally received the
recognition for his life's work that he undoubtedly deserved.
However, a question comes to mind: To what extent do people living
in this river valley today understand the spiritual significance of the
work of Laestadius? The Jews during the time of Jesus honored
Abraham, "We have Abraham to our father" (Matthew 3:9). They
valued their historical prophets but they hated our Lord. Martin
Luther is acceptable today as a spiritual advisor to almost all of
Christendom, but are Luther's teachings acceptable to the "pretentious
pagans" of our day?

In this article, I will focus on Laestadius as a revivalist. I will
examine the topic from five different perspectives and attempt to
compare them to the situation in our Finnish Evangelical Lutheran
Church today.

ROWING AGAINST THE CURRENT

It is said that dead fish travel with the current while live fish
struggle against the current. Sometimes fish that have been swimming
against the current for a long time act as if they are deranged or
disturbed. In church history, the prophets and church reformers have
always rowed against the current. They have not chosen their role in
life. This role was assigned to them in God's plan for the world. They

declared God's will to the people of their day because they had an inner compulsion to do so. The Old Testament prophets are a good example. The Hebrew word for prophet, *nabi,* actually means "crier," one who shouts or proclaims. The prophets were compelled to proclaim, or cry out, the will of God to the people of their day—and were discriminated against, pushed aside and out of the mainstream. Jeremiah felt that he had been born "a man of strife and contention" (Jeremiah 15:10). John the Baptist in the dawn of the New Covenant was such a "crying voice." He prepared the way for the Lord. He did not bow down to idols, and we know the results. Church history tells us about Jan Hus and Girolamo Savonarola, the religious reformers and great revivalists. They were all condemned by public opinion and often also by the prevailing organized religion, but their names have remained in history. Who remembers the names of the popes in power during Luther's time? How much have the bishops of Härnösand in the early 1800s been spoken about in the year 2000! We also notice from the life of Laestadius that the same thing still appears to be true. Spiritual awakening is not initiated by the Bishop's Council! Our church tolerates pastors with almost every possible heretical teaching, but if someone truly takes the Bible seriously or begins to rock the National Church [of Finland] boat, the swords are drawn.

Laestadius was a voice crying in the wilderness of his day—the John the Baptist of the Arctic area of Scandinavia. He rowed against the current. He was hated by the world and the State Church [of Sweden]. He recognized this himself, and there was nothing strange about it.

> As soon as the voice of the crier starts crying about repentance, the wolves begin to howl, the bears begin to growl...so that the voice of the chickadee cannot be heard in that place where this amazing sound is coming from.

> Why was Pietism hated? It was because it revealed the hypocrisy of the spiritual fathers and their lack of faithfulness toward Christ. For what reason was the Conventicle Act later revived and made more severe? This was done because the latter prelates feared the Readers. Why were the Readers feared? It was because the Readers disturbed the consciences of the spiritually indifferent and ungodly multitudes. (Laestadius)

THE TENSION BETWEEN BELIEF AND UNBELIEF

The proclamation of Laestadius had a specific aim. It was the same as Apostle Paul's: "We persuade men [to believe]!" (2 Corinthians 5:11). Not all the baptized people of Karesuando had remained in the covenant of baptism. The fruits of their lives revealed this. Laestadius directed his biting and sharp repentance sermons at everybody. You must change! God's Word does not change! God is not the problem—you are!

Laestadius divided his listeners into three categories: the spiritually indifferent [nominal church members and the ungodly], the awakened, and the believers. Living faith was not mere knowledge that I have once been baptized as a child. Although we give baptism its due, we must still dare to say today that the person who has fallen away or forsaken the grace of baptism cannot partake of its blessing. That is why repentance is necessary.

Laestadius's method of dividing listeners according to the condition of their souls is not in the least fashionable today. In our churches, all those who attend are considered true Christians, as if entering a church building makes them holy even though their daily life is ungodly and they break all of the commandments. A person's spiritual condition depends on the revelation of the truth of God's Word to the individual's conscience. Even fire cannot burn this truth. I believe that the homiletics professors of today in the Swedish schools of theology would fail Laestadius in practice preaching, and Peter would not likely receive a good grade on his Pentecost sermon either.

> Woe unto you, scribes and Pharisees, hypocrites! Because ye build the tombs of the prophets, and garnish the sepulchres of the righteous, and say, if we had been in the days of our father, we would not have been partakers with them in the blood of the prophets. Ye serpents, ye generation of vipers, how can ye escape the damnation of hell?" (Matthew 23:29-31,33).

BAPTISM IS NOT EFFECTIVE WITHOUT FAITH

I have already alluded to the teaching of Laestadius that baptism does not do a spiritually indifferent person any good if he does not have a personal faith. Do not misunderstand me. Laestadius did not look down on the sacraments. They are the means of grace established by Jesus himself. Let us not rise up against the Small Catechism. Whether people today live as baptized persons are supposed to is a different story. The preacher, Matti Suo (1861-1927) has reminded us that he who is baptized is obligated to believe. The Bible does not teach that baptism is a magic rite in which salvation is automatic. "He that believeth not shall be damned" (Mark 16:16). By faith we claim the gifts of baptism, and subsequently the true significance of this means of grace is revealed. Laestadius warned seriously against trusting in baptism in a condition of spiritual indifference.

> ...So great is their pride that the supporters of dead faith must rely on their baptism and first communion in order to avoid responsibility for their neglect of contrition, repentance, conversion and new birth (Laestadius).

The church was controlled by the tyranny of the ungodly. The believers, who were the true congregation, were discriminated against.

> The door to the sheepfold is wide open. They not only let in the goats and the rams, but also the dogs and pigs. The sheep are left to stand outside. The swineherds of our day fatten the swine.... But the sheep are despised and called separatists. Thus they want to make it appear that the separatists have separated themselves from the fellowship of the church. But then, what good would it do them to enter the pigsty. (Laestadius)

In his time, Professor Antti J. Pietilä (1878-1932) reminded people of the importance of repentance and conversion as follows:

> Even the most cultured and highly educated members of society have no way to the Kingdom of God besides repentance. The person who does not go in through this gate cannot in the full sense of the word partake of the gifts offered by the Christian faith, the broad vistas into life that it opens up, its life-giving power, and the holy enthusiasm engendered by it... The lifeblood of Christianity, its sustaining power, and the promise of life and peace with God therein is an unknown world to us unless we have repented.

CONCRETE SINS

The characteristic of the proclamation of Laestadius in which he strongly differs from most of the preachers of our day is his directness and concreteness. He mentioned sins by name. It has been said, "household discussions and the secrets of the back room were brought to the pulpit." Laestadius struck with the hammer of the law directly at people's consciences, and they were unable to defend themselves. We know that the repentance sermons of Laestadius were aimed at drunkenness, adultery, reindeer theft, etc. What would the Trumpet of the North proclaim today to Finns living in the power of a selfish, greedy, profiteering spirit? Or to the sophisticated Church of Sweden which has made women's ordination and the equal rights law its new creed and can now give homosexual couples the blessing of the church!

What delightful criticism might he direct at the liturgical renewal in our church–as if the movements of the pastor inside the altar rail or outside of it could be the key to spiritual renewal. Or what would he think of the elite society women who admire the icons and long for the quietness of the convents of the Orthodox Church without even giving a thought to the fact that women's ordination would never be considered in that church.

As for Laestadians of today, it is scary to even think of what he would have to say to us who are guilty before the Lord of being quarrelsome, hard, proud, and divided into eighteen groups. How would he view the revival movements of our day which so easily change from revivals to organizations? Would the evangelist of northern Scandinavia have something to say to those who think that true Christianity is the intellectual, ideological and mechanical reiteration of so-called orthodox teaching? In the 17th century orthodox doctrine was preached, but the people slept in church! Let us allow Laestadius to speak:

> Our most notable preachers do not endeavor to tear, cut, scrape or thrash the Old Adam with the hammer of the law or bare the sword of truth. They do not dare to puncture the Old Adam's poison sac with the blade of truth. They do not have the courage to lance the stinking boils of sin. Neither do they dare to cut away the dead flesh of the conscience so that the sensitive conscience of the old man would not have to bleed and sting until eternity. Instead of puncturing the festering boil, these spiritual quacks place soft poultices on the sinner's stinking boils; instead of cutting away the dead flesh from the conscience, they pour the devil's brew into the wounds of the conscience; instead of scraping, cutting and exposing the rock hard heart, they cover everything with fleece and make the cup clean on the outside (Laestadius).

The exclusive aim of the repentance sermon was to reveal grace to the sinner and to make Christ known. A short quotation from Laestadius: "All you beggars remove the rags of self-righteousness and clothe yourselves in the righteousness of Christ by faith."

COURAGE AND FIRM FAITH

Finally, I want to call your attention to a trait of Laestadius that we could emulate. He was an unbelievably courageous man! He was not afraid of people, neither secular nor religious rulers. Using today's terminology, he was not afraid of public opinion! You can be sure he encountered lots of opposition. Mud was thrown in his face, but Laestadius knew how to give it back. He did not seek his own glory but the glory of the One who had commissioned him. He dared to defy the powers-that-be of his time with the sword of God's Word! And this sword pierced! When the great awakening broke out in Karesuando in the early spring of 1846, it is unlikely that the pastor of the small, unimportant congregation thought this small stream would develop into a current that would roar like a flood over visible and invisible boundaries. The spiritual legacy of Laestadius has been tremendous. In recent years, the international connections of the "Christianity of the Nordic countries" have been often noted. Senator Kaarlo Castrén (1860-1938), a famous Finnish politician, wrote in his well-known biography of Laestadius (1932) as follows:

The amazing awakening rushed down the Arctic mountains like an avalanche

From my earliest childhood—the end of the 1860s or the beginning of the 1870s—I recall how along the Tornio River

Valley this amazing awakening rushed down the arctic mountains like an avalanche, and I imagine I can still hear the mighty sound as of wings beating. In the satellite congregation of the Turtola Parish where I was born people talked about the complete social upheaval brought about by this revival in the wide-ranging village of Pello, which was located some twenty miles north of the church village. The villagers, with rare exceptions, had renounced their sinful life, confessed their sins, compensated for any damage they had done to their fellow men, and set out on the narrow way. From Pello the awakening continued south to the village of Juoksenki, by-passing the church village, and the change it brought about was equally astonishing and radical. Soon the church village also came under the same influence. People asked to have their sins forgiven and were assured of forgiveness. The preachers and other brothers and sisters in faith absolved them in the Name of the Savior, and happiness and bliss radiated from the eyes of those who had been pardoned.

It is true that Laestadianism has spread further than any other revival born in the Scandinavian countries, in spite of the divisions. Unfortunately those of us who preach today, pastors and laymen, do not willingly submit to the role of the cross bearer. Conforming, adapting, and the pursuit of easy alternatives—it is so typical of us! We make carefully considered decisions, we want to be moderate, and we certainly are not fanatics!

People today select their teachers to please their itching ears. They want to avoid the first step in the order of grace, which is being awakened, until they reach hell—but unfortunately then it is too late! We see the spiritual and religious condition of our people. We know the anxiety and distress of our youth! We see the direction in which the sophisticated Euro culture is taking us! That is why we need preachers like Laestadius! We like to speak about the need for revival, and we even pray for it. But if God were to give Finland a great national revival, what would happen? Revival is not likely to come with dogmatic books under its arm. Perhaps we would consider it heretical and a fanaticism to be avoided! Then, once it started to make sense, every organization would begin to draw these sincere individuals into their own group. How horrible! And finally some group would explain that all spirituality up to this point was only imaginary; the true Kingdom of God is only in the one right group. The Holy Spirit is there and only there! This is what happened ten years ago when the spiritual rebuilding of the Ingrian church began. What spiritual panic—all the revival movements in Finland wanted their own group presence in Russia. Fortunately the Ingrian church is standing on its own feet and is moving forward spiritually. God can give us a revival and nurture it—in spite of human nature. This vision gives us hope!

Translated by Miriam Yliniemi

8

The Main Features of the Proclamation of Lars Levi Laestadius

Jouko Talonen

What were the main features of the proclamation of Laestadius? What can we learn from Laestadius today? It is written in Hebrews 13:7, "Remember your leaders, who spoke the word of God to you. Consider the outcome of their way of life and imitate their faith."

THE MESSAGE OF LAESTADIUS

What was the central focus of the message of Lars Levi Leastadius? What was his doctrinal understanding? First we must note that Laestadius did not establish any movement as such. He served in the pastorate, and the early revival was born at the base of his pulpit inside the State Church of Sweden. "Lapp Mary" (Milla Clementsdotter), who had an important role in the spiritual development of Laestadius, belonged to the "Readers" revival movement. Her spiritual father, Pehr Brandell (1781-1841), was a powerful preacher, a Pastor in Nora, Ångermanland. Brandell emphasized the Gospel and was a moderate who mainly identified with the "Old Readers." The spiritual awakening began in the Nora parish in 1819. "The fires of awakening" burned in Ångermanland 1820 to 1830s. The lives of many people were changed. The movement had a pietistic as well as Moravian tone. By adding to these influences the church piety of

The Pajala Church pulpit from which Laestadius preached

Laestadius's mother, the influence of the New Readers, his knowledge of Luther and orthodox theology, we get a general picture of the influences that shaped the doctrine and proclamation of Laestadius.

Laestadius, however, did not create a cohesive system. In his proclamation and teaching, there is a certain tension between the pietistic influences and the orthodox Lutheran views he was taught by the Theological Faculty of the Uppsala University. In spite of this, certain aspects in his understanding of Christianity have received emphasis, more or less leaving their mark on the movement that bears his name.

In his major religious philosophical work, *Dårhushjonet* [translated into English as *The Bedlamite*], Laestadius attempted to prove that there was a distinct system, a "red thread" underlying his proclamation. The mystery of atonement intrigued him, driving him continually deeper into contemplation of this mystery, which even the angels desired to look into. The natural man was controlled by passions such as selfishness, pride, greed, anger, envy, the devil of adultery, and the spirit of lying. These passions also affected a person physically; their effect was felt in the conscience and will.

Laestadius differentiated between living and dead faith. For him, a life of faith was not only doctrine and outward forms, but first and foremost, something experienced and felt in the human heart. The experience of the order of salvation and the moment one experienced the grace of God were "mountain top" experiences to be felt. Living faith was awakening, repentance and the receiving of grace, which was explicitly felt. Living faith had both an objective (God's Word, means of grace) as well as a subjective (order of salvation) basis. Dead faith was blind faith in authority and based only on objective outward foundations. The fear and distress caused by the Law, or godly sorrow, was a prerequisite or condition of living faith.

It is true that a person cannot merit grace by his contrition and repentance; on the other hand, it is also forever true that when a mother gives birth, she experiences distress and no one can be born again without this spiritual distress. The heart must be prepared to receive living faith by sincere remorse and repentance. Therefore, the old man must experience sorrow and distress before a new man can be born. This argument is not only supported by the repentance of David, Peter, and the sinful woman but also Luther's own experience although the rationalists have ridiculed Luther's reflections. But we contend that no one can receive living faith without contrition and repentance. To the doubting we must say, "don't ponder—believe," but not to those who invent their own faith (Laestadius).

The means of grace were not beneficial unless a person had experiential faith. Laestadius's view of the sacraments, which can be discussed at length, firmly related to the question of living and dead faith.

But even the unsophisticated person, who does not feel he has sufficient mental capacity to process all the explanations, finds his faith failing him in life's most important moment when he is lacking a subjective basis for his conviction. He will surely seek power to believe from the sacraments, but that means alone, being purely objective, is not sufficient to calm the conscience. Since he has not gone through the proper order of salvation, he lacks an objective foundation for his conviction, the witness of the Holy Spirit that he is a child of God. When a person claims to himself the word of reconciliation without preceding contrition, repentance and conversion, new birth etc., it becomes simply dead faith and blind belief in authority, founded only on objective principles. It is dead since, according to the testimony of James, it is without works. It is not followed by a change of mind, and it does not renew the heart. It is blind, for it lacks a sense of life and grace. The witness of the Holy Spirit is altogether missing. In short, a faith based merely on opinion, imagination and illusion, without sufficient foundation, leaves a miserable person in despair at a decisive moment (Laestadius).

Living and dead faith were recognized by their fruits. The fruits produced by those who professed dead faith could be like this:

In the life and practice of dead faith there are always contradictions: They pretend to be devout in church but very frivolous in places of entertainment, weep in church and ridicule behind the church, are godly in church and ungodly in the tavern; they pretend to be penitent at the altar but fight at the bar. They bless in the church and curse behind the church; they are moral in the church and adulterers and fornicators behind the church. Briefly said, a person who has a dead faith in his skull can be godly and ungodly on the same day. In one place he is honorable and in another a scoundrel. He blesses and curses, says prayers, and practices witchcraft the same day (Laestadius).

In order that the indifferent as well as the confessors of dead faith would receive living faith, repentance must be preached. The sermons of Laestadius followed the typical thought pattern of revival Christianity: the indifferent, the awakened, and the believers are separate concepts. The grace of Christ had to be revealed to those whose consciences were distressed. The sole purpose of the preaching of the Law was that grace could be revealed to the sinner. In this regard Laestadius represented passion mysticism: Even the hardest heart must break at the vision of the thorn-crowned Savior hanging on the cross. Although the Law was to be declared unconditionally, a sinner had to be able to taste at least a drop of grace so that the heart would be broken and the burden of sin could be lifted from the shoulders. God's power was in the Gospel. Laestadius considered the confession of sins, not only to the confessor father, but also to those against whom the repentant person had transgressed to the extent that it was possible, an important fruit of faith. The fight of faith was struggle and pain but also joy due to that righteousness which was fully prepared by our Savior.

Laestadius related critically to the Church and its pastors. His appraisal of the condition of the Church of Sweden was sharp and even sarcastic. The bishop of Northern Sweden was only lightly criticized; he was the one that endeavored to relate to the Pastor of Karesuando in an objective manner. In relation to society and politics, Laestadius represented the role of keen observer. In many respects he was a conservative: He did not approve of a republic or a democracy. Instead, he spoke of the King with respect. He demanded freedom of religion and that the clergy be removed from representation in Parliament. Laestadius had a social concern for the poor, but he saw poverty partially as a result of sin. Laestadius and his wife, Brita Kajsa, are remembered for helping the poor. He did not speak out on social justice, but he practiced it in everyday life, as the pietists generally did. Laestadius could relate to the ways of the world with indifference; it did not matter to a Christian whether the ruler was Nero or Robespierre, whether he paid his taxes to the American President or the Sultan of Turkey. The main thing was that he lived a life obedient to the law of the land and was concerned about his salvation. One could not expect political action to help in changing people and society. Spiritual awakening, on the other hand, was necessary.

LAESTADIUS TODAY

What would Laestadius preach to us today? A revival movement is in continuous danger of turning into a movement that "lulls people to sleep." It can become absorbed in preserving its own traditions and lose its "salt." Is our Christianity still alive? Are we as individuals in living faith? Each one of us has a reason to pause and face these questions. We do not preach Laestadius or the traditions of our revival but the crucified and risen Christ! In our time, we must be bearers of the torch of truth and the light of the Gospel. L.P. Tapaninen (1893-1982), who was Bishop of Oulu 1963-1965, wrote in 1943:

> Christianity is in constant danger of attempting to assimilate into the lifestyle of the world and trying to avoid offences and conflicts. Thus is born the "light Christianity" which is not "dangerous" to anyone. It, too, can preach powerfully against sin, but as if by secret agreement the sword of the Word is wrapped in sufficient layers of cotton that it does not truly offend anyone.

This is the question for all of us, as preachers of the Word as well as listeners, in this phase of church history. Have we perhaps adapted into this general pattern—the Bible is good, the Church Confessions are good, church law is good—as long as in practice it makes no difference in our lives? Do we present a clear message of the Law and Gospel arising from a conscience bound to the Word of God? Confusing the Law and Gospel continues to be a danger in our churches. In this regard, Laestadius has something to offer to us. Is it not true that church history continually repeats itself, and even today, the pastors committed to the ministry like Laestadius end up in difficulties? Traditions do not help unless they are alive. To admire the revival of the past does not benefit us if in reality we are against the preaching of the Law and the signs of revival. On which side do we stand on the church battles of today? I think Lars Levi, the Trumpet of the North, would present these very questions to us 139 years after his death.

The goal of the Christian is still the land of glory. Even though we remember those teachers who have spoken the Word of God to us, we are before all else to follow the Lord Jesus Christ. Laestadius encouraged the travelers on the road to heaven in his day as follows:

Pay attention to the star of heaven, you weary travelers! Do not become weary in watching and fighting the good fight of faith; do not look down, but look up to where the star shines and follow that star.

Translated by Miriam Yliniemi from the January 2000 issue of the Rauhan Sana

9

True Christianity

FREES US FROM THE BONDAGE OF THE LETTER AND BINDS US TO GOD'S WORD

Sermon by Lars Levi Laestadius on the occasion of his inspection in Sorsele—1/27/1844

"Now this I say, that every one of you saith, I am of Paul; and I of Apollos; and I of Cephas; and I of Christ. Is Christ divided? Was Paul crucified for you? Or were ye baptized in the name of Paul?" (I Corinthians 1:12-13).

Apostle Paul had heard rumors and his traveling companions had related to him that the Corinthian Christians were divided into factions, each one considering itself to be wiser than the other. When some had heard Paul preach, they preferred him; others had heard Apollo, and others Peter, and finally there were a few who had heard the Savior himself preaching.

What took place among the Corinthian Christians often happens in our day: one prefers one preacher over another since preachers are not alike in the way they express themselves and in their manner of speech. In that day the preachers were not alike either in their mannerisms or use of words even though they worked from the same foundation and spoke about the same subject, namely the crucified Christ. This gave the Corinthians a reason to divide into factions and say: I am of Paul, I of Apollos, I of Cephas and I of Christ. The same happens today; when spiritual unity is broken, we begin to weigh words and split hairs. Factions and divisions develop in the congregation. This has occurred from the time of Paul until today.

Paul is pointing out to the Corinthian Christians that this type of doctrinal division and true Christian unity cannot exist together. That is why he imitates their words and ends by saying: Is Paul crucified on your behalf or have you been baptized in the name of Paul? Paul portrays to them how he has humbly and simply preached Christ and Him crucified without the wisdom of the world. He continues in the third chapter, third verse, "For you are yet carnal: for whereas there is among you envying, strife, and divisions, are ye not carnal, and walk as men?" The greatest calamity that the evil enemy of the soul brought to the Christian Church was the carnal spirit of discord. This appeared among the Corinthians during Paul's time and became even more common immediately after the time of the Apostles among those who still seriously sought the grace of Christ.

Even during the great persecution, when the hatchet of the pagans shed the blood of Christians, there were numerous schisms and factions. Each group believed itself to be better than the others, even though they all fought in behalf of the same cause. More factions appeared at the end of the persecutions. The various factions began to persecute each other and condemn the others as heretics, without cause. One faction said: I am right and another I am right; the third and fourth said the same. Who was right? I believe that the one that never involved itself in these semantic arguments but simply remained in the written Word of Christ was right. They often fought fiercely with anger and bitterness over a single religious detail. Who was right? Perhaps he who least weighed his words or letters.

Even in the Lutheran Church of our day there are an endless number of factions that all believe themselves to be right: Moravians, Quakers, Methodists, and Pietists—Who is right? Perhaps the one that least shouts and brags about his doctrine of faith! True Christianity is not in empty words but in spirit and truth. It is in the inward man which is in spiritual unity with the mind of God. In true Christianity the question is not whether there is one letter more or less in the outward confession, but whether the inward spiritual life within the heart rests upon the redeeming grace of Christ.

Whether you are a Jew, Greek, or Lutheran; whether you are a Catholic, Reformed, Pietist, Moravian, or Quaker; A New Reader, Old Reader or whoever; do you believe that dead faith in the letter of the law which your fathers have spelled out before you, and you have followed, will save your soul from condemnation? Do you believe so because you think you literally possess the true confession even though you have no real spirit and life in the hidden recesses of your heart? True faith expresses itself in unity of faith and love. Do you think that God's Spirit allows himself to be shackled and bound by the bolts and locks of dead letters. No thanks, my friend! Christianity does not allow itself to be bound into this or that confession, which is still the work of man no matter how pure and orthodox the doctrine. No, true Christianity is itself free, and makes us free, as the spirit is free which awakens true Christianity. It brings freedom from slavery to the letter of the law. "For, brethren, ye have been called unto liberty" (Galatians 5:13) not into fleshly freedom that the children of this world praise and strive for but into a spiritual freedom which is the essence of the Christian life, "for the letter killeth, but the spirit giveth life" (II Corinthians 3:6).

Therefore, it is not surprising that the Apostle had to encourage the Corinthian Christians to avoid foolish verbal disputes which are not constructive but just the opposite—they destroy and suffocate the spirit and life of Christianity. Therefore Paul says: You are still carnal when you say, "I am of Paul; and I of Apollos; and I of Cephas; and I of Christ. Is Christ divided? Was Paul crucified for you?"

Today it is necessary to repeat and explain the same words. Christianity has been muddled by the many factions and schisms which stand as yoked oxen enslaved by the letter and say: I am a Calvinist, I am a Lutheran, I am a Pietist, I am a Quaker, I am a Moravian, I am a New Reader, and I am an Old Reader. Do you think that God's Spirit would allow himself to be tied to the letter or outward confession? Do you think that a true Christian allows himself to be tied to the dead letter as a dog to a concrete pillar? Do you think that God cannot awaken the Turk and the heathen as well as a Lutheran or a Quaker from the sleep of sin to seek grace? "I say unto you, that God is able of these stones to raise up children unto Abraham" (Matthew 3: 9). This is what John said to the Jews who believed they had the true faith while they were in slavery to the letter of the law.

If Paul were to arise today from the bright morning of Christianity, or John the Baptist were to awaken from the new moon of Christian faith, or Luther were to raise his head from a Christian faith which was soon extinguished in the ruins of the evening dusk—what do you think these men would say upon seeing Christendom split into so many schisms and factions which all think they have the right doctrine? They would surely lament and shed bitter tears over the horrible blindness and terrible darkness with which the enemy of the soul has overcome the blind masses of the world. They go as a herd of swine chased by wolves into a bottomless pit or become entrapped in the web of Satan by being bound under the iron yoke of a dead letter. I do not want to express all my thoughts about the terrible bondage in which the evil enemy binds the conscience of poor souls when they are weighed down by the bondage of the letter. From this follows everlasting bondage.

Under this bondage of Satan, many that have a tender conscience become exhausted when after they are awakened they begin to weigh words and split hairs. This creates factions and doctrinal differences leading to confusion in the core of Christian faith. The spirit and life are extinguished. Living faith turns into a dead letter. The love toward God becomes a cloak of false righteousness. Spiritual pride, the unbearable odor and stench of Satan contaminates preciously redeemed souls with the poison of hypocrisy.

When a person skips over the order of grace and moves directly from a spiritually indifferent state to spiritual self-confidence, then the devil smiles sweetly, for he has won the game. Then the unclean spirit enters the lobby of the hypocritical heart bringing seven other spirits with him, which are seven times worse than he is. Then he and his companions of darkness can rule freely and create chaos like a hungry wolf in a sheepfold, tearing and destroying the helpless sheep. The cataract of false righteousness grows as the scales of a dragon on the eyelids, and it shows its bloodthirsty teeth to everyone who does not voluntarily choose to crawl into his blood red throat.

Dear children, watch out for wolves in sheep's clothing, who want to swallow your souls alive. They approach you cautiously with beautiful words and want to entice you away from the simplicity of Christ referring to their inner light which is not in the Word. When they should show their faith and love toward God and their neighbor by sacrificing a small portion of their earthly goods, they creep away with their tails between their legs like timid dogs. Watch out for these bloated frogs! Spiritual pride has caused them to swell. They crawl over the order of grace and wish to deceive others so they would do the same. But from their fruits you shall know them. The person with the greatest false righteousness finally becomes the greatest deceiver.

I consider this warning most necessary for this congregation where one group has slipped into the terrible darkness of fleshly indifference and the other group weighed down by slavery to the letter has been bound by a knot on their conscience which is difficult to open. No man can untie it unless God, who is gracious toward well-intentioned but lost souls, unties this difficult knot and loosens their tender consciences from the bondage of the letter and lets them taste of the life of spiritual freedom and its essence. Surely there are many here that in all sincerity study the Word, seeking grace, and pray in the stillness of the night with sighs and prayers. In the midst of the howling wolf pack, it is nevertheless difficult for a seriously seeking soul to find the middle road, the narrow gate, which leads home. The wolves howl with all their might, each trying to outdo the other. These are the great saloonkeeper, the great drunkard, the great hypocrite, the fighter, the miser, the adulterer, the dance master, and the bloodsucker or bloodhound. There is a great variety of animals which rise from the bottomless pit and race around each other. One is bleating, another growling, the third howling and barking, the fourth with superstitious notes and sinful whisperings trying to entice the lonely, grace-seeking soul who endeavors to reach the narrow gate of heaven. It sounds like howling from the bottomless pit. It is a great miracle of God if the lonely, seriously seeking soul does not lose his way and stray from the narrow path that finally leads to heaven's gate.

Dear Soul! You, who truly seek grace and the narrow gate of heaven, do not stray from the road. Do not allow the attractive enticements of sin to lead you away from the narrow pathway. Do not listen to those who whisper in your ears, twisting and turning God's clear Word to their own condemnation, but hold fast to the Word. Hold firmly to the anchor and do not let go of your grip on the rock of your salvation, Christ. Do not lose sight of that star which leads to Bethlehem, the Promised Land. If you lose sight of this, you are eternally lost. That star is God's revealed Word. If you wish to find

Laestadius often spoke at the parsonage and other homes where people gathered for services

Christ, follow that star, or you will not find Him. Then you will be your own pastor and your own king. I say no more! He who has even a slight experience of the way of grace understands me well; he, who does not will not understand, for he is blinded by Satan.

May God give grace to those few lonely, grace-seeking souls in this congregation who are like sheep without a shepherd. May God give His grace, peace, and eternal life through the merits of Jesus Christ to those who are lonely and spiritually poor, seeking diligently and honestly for the grace that saves by faith and love in the Lord Jesus Christ. Amen.

Translator's note: This sermon is interesting in that it was apparently found later and published for the first time in January 1994 in the *Rauhan Side*, the Finnish publication of the group which is in fellowship with the Old Apostolic Lutheran Church in America. This was a full 150 years after it was first preached. It was also printed in the October 1998 issue of the *Rauhan Sana* which is the group in fellowship with the Apostolic Lutheran Church of America. The following is a well-researched description of the audience that first heard this message written by Seppo Leivo.

THE READERS OF SORSELE

Seppo Leivo

In reading this sermon by Laestadius the question arises: What was his audience like and why did he speak like this? This sermon, which was preached on January 27, 1844, awakens our curiosity. Laestadius had met Lapp Mary about four weeks earlier. In this sermon we sense some of the freedom, confidence and faith that he had received.

The sermon was intended specifically for the people of Sorsele. The spiritual life of this congregation in southern Lapland had the stamp of the New Readers movement. It was born in the early 1800s and clearly differed from the earlier Old Readers. If we were to make a simplistic comparison of the New Readers to other spirituality of that day, we could say: that the prevailing church teaching at that time was based mainly on virtues and values; the Old Readers were focused on their walk based on their own repentance; the New Readers emphasized the fact that they were helpless in relation to faith and man's only possibility was to claim the redemptive work of Christ by faith. They read Luther's books diligently and became known for their fight against the new church books (handbooks, catechism and hymn book). They knew that the new books clearly differed from the Lutheran Confessions and damaged the church. This is how it unquestionably was.

The New Readers had different modes of expression in different localities. Some were more moderate like Pehr Brandell; some were very severe and harsh. The New Readers in Sorsele had perhaps become more harsh and severe than anywhere else. In addition to that, they had divided into two groups fighting against each other. One of the groups received wide notoriety because of the unusually radical behavior of two central figures, Margaret Mårtendotter and Pehr Köngsson. The situation was delicate for Laestadius because they were his blood relatives being cousins on his mother's side. Their followers were also mainly relatives of Laestadius. The soul of the movement was Margaret or "Mother Greta." These Readers did not approve of baptism performed according to the church handbook; therefore, they baptized their own children. They avoided going to communion and held their own services at the same time as worship services were conducted in church, etc. Especially "Mother-Greta" felt an inward need to proclaim judgment, very vocally, on these books and pastors. This happened even during worship services at the church, and once she even threatened to burn the church. Her faith leaned heavily on her own visions and revelations. Many individual things that they considered vanity, such as a hair comb and coffee, were severely judged. All these peculiar issues had become such a central focus in Sorsele that they threatened to obscure the essence or core of Christian faith.

The inspection sermon of Laestadius reflects in plain words his criticism of the Reader group because of their judgmental spirit toward one another and their semantic arguments. At the same time he rebuked them for their blind orthodoxy [emphasis on right doctrine], spiritual pride, hypocrisy, and for the fact that they set their own inner light above the Bible. On the other hand, Laestadius related to them with warm understanding and spent the day after his inspection tour with the Readers. He discussed their problems and tried to reconcile their differences. He also rewrote their lengthy letter to the church leadership explaining their religious viewpoints and requesting, among other things, that the old church handbook be used again in worship services.   Although Laestadius himself criticized the church rather severely, he considered it a mistake that the Readers and other awakened made major issues of secondary matters.   Laestadius always wanted to emphasize living faith and Christianity of the heart and keep that at the forefront.

By the time of the inspection, the heat of the battle had dissipated to some degree.   In her old age Greta said that many things which she preached about were only secondary issues with which pride, her own flesh, and the enemy of the soul filled her, robbing her of the most important thing, which is faith in Christ and His presence.

Translated by Miriam Yliniemi

10

Parables by Laestadius

Laestadius was noted for his amazing mastery of language and his allegorical expression. He explained spiritual matters by taking illustrations from the everyday lives of the people and their surroundings. He often wove these into his sermons without further explanation.

His messages were conversations from heart to heart. They contained austerity, irony, judgment, persuasion, tenderness, love, good humor and sarcastic satire. He was a master in the use of unique expressions, parables from everyday life, and Lapp mythology. His Scripture quotations reached the intended target. He knew the rhythm of words and phrases. He repeated and accentuated. Often, his sermons concluded in a powerful, consoling, poetically beautiful, uplifting tone.[5]

The following selections are translated from *Katso Jumalan Karitsa (Behold the Lamb of God),* excerpts from the sermons of Laestadius, compiled by Pekka Lappalainen in 1978. Note the word pictures.

SHEPHERD DOGS

The sheep follow the shepherd and know his voice. The sheep also recognize one another from their voice and scent. But all sheep are not so obedient that they will immediately come to the shepherd. Some sheep are proud and escape into the woods; therefore the shepherd sends his dogs to gather these straying sheep into the flock. A shepherd, who has many sheep, cannot get along without dogs.

We know that an ordinary dog is more valuable to his Master than a lazy servant. We also know that a Master values a good dog who is diligent in barking and gathering scattered sheep and has a keen nose for detecting the scent of wild animals.

---

[5] L.L. Laestadius. *Katso Jumalan Karitsa.* compiled by Pekka Lappalainen. Jyväskylä, Finland 1978.

A lazy dog is one that will crawl under the bed and think he can stay there when the Master calls him to go with him. What does a Master do to a dog that never barks? I think that mute dogs that never bark will probably be hanged.

The way the dog is trained is very important. Some dogs bark aimlessly in the midst of the flock. They scatter more than they gather. Some go to the front of the flock and bark. But the best sheep dog is one that barks from the rear of the flock.

When the goats come to steal the food of the sheep, the Master sends his dog to chase the goats away and they bleat pitifully if the dog bites them. However, if the dog begins to bite the sheep, his teeth will be filed down.

The dogs chase the sheep from the mountains of pride to the valley of humility. If the sheep climb from the meadow of morality to Mount Sinai, the Master sends his dogs to drive the sheep from Mount Sinai to the hill of Golgotha, where they can rest awhile and behold how the Good Shepherd in that great struggle gives his life for the sheep.

On the Hill of Golgotha some drops of reconciling blood will sprinkle on the sheep. The wolf, who fears the blood of the Lamb of God, does not dare touch the sheep as long as they rest on Golgotha since the blood of the slain Lamb of God is a deadly poison to the wolf. If this blood clings to his teeth, the teeth become dull and fall out. ... Even the scent of the Blood of the Son of God makes the wolf howl. The wolf cubs have the same nature. They howl pitifully if they detect the scent of the sheep upon which the blood of the Lamb of God has been sprinkled.

The wolf is not only angry at the shepherd but also at the dogs whom the shepherd has sent to gather the sheep. The wolf is not angry at mute dogs that do not bark at anyone. All the wolf cubs are angry at the dogs that diligently bark because these are the ones that prevent the hungry wolves from getting their meat. The hungry wolf cannot tear and maul the sheep as long as the shepherd dog returns the straying sheep to the shepherd...

It is not pleasant to the old Adam to be a dog. When the goats and rams butt the dogs and the sheep are scattered and running after mushrooms, even the dogs become tired and exhausted.

Do you not see that the sheep have an advantage over the dogs? The sheep are led into a shelter when the Great Shepherd has gathered them with His dogs. The dogs are given bones and broth and then sent to the porch to bark at thieves. Therefore, the position of a dog is not pleasing to the old Adam.   Nevertheless, do not crawl under the bed, you goat and sheep dogs, but be diligent in barking at the beasts of the forest, so that the Master can hunt down the beasts and take care of the goats which come to eat the food of the sheep, the scattered sheep which do not wish to stay with the flock, and the fat sheep that butt and shove the weaker ones.   The Master knows well that your job is not easy.

The Shepherd holds you in high esteem even though He only gives you broth and bones and may have to send you out of the warm shelter to bark at thieves.

However, we are assured that when frosty weather comes and you begin to whine and scratch the door, the Master will say to His servants, "Let the dogs in."   Then you can be in the Master's house and rest until morning.   There you can stay next to that fire which Jesus came to kindle on the earth...

You few souls who have realized that a household cannot get along without a dog, pray to the rich, great and high Master of the house that He who feeds the dogs and the thieves who come to beg for food from Him would help me, a wretched dog, hated by the thieves of grace, to be a faithful house dog.   May I be diligent in barking at thieves so that no one could steal grace goods from the Heavenly Master's storehouse because of my laziness...

Also, if possible, that I would be a sheep dog suitable for shepherding and keeping the flock together when the proud sheep begin running too fast, scattering, trampling the pasture, and butting the leaner sheep until the Chief Shepherd gathers them into the sheepfold when the sun sets and the door is closed.

FISHERMEN

It appears as if the whole keg of fish is now rotting.   This is perhaps caused by the fishermen being too lazy to check their nets. They do cast their nets into the sea according to the command of the Savior but they are negligent about checking them.   If a fish is caught in the net, it dies there.   If the fishermen are not diligent in checking their nets the dead fish soon rot in the warm water.

Secondly, the fishermen are blind.   When they should be gathering the fish into containers, they do not have the knowledge to sort the fish and throw out the spoiled ones, instead, they mix the fresh fish and the spoiled fish in the same containers, even though the Savior has said that the spoiled fish should be cast away...

Thirdly, the fishermen of today are without salt or their salt is no longer salty. It has lost its savor, as the Savior says to his disciples, "Ye are the salt of the earth: but if the salt have lost his savour, wherewith shall it be salted?" ... The fish will soon rot no matter how much salt is used if the salt is no good. It is not a wonder if the fish spoil when they are first allowed to rot in the net and then salted with poor salt. ...

We thank our heavenly Father for those few fish already caught and hope that the fishermen will become more diligent in trying their nets and obtaining salt that has not lost its savor. We hope that not many of the fish that have already been caught in the net of the Holy Spirit become spoiled.

We hope for a greater catch of fish in the future as the fishermen cast their nets according to the command of Jesus from the right side of the boat. Peter was amazed at the great catch of fish that he received in one day, from one draught.... The more he saw the blessing of God that followed his work, the more he felt his sinfulness. The more he experienced God's grace, the more humble he became.

Oh that all those on the same road as Peter who have themselves experienced God's grace and His merciful love would unite in prayer to our Lord Jesus Christ that all spiritual fishermen would be successful in catching souls from the world and from the power of the devil....

Dear Savior, be our advisor on how to cast and draw the net so that even a few fish might be released from the net of Satan and through your Holy Word become enclosed within the net of the Holy Spirit.

THE NET

The net of the Holy Spirit is not woven of fine, soft, silk thread like the net used by Satan to catch fish... The net of the Holy Spirit is of strong cord made of the best hemp fiber available. It is so strong that the scales are pulled off the fish that swims into this net. Therefore, the proud fish fear the net of the Holy Spirit. They know instinctively that this net will hold no matter how large the fish that is caught.

The fish do not very willingly enter into the net of the Holy Spirit. The fish do not get caught at first, even though the fishermen draw in the net. Certain fish, which are very proud, go over the net and spring to the surface and show their tail to the fishermen. Some fish sink into the mud and allow the net to pass over them. Often the fishermen may work all night and catch nothing.

Some fishermen do not care much about catching souls for the Kingdom of Heaven, especially those who are only fishing for wages. They borrow silk thread from the prince of this world and make delicate nets. They use liquor for the upper portion and the honor of the world for the lower portion with natural inclinations and empty tears bringing up the rear. This type of net is light and easy to draw, but it catches no fish. Their net is surely full of fish, but when the rear of the net is brought to shore, it is empty...

The net of the Holy Spirit used by spiritual fishermen to catch souls for the Kingdom of Heaven is woven of the strongest hemp, whereas the nets of Satan are fine and soft as a spider's web. A sinner does not know when and how he got entangled into the nets of Satan....Fish entrapped in Satan's net can spend their time in the lust of the flesh and sensual pleasures....But the nets of the Holy Spirit are felt in the depths of the heart.

The person caught in the net of the Holy Spirit immediately becomes powerless. The heart begins to ache. He has such a deep longing that his heart is about to break. He is no longer able to swim in sin. He is no longer able to drink liquor, curse or fight. The intent of the Holy Spirit is to cause a sorrow pleasing to God which leads to repentance unto salvation through contrition, repentance, conversion and new birth.

May the Lord Jesus Christ give all spiritual fishermen success in catching fish for the Kingdom of Heaven. May the net of Satan break and the net of the Holy Spirit enclose a great multitude of fish when we launch out into the deep and let down the nets for a draught.

Translated by Miriam Yliniemi.

11

Juhani Raattamaa

(1811-1899)

Uuras Saarnivaara

THE GREATEST LAY LEADER OF THE LAESTADIAN MOVEMENT

By the last years of Laestadius's life the leadership of the revival movement was essentially in the hands of Juhani Raattamaa. After Laestadius's death Raattamaa was known and acknowledged as the spiritual leader of the movement. The Chief Shepherd Himself had assigned him to this demanding and difficult post, preparing him with the necessary gifts, both natural and spiritual.

CHILDHOOD, YOUTH AND CONVERSION

Juhani Raattamaa was born in 1811 in the Kuttainen village of Karesuando the son of a pioneer farmer and juryman (member of a standing jury). His father was a "God-fearing" man who tried to follow the requirements of God's law. When he discovered that it was impossible, he came to the conclusion that only those who died in infancy had any hope of inheriting eternal life. This was before the beginning of the Laestadian revival. His mother was a gentle, pious woman who often spoke to her children  about God, death, judgment and heaven. "My mother's loving, warmhearted teachings touched my heart," Raattamaa said later, "but they did not lead me to true repentance and salvation."

At fifteen years of age Raattamaa became seriously ill. His conscience began to accuse him of his sins, and he felt as if death and hell had opened their jaws to swallow him. In vain his father tried to comfort him by saying that God's grace was for the penitent. "I'm not penitent enough," the boy said. For a long time after recovering from his illness, he was so depressed that people were concerned for his sanity. While in confirmation class, he confessed his sins to Laestadius, but he did not experience release from guilt or come to faith. No wonder: this took place in 1829, a time when the way to life and salvation was still unknown to Laestadius himself.

During the confirmation instruction, Laestadius was impressed by Raattamaa's exceptional talents. He felt that the boy would make an excellent teacher, catechist, for one of his circuit schools. Because the Sami people [Lapps; indigenous people of Lapland] moved from place to place with their reindeer herds, it was impossible to establish permanent schools. The catechists traveled with them, teaching the Sami children to read and write. At the same time, they taught them the basic truths of Christianity and their civic obligations.

There were no teachers' colleges in Lapland, so Laestadius had to provide the necessary training for the teachers himself. Raattamaa became such a skillful teacher that Laestadius said, "The Savior says that the disciple is not greater than his master, but I have to say in this case that the disciple is indeed superior to his master." Raattamaa had one failing, however: he had a tendency to drink. Lacstadius rebuked him for this vice many times but without success. After the revival began, Raattamaa himself understood that it was a sin, and he begged for forgiveness every time he succumbed to temptation. He did not, however, succeed in overcoming the habit until he had experienced new birth soon after the revival started. This is what he says:

Many and long were the occasions when I listened to his [Laestadius's] advice and spiritual counsel. At times it was as if the Gospel bell were ringing in a joyful day of freedom to my soul—but then again I felt like I was a slave under a yoke, as if a noose were tightened around my neck and I was choking. During happier times I even preached to others, proclaiming repentance and conversion, but in between I was appalled at myself. For about a year I was tossed back and forth between faith to unbelief. Then dawned the unforgettable day when I received the grace to look with the eyes of the spirit upon the bloody and thorn-crowned King. The sufferings of Christ produced in me a living power that I had never known before; I believed that now my sins were forgiven in the blood that was sprinkled on my heart. An unspeakable sense of the risen and living Lord Jesus overwhelmed me. That which I had been seeking from afar was now present within me and brought joy and peace to my soul. I was ashamed of my unbelief and realized that before this I had never believed with my whole heart.

This change took place in the beginning of 1846 while Raattamaa was listening to Laestadius's sermon in the Karesuando church. New anxieties began to oppress him soon afterwards, and while struggling with these, he fasted and prayed. As he was lying on a reindeer skin in his room one day, he saw a door opening and the devil himself coming towards him. Terrified, he jumped up, but then the assurance of Jesus' atonement overwhelmed him and he cried out: "Come on, Satan, if you dare. Jesus is living in my heart." At that, the devil withdrew. Raattamaa heard these words spoken in a clear voice: "My grace is sufficient for thee: for my strength is made perfect in weakness." A sense of God's grace and love filled his heart. He entered into life in the power of the risen Christ and the Holy Spirit.

AS A CATECHIST

In 1847 Laestadius wrote to the Swedish Mission Society and proposed that a mission school be established in the Lainio village of Jukkasjärvi parish and that Raattamaa be appointed as its teacher. His proposal was approved, and from the beginning of 1848, Raattamaa taught in the Lainio school. As it turned out, the "mission schools" in the area were not maintained or supervised by the Swedish Mission Society. They operated entirely in the service of the Laestadian movement and were maintained partly by the state and partly by contributions from believers of the Laestadian movement. Laestadius was in charge of their organization and supervision for the eleven years during which he served as inspector of the Tornio [Torne region] parishes and also as superintendent of the school system. Thus, he was able to establish these schools strategically in places that appeared beneficial to the spread of the revival at any given time. Several schools were operating simultaneously with suitable teachers who had come to faith through the revival movement. These schools presented an excellent means for spreading the revival, because the Conventicle Act prohibiting devotional meetings led by laymen was not applied to devotional periods in schools. The student body included teenagers and adults who attended the devotional meetings held there. In addition, the fact that Laestadius was in charge of the church work and educational system in these parts was an advantage.

Reinholm Vormbaum, the director of the Kaiserswerth Deaconess Institute in Germany, visited Raattamaa's school. He gives the following account of his visit:

> Raattamaa conducts his school in a shabby, dimly lit thatch-roofed cottage. There the children sit day in and day out learning to sound out words and recite from memory. The most advanced fluently read the sacred Word of God from the Bible in a high-pitched voice, and Raattamaa explains it simply and in a way that children can understand. The children listen most intently and eagerly. In fact, the children display a remarkably good knowledge and understanding of the basic truths of Christianity. The teacher himself carries out his vocation with marvelous seriousness, diligence, love, and patience, and for that reason he very rarely needs to use physical punishment with his pupils. Even some adults who have never been taught before have become very eager to learn in order to read and understand the Word of God for themselves. When he explains the Holy Bible or otherwise talks about the way of salvation, it is done in a sweet and gentle manner so easy to understand that the hearers' attention is riveted on him the whole time. His neighbors say that they wonder when he rests, for he spends his nights in conversations with them, teaching them as well as older and younger people who have not had an opportunity to meet with him during the day. He starts and ends every school day with a devotional service which includes hymn singing, readings and admonitions to the people.

Laestadius describes Raattamaa and his work thus:

> He labored unceasingly day and night. He only slept for a few hours towards morning, and it was truly amazing that he did not become completely exhausted. But he has a good constitution and good health and is in his prime; he has a high forehead, large and lively eyes, a voice that is powerful but also resonant and resilient. He has the ability to modulate his voice to fit the subject covered. He takes the smallest children onto his lap, hugs them and talks to them in a touching manner which goes straight to their hearts, and before long the children are in tears. He has never had to use the switch.

Villagers in large numbers came to the school to attend Raattamaa's evening meetings where hymns were sung, Laestadius's sermons were read, and prayers were raised up. An important part of these meetings were the discussions afterwards which often lasted till the wee hours of the morning.

After Raattamaa had been working in Lainio for about a month, the largest liquor dealers in the village were pricked in their consciences. Here is Laestadius's account:

> An intense battle and struggle commenced against the liquor dragon, which had its own soldiers and representatives in the school. The most educated tried to defend the usefulness and need for liquor with Bible verses, but Raattamaa was so well versed in the Bible that he was able to contradict them with other Bible verses. At last a few tavern keepers were so shaken that they decided to pour out their liquor on the ground.

According to Laestadius, many Sami were aghast at such "waste of God's grain." But it turned out that when news of these events spread to neighboring parishes, great numbers of people went to Lainio to see this remarkable teacher. Some came to argue with him, but many of them had to leave with broken hearts and the feeling that they did not yet have a gracious God or true Christianity.

THE "DISCOVERY" OF ABSOLUTION

The revival spread from Lainio like wildfire, and many other "mission schools" were also centers for spreading it. Broken by the proclamation of Laestadius, Raattamaa and many others, people who had lived in godlessness and indifference often writhed on the floor in their inner torment. For nearly eight years, from the beginning of the revival, the Gospel was proclaimed generally to the penitent and the merciful heart of the Heavenly Father was made clear to them. Many came to faith by this means and rejoiced. Some, however, did not receive an assurance of forgiveness and personal faith in this way. When many convicted souls enquired about the way to peace, Raattamaa felt the necessity of finding a better and more effective means for helping them. He had often read the chapter on confession and absolution in Luther's Small Catechism and even taught it to others, but he had not had the courage to put it into practice. He was further enlightened and assisted in this matter by Luther's sermon for the first Sunday after Easter in his Church Postil, where the Reformer explains Jesus's words in John 20:21-23: "As my Father hath sent me, even so send I you... Receive ye the Holy Ghost: Whose soever sins ye remit, they are remitted unto them; and whose soever sins ye retain, they are retained." The Reformer further said:

> But if absolution is to be proper and powerful, it must be founded on the command of Christ, which is as follows: I absolve you from all of your sins, not in my own name or in the name of some saint, neither for the sake of any human merit, but in the name of Christ and by the power of His command, whereby He has commanded me to say to you that your sins are forgiven you; thus it is not I but He Himself who forgives you your sins by means of my mouth; and it is your duty to receive this and always believe it, not as the words of mere men but as if you had heard it from the mouth of Christ the Lord Himself.

> For although only God has the power to forgive sins, we must know, however, that he exercises that power through this external office.... He relegates the remission of sins to this public word and office in order that it would always be with us, in our hearts and on our lips. There we shall find the forgiveness of sins and deliverance from sins. We should know that wherever we hear such words proclaimed to us at the command of Christ, there we are bound to believe them just as if Christ Himself had declared them to us.

> If you are sorrowful and under the burden of sin and fear of death, which is God's eternal punishment for sin, and you hear from your pastor - or if you don't have one, from a nearby Christian - words of consolation that sound like this: "Dear friend, be of good cheer..., for Christ...came for sinners..., commanded His servants who have been called to the office for this purpose, and in cases of need, every Christian, to console one another on His behalf and absolve one another in His name.... For this reason you should believe him...as if Christ Himself were present, laying His hand on you and declaring absolution to you.... Christ ordained a comfortable kingdom on earth in saying, "As the Father hath sent me, even so send I you." Here He consecrated us all priests to proclaim to one another the forgiveness of sins.

Encouraged by these teachings of Luther, Raattamaa pronounced absolution in the name and blood of Jesus for the first time early in the year 1853 to a woman who was under conviction of sin.[6] This took place in the Markettavaara village of Gällivare parish where the mission school was located at that time. Pastor Aatu Laitinen (Raattamaa's younger contemporary) tells about this event:

An awakened woman servant who had to be home at a certain time was present at the meeting. The time approached for her to leave and her distress increased because she had to leave with her burden of sin. Then Raattamaa asked her whether she believed that they were people of God. To that the servant said she did. Did she believe it to be the grace of God if they were to testify to her on God's behalf that her sins were forgiven; she promised to believe that, too. At that Raattamaa laid his hands on her and pronounced upon this grieving soul that most precious divine assurance that can be pronounced to a human being on this earth. And the effect was immediately evident in the servant's great joy. And so she went home rejoicing like the Ethiopian eunuch of long ago. Raattamaa says that from that day forward, he was convinced that the keys of the kingdom of heaven are to be used in the church of God for the salvation of people.

Raattamaa reported this incident to Laestadius. The latter studied the Bible, the Lutheran Confessions, and Luther's writings and came to the conclusion that Raattamaa had acted properly. After this the use of absolution in the church, that is, in the fellowship of believers, became very central in the Laestadian movement. It was used generally in sermons and individually in confession. Through the influence of this movement it has also come into widespread use elsewhere, especially in Finnish Christian circles, bringing to thousands release and a saving knowledge of Christ.

Raattamaa emphasized that it is necessary for a person through the preaching of repentance, that is the law, to taste in his conscience the holy wrath of God and thus experience such fears in his conscience that his heart would open up to accept and embrace the grace of forgiveness. But only at the foot of the cross, when the individual has a

---

[6] Raattamaa wrote about this in the *Kristillinen Kuukauslehti [Christian Monthly]* 1881, p. 180: "The spiritual movement had been spreading for six years before I truly came to embrace freedom. From that time forward we, along with some brothers and sisters, started using the Keys of the Kingdom of Heaven. People under conviction [of sin] began to experience freedom, and prisoners of unbelief were loosed from their bonds."

revelation of the sufferings and bloody sacrifice of Christ, does his heart truly break and melt. Mere preaching of the law does not bring this about. The person who is under conviction and humbles himself to repent receives the grace of justification and salvation when he hears and believes the Gospel of atonement for his sins and forgiveness in the name and blood of Jesus. A person experiences new birth when the Holy Spirit reveals this grace to his heart, thus igniting faith. The book W*ritings of the Elders of Our Time* contains Raattamaa's explanation:

> This, then, is the place where the new birth occurs: Come, stony heart, and stay at the foot of the cross to pray that the Spirit of the Lord would illuminate in your heart how you have nailed God's only Son to the cross with your sins and pierced his veins with your sin spear, causing them to bleed. But unbelief enters the hearts of many while they are looking at it,...and then the Lord must send verbal preachers. The Lord Himself explained what the Scriptures said about His sufferings and resurrection, and even now he sends people in His name and power to rightly explain the Scriptures to awakened consciences and assure them all of the forgiveness of sins in the blood of Jesus. Even now he commands us to proclaim to the penitent the forgiveness of sins, just as all of you who have come to a living knowledge of the Lord Jesus through faith have come to know and feel it in your hearts.

A person whose conscience is awakened may indeed read the Bible and pray because he feels an inner compulsion to do so, but he also needs to have the Holy Spirit which, through the "spoken word" within the Christian fellowship, reveals to him the Scriptural Gospel of Jesus's atonement for sin and forgiveness in His blood. In the same book Raattamaa says, "Servants are needed to clothe the prodigal son in his father's house so that he may comprehend and preserve the freedom in his conscience."

The believer still retains his corrupt flesh against which he must struggle in daily contrition and repentance putting it to death through the Holy Spirit. He may, nevertheless, continue to believe in Christ as his righteousness and have assurance through His blood. Raattamaa says:

> Let us walk in the Spirit during this brief time knowing that the Old Adam and the works of the flesh must be put to death through the Spirit. For that reason we are breakers of the law day after day. But Christ's fulfillment of the law is the special perfection of us

believers [a perfection which is our own]. It is God's gift to us that we sinners are holy and righteous, even fulfillers of the law through Christ. Let us then take possession of His innocence as our own innocence and His righteousness as our own righteousness.

Raattamaa and Laestadius felt a kinship of spirit to the very end. They had a harmonious relationship in spite of the fact that they had different emphases in their understanding of Christianity. Aatu Laitinen writes:

Laestadius was first and foremost a preacher of repentance, a John the Baptist, under whose passionate preaching people were awakened and were thrust into such distress over their sins that Raattamaa considered it—at least during Laestadius's lifetime—to be his main calling to bind up the wounded, console the grieving, and raise up the awakened from their terrible anguish and affliction by means of God's promises of grace.

Laestadius and Raattamaa thus complemented each other in a superb way. Each of them worked for the salvation of souls in accordance with the talent he had received. One of the differences between them was that Laestadius emphasized the importance of avoiding manifestations of worldliness in external things such as dress, whereas to Raattamaa, the most important thing was the state of the heart, which in itself had an effect on the outward life. The latter's way of thinking is illustrated by the following recorded conversation between him and a certain lay preacher who emphasized a denial of the world in external things:

Must the people from the town of Rovaniemi as well as others be like us Laplanders? asks Raattamaa. The man: Certainly not. Raattamaa: How is it, then, that you expect the officials and the gentry to look like the poor laborers and farmers? Answer: But the Apostle doesn't recognize any difference between the gentleman and the farmer.—Raattamaa says: Luther does, though, and even the Apostle says, Submit yourselves to every ordinance of man for the Lord's sake. They should at least be allowed to keep the clothes that they had when they became Christians, because it would be too great a loss if they had to destroy them. The important thing is that vanity and extravagance are removed. If too much is required of them, they will be afraid of Christianity. We must permit them to behave differently from us in accordance with their means. I place so little importance on external things. Just so they have become Christians in their hearts.

AS LEADER OF THE REVIVAL MOVEMENT

After Laestadius died in 1861, Juhani Raattamaa became the preacher and leader who was generally trusted and who had more spiritual authority than anybody else. Under his leadership most of the movement became more evangelical than it had been when it was dependent on Laestadius. Raattamaa had a special talent for leadership. He did not lord it over the people but rather governed by the Holy Spirit. When he was not on "mission trips," he lived in his home in Saivonmuotka village in Karesuando parish. This village became the center of the Laestadian movement for nearly four decades after the death of Laestadius. Raattamaa wrote hundreds of letters from there, in which he gave advice regarding Christianity and direction in practical matters relating to the movement. His farm was the largest and best cultivated in the village. When he was at home, friends gathered there even from long distances. Hjalmar Westeson writes:

> If some traveler came to Saivo, be it night or day, he could always be certain of receiving lodging at Raattamaa's house. It was not in the least unusual for the old man himself to take the container of *viili* (a cultured milk similar to yogurt) down from the milk shelf and a loaf of bread from the table drawer. He was obviously happy to see visitors in his home, be they rich or poor.

The Raattamaa house in Saivomuotka

Oskar Immanuel Heikel tells about his visit to Raattamaa's home:

> We did not reach Saivonmuotka until the wee hours of the morning. We stayed there for eleven hours, during which time old

Raattamaa talked to me diligently about the teachings of the Bible regarding new birth and explained the parable of the Good Samaritan and other doctrines of Christianity.

During Raattamaa's time, there was much talk about the "spiritual government" of the congregation composed of preachers together with other Christians who were enlightened by God's word. Raattamaa explained spiritual government thus:

It is the office of the Holy Spirit which the congregation executes in the Lord's name, not only through the preaching office. Govern then, dear brothers, according to Christ's teachings and ordinances, and the church will hold together. If disagreements and quarrels separate preachers, let the church decide between them and govern them, ...and those preachers are proper who listen to the Church, which has received the Holy Spirit...God is the master of the church and the home and Christ the head of the church, but preachers are not like beasts of burden or servants. Let us content ourselves with this high calling, to be allowed to be man and woman servants of God and His church. O you Finnish preachers, work to keep God's flock together no matter how far it spreads. It is my belief that the church will hold together as long as it is governed according to Christ's teachings and ordinances.

As emigrants from Finland as well as the other Scandinavian countries went to America in ever-increasing numbers, there were Laestadian believers among them. A large flood of immigrants from the Laestadian areas of Scandinavia began to arrive in the 1850's and then increased as the turn of the century approached. The first church to be organized by Laestadian Christians was established in the Copper Country of Upper Michigan in 1872, and it was called "Apostolic Lutheran." Since that time American followers of Laestadius called themselves "Apostolic Lutherans." Raattamaa kept in close touch with the brothers and sisters in faith living in the New World both by letter and by sending preachers to them. During the last decades of his life, dissension and divisions began to appear within the revival movement, primarily in America. Raattamaa repeatedly urged the believers to love one another and maintain unity "in order that the Lord's flock might stay together." He realized that making radical judgments would only worsen the situation and promote division. He avoided them himself and warned others against "making radical judgments when serious disagreements developed" so that the flock of believers would not split into factions. After divisions developed, Raattamaa acknowledged that both sides in the dispute included true believers. Unfortunately, this principle and example of Raattamaa has not always been followed in the Laestadian movement.

Raattamaa's open-mindedness extended to other revival movements as well, and he acknowledged that God was working within them. He often expressed the wish "that all of the revival movements would join together in one sheepfold according to the Word of the Lord." In 1871 he wrote, "Let us hope that all of the revival movements will some day be united, those which have left the state church as well as the Baptists, Methodists, Hedbergians, and even those living Christians who have separated themselves from the world but live within the [state] church, so that all of them would love one another, be they called by whatever name; since the leaven in all the bread mixing bowls is similar, let the bakers mix the dough into one batch." Raattamaa's close friend, J. Takkinen, wrote to Bishop F. L. Schaumann, "We don't want to say that there isn't any Christianity anywhere besides our group." Another close preacher brother of Raattamaa's, Erkki Antti Juhonpieti, wrote a letter together with O. Lindstedt to "our brother Moody," telling him "that he even has brothers and sisters this far away in the North." Aatu Laitinen wrote, "If all born-again Christians were to know about each other, surely the Lord's true dough would be larger than what is now evident. For they would surely recognize us as brothers, and we would understand that we are one in the Spirit."

Raattamaa and those who were in agreement with him were of the opinion that people who believed according to the Bible, be they in whatever church or group, will be saved. The outward church or organization does not determine whether somebody is a child of God; what determines that is whether he is born again and whether he has the right faith and doctrine.

When a distrust and rejection of the state church and its pastors cropped up in some Laestadian circles, Raattamaa did not join in. It did not make any difference to him whether an individual was a pastor of the state church or a layman. What was important was whether he was a believer, a Christian. His ideal was a living community of believers within the national church, with the revival movement and the church supporting each other in leading people to the way of the Lord.

With regard to the question about the relevance of God's law to the Christian as a guiding principle for his life, which has aroused much controversy in the Laestadian movement, Raattamaa's stand was Biblical: The law of Moses is not a guide, but the law of Christ is. He wrote, "Let us adhere to the teaching of the prophets, Christ and the apostles, even the law of Christ, that we should love one another in the hope that through the blood of Christ we might retain the victory until the end." Within Christ's church there should not only be the preaching of grace and the Gospel of forgiveness. There should also be the teaching of how Christians should live, seeking to please God in all things, doing His will. For that reason those who proclaim "the Gospel leaving out words of advice, admonition and correction to the Christians" do not preach properly. Raattamaa's letters and speeches to the believers include plenty of admonition, instruction and exhortation to repentance for sins and shortcomings relating to their pilgrimage and sanctification.

For Raattamaa God's church which is composed of born-again children of God was the most important thing. The external church organization, be it the so-called "state church" or other denomination was of relative indifference to him. In the "Old Country" he and the Laestadians in general were content to belong the state church; but in America, due to circumstances beyond their control, the Laestadian Christians established independent congregations. Raattamaa wrote, "We here in Europe receive the sacraments from official pastors, as the law here requires." But in America, Laestadian Christians (who had begun calling themselves "Apostolic Lutherans") had the freedom to do otherwise. Raattamaa wrote to them, "You know, of course, that the church of Christ is made up of humble and broken hearts. Let us, then, build up God's temple with Gospel sermons about the blood of Christ, working with hearts so that through the blood of the Lamb they would remain cleansed of the sin that always clings to us." Raattamaa's thinking was: Since Christ's true church is the body of people who believe in Him, which is built up by the preaching of the Gospel, outward organization is not important and could be different in different countries. "We approve of the brothers in America establishing lay churches [congregations served by lay preachers] all over the free country of America so that even the poor may hear God's Word for free [without church taxes]."

The Karesuando church, to which Raattamaa belonged, was the cradle of the Laestadian revival movement, and it was dear to him even after Laestadius was no longer preaching there. When he was home, he regularly attended Sunday worship services in the church. He was frequently seen kneeling in prayer both at home and in church which at that time was the custom of the old Christians in Lapland. Several months before he died, Raattamaa wrote:

> I saw this Christianity sprout from a mustard seed in poor and barren Lapland over fifty years ago, and now it is like a tree whose branches have spread over the oceans all the way to America—so that we have to exclaim: O Emmanuel, how abundant is your mercy.

THE END OF HIS JOURNEY

Raattamaa's immortal spirit went home to the Lord in 1899. Wilderness folk of Lapland came in large numbers to attend his funeral. The people in the funeral procession, which was almost a mile long, had the same goal as he did, to preserve their garments white through the blood of the Lamb and to reach that place one day where the Savior is with all of His saints.

From Uuras Saarnivaara. *He elivät Jumalan voimassa [They Lived in the Power of God]* Suolahti, Finland: Ev. lut. Herätysseura, 1975. Translated by Rodger and Aila Foltz.

12

Erkki Antti Juhonpieti

(1814-1900)

Miriam Yliniemi

Erkki Antti Juhonpieti, also known as Erik Anders Andersson, was one of the most important lay preachers of the Laestadian movement. He was born March 25, 1814, in Pajala, Sweden. Erkki Antti served as a teacher and missionary for Pastor Laestadius. After the death of Laestadius, Erkki Antti became Raattamaa's working companion. He was known as an evangelical "preacher of faith." He died on November 2, 1900.

INTRODUCTION

Erkki Antti Juhonpieti was a landless craftsman who lived in Pajala, a Finnish-speaking area of northern Sweden. He was especially skilled at making spinning wheels. When Laestadius became the pastor of the Pajala parish, Erkki Antti became his assistant in the revival ministry. It has been related that Pastor Laestadius encouraged him to leave the spinning wheel making to other carpenters and begin preaching. After the death of Laestadius in 1861, Juhani Raattamaa became the leader of the movement. Erkki Antti was the most famous working companion of Raattamaa.

Erkki Antti was generally looked upon as an evangelical "preacher of faith." When, at the turn of the twentieth century, the Laestadian movement broke up into three main groups, Erkki Antti was considered one of the fathers of the largest so-called Conservative Laestadians. The two other groups were called the Firstborns and the New Awakenists.

CHILDHOOD AND YOUTH

Erkki Antti was born as the middle child in a family of thirteen children. His parents were honest citizens who could read and write, but his father was an alcoholic. He attributes his awakening, which took place at the age of thirty, to the influence of his mother and the work of Laestadius. Erkki Antti writes about his childhood and awakening in his autobiography (1880) as follows:

During my childhood, we had a good farm and a good standard of living even though my father was a notorious drunkard. He was merciless and harsh when he had been drinking, but honest in all his dealings when he was sober. Even while he was drunk, he didn't do anything bad other than rage about the fact that no one would do what he wanted them to do. Therefore, we always had to be like slaves. Mother was very quiet and also enslaved. My parents made sure that we learned how to read when we were small children. When mother was alive and we were with her in the bedroom, she often spoke to us about the joy in heaven as well as the anguish of those condemned to hell. Her outward manner was as calm as any Christian's ever was. This left pricks on my conscience that will remain with me the rest of my life. When mother died, I was almost eleven years old. Father remarried and we were under even greater bondage. With mother gone, we had no refuge. Then came the hard years of total crop failure and with it poverty to our home.

Finally, when I had turned eighteen, I left home to become a hired hand, and so I ended up completely in the world. I knew how to live to please the world; therefore, I fell even deeper into the ways of the world. In the midst of my life of sin, the spirit of God pursued my conscience and said, what will follow this life? In recalling the words of my mother, I often became so distressed that I had to go to a hiding place to weep. Sometimes I was visibly distressed in my conscience but what could I do when I had no one to guide me? I did not have the Holy Spirit because of my unbelief, so I remained in bondage to sin. My favorite outward sinful habits were playing cards and dancing. When I was not involved in these, I secretly practiced sins that I am ashamed even to mention.

Then the powerful awakening cry of Laestadius began to be heard. His message was brought forth in a most terrifying way. My mother's words had affected me in such a way that when I turned thirty years of age, the Spirit of the Lord again spoke to my conscience: "You are now thirty years old and even if you live long you barely have another thirty years left, and these thirty have gone as though they were stolen. What will follow this life?" I decided that my life must change now.

From that time on, I began to read the Book more, seeking a way to heaven, but sin overcame me over and over again. I truly worked to find salvation but, even by reading, I could not find a better way than: if I could live without sin, perhaps God would be merciful to me. When I endeavored to make repentance for a time, sin again overcame me. Sometimes, the thought came that perhaps God has not even created me for heaven since I cannot live a better life, but I will try anyway, for it is bad to go to hell. I continued in this and read from cover to cover all the religious books available in Finnish. This went on for nearly five years.

When that madness, as it was called, began to be heard, I had come to understand, through my reading, that true Christianity has always been considered madness by the world. I thought: this must be the truth, since it is madness in the eyes of the world. I decided that this would be the day of my true conversion. It doesn't matter if the world considers me mad or wise as long as I am right before God. I began to pray continuously that God would make me the kind of Christian who would be saved, regardless of how it appeared to others, if only I was right before God. There were no true Christians here [Pajala] yet, and Laestadius was still in Karesuando. I always prayed for this in secret. Then my detailed file of sin opened up before me, and I became the greatest sinner among sinners. I marveled that the earth could bear me. Unbelief burdened me with the thought that I had committed the sin against the Holy Spirit which will not be forgiven in this life or the life to come because I had neglected so many promptings of God. Perhaps God no longer cares for me. Then came bitter regret over the wasted time of grace. The weight of ten thousand talents lay on my shoulders, and this bondage was far more cruel than that which I experienced in my youth with my father and stepmother. Secret Christianity no longer sufficed, for sin had become exceedingly great and could not remain concealed.

CONVERSION AND NEW BIRTH

Erkki Antti's conversion experience, five years later, is similar to that of other Laestadian elders in that when he was distressed by the judgment of God, he saw the crucified Savior and experienced new birth as the breaking of the heart in which the cleansing fire went "through his being." His experience differed from the usual in one important way: He experienced peace and a saving faith through the reading of a book by the German author David Hollatz (died 1771) entitled *The Order of Grace unto Salvation.* This well-known devotional book was especially popular among the Moravians in the 1700s. The book is written as conversations between a Soul and Teacher. It had been translated into Finnish and had five printings done in Oulu between 1832-1849. Records indicate that Laestadius had ordered fifty copies of this book for distribution in his parish. In spite of this beginning, Erkki Antti taught that the congregation of believers and the oral declaration of the forgiveness of sins were essential.

Erkki Antti gives the early part of 1849 as the time when he was born again and received the Holy Spirit. He was thirty-four years of age when he committed his gifts to the service of the revival, and that became his life work. He continues in his autobiography about his conversion experience as follows:

I was in my thirty-fifth year when on Epiphany a penitent man named Heikka Erkki from this same village visited me. We discussed how to become saved, as we understood it. He left for home in the evening, and I was in great distress about my salvation, for death and judgment were right before me. Then the Savior appeared to me on the cross which brought great distress to my conscience. If only I could be saved before death cut the thin cord stretched over the burning fire and brimstone of hell on which I was standing. I trembled with great alarm over the fact that this thin cord might break and no one would rescue me and I must sink into the deep. I saw the surging fire and brimstone and the unfortunate ones who were writhing there. I am not able to write this without weeping. When I consider from what awful fate the Eternal Lover has snatched me, tears of sorrow still come to my eyes. Today, when I think about what the other Christians and I have become through the precious Blood of Jesus, I cannot restrain the tears of joy and gratitude. In my distressing situation, I read and prayed that God would help me, if He could find a place in my heart.

One day I was alone in the rear cottage of Vanhatalo, where I lived at that time, reading a book entitled *Armon järjestys* (*The Order of Grace*). After reading the "First Conversation," I was stripped naked of my own holiness. As I was reading the last part of the "Second Conversation," the gracious promises of the Gospel opened up to me, that if you believe on the Lord Jesus you are saved.

Now came the feeling of my unworthiness. How is it possible for me to believe when I have not yet been properly contrite or repentant? Would I not become a hypocrite and so on? But the Spirit of God, who is the author and finisher of our faith, entered me through that written word saying that if you don't believe, you will go to hell no matter how penitent you may be. My fear was great but I had a little hope. Then I grasped a firm hold on the gracious promises of God, and to the extent that I believed I felt peace and rest. I also felt joy for the first time and was able to see Jesus in His triumphal glory when I was able to believe myself saved.

I do not recall anything else, but I do remember that I was filled with joy and paced the floor in gratitude, and I went into the main house to tell the others about the great grace that had taken place in me. I distinctly felt that a purifying fire went through my whole being three times when my heart was broken by faith in the blood of Jesus. After this, I knew nothing of sin for about a week.

Erkki Antti was sensitive and tenderhearted. He revealed his inner thoughts and feelings in his writings. Visions and dreams played a significant role in his life, as can be seen as he continues his story.

When I again sank into a consciousness of my corruption, many doubtful thoughts came. I wondered if I was even on the right road…. But I will mention that several times I was shown the blessedness of heaven in such great measure that, due to my joy, I did not know if my spirit would return to this world. At other times, when overcome by the love of God, I often thought that perhaps I was already on my way to the wedding of the Lamb.

106   *A Godly Heritage*

During the early phase of the revival, under feelings of grace, I was allowed to see some prophets. I have also seen Laestadius, the Apostles, and finally the Savior in triumphal glory. At that time I heard the same testimony, first from Laestadius, then the Apostles and the prophets. But seeing the Savior melted the core of my being so that I could no longer look at anything, for I lay totally powerless, like a heap of foam. It was as though the love of God dissolved me so that for a time I did not know if I even had a body.

Some well-respected brothers were oppressing me at the time when the last-mentioned revelation came to me. In my fight of faith, I have felt the corruption of sin in my members in so many ways that I cannot enumerate them. I have also felt the peace and love of God, sometimes in lesser and sometimes in greater measure, as God in His wisdom has ordained for me. I have kept the faith even though feelings have fluctuated. The foundation of our salvation is not in our feelings, but the precious merit of Jesus is our complete redemption from punishment for sin as well as the fulfillment of the law.

REVIVAL WORKER

Immediately after his conversion experience, he began speaking about his faith. When Laestadius assumed the pastorate in Pajala, Erkki Antti began to assist him by helping with the confirmation classes. He was one of the more literate men of the area. He was known to be an avid reader which is evident from his conversion experience as well as from his letter writing and the books left at his death. He soon was given broader responsibilities when he was assigned in the circuit mission schools to instructing children during the day as well as adults who came in the evenings to learn more about this "strange new message."

Erkki Antti's great influence was based on his warm-hearted nature, clear manner of speaking, and his broad knowledge of the Bible. This can be seen from his use of many biblical quotations in his letters. His gentle, mild manner made him an exceptional comforter of the sorrowful. By his special gifts of faith, grace, and love he was able to reach those struggling under the law and self-righteousness and reveal the power of faith in Christ, bringing peace to many. However, he did receive criticism on being too evangelical. Some have suggested that Erkki Antti's influence changed the movement in a more evangelical direction. Most of this criticism was in the early 1870's. Researchers have not been able to prove from his letters that his position differed in any significant way from the prevailing Laestadian view of that day. He appeared to have the full support and respect of Raattamaa and the other early Elders.

He never married and was consequently free to travel. In midlife he lost one eye while working on a millstone. In his later years, he was described as short and stout with a husky voice. He loved children and spoke with them at services often asking them, "Are you a Christian?" He continues in his autobiography as follows:

When God taught me to believe my sins forgiven in spite of my unworthiness, the Holy Spirit came to live within me. I could no longer refrain from speaking about Christianity. I saw that the whole world was going to hell in the false hope that their knowledge of Christian doctrine [would save them] without a change of heart and mind.

When the late Laestadius became our pastor in the early spring, I spoke in the presence of him and everyone listening according to what the Spirit gave me to say at any particular time. Laestadius was pleased with me and began to ask me to be his companion and driver to parish catechetical meetings, inspection tours, and to teach children.

One summer after I had been a Christian for two or three years, the Christians of Pello came to the Pajala church on Midsummer Day to ask the Pastor to provide them with a schoolteacher, for they too needed to be saved. Laestadius said, "Erkki Antti can go with you to teach you." To me it seemed impossible to even think about it; who was I for such an important task? I said, "Dear Pastor, I do not have the gifts for such a position." He bound me to this with words from the Bible. Finally, I agreed to go, but I thought to myself that the Pastor would soon see that I do not have the gifts required for the job.

After I had held meetings in Pello for two weeks, the people under the law were released by faith in the Lord Jesus to enjoy the power of the forgiveness of sins and freedom and peace in God.

After that I was called even further down the Tornio Valley. People also came from Finland, and the Lord effected powerful awakenings even through my mouth in Finland, Sweden and also in Norway.

The Tornio River Valley south of Pajala became the most important field of work for Erkki Antti as early as the 1850s. Almost every winter, until the end of his life, he made a long preaching tour down the river valley and back. In addition, he often visited the nearest villages in the Muonio district and Karesuando, where Juhani Raattamaa lived. Beyond the Tornio River Valley, Erkki Antti's preaching of faith achieved crucial importance in two areas in the 1860s: Kittilä in northern Finland, and Vadsø (Vesisaari) in northern Norway.

CONTACTS WITH AMERICA

Laestadianism spread rapidly in the twenty years following the death of Pastor Laestadius. The rapid expansion is attributed to the converts who enthusiastically testified of the work of God in their lives to everyone they came into contact with as they moved about. By the 1870s, it had spread to many areas in southern Finland as well as the USA.

It is interesting to note that Erkki Antti and the other northern elders knew more about the Laestadians in northern Norway and the USA than about those living south of Oulu in Finland. These two areas were familiar to them because most of the early Finnish emigrants were natives of the Tornio River Valley who had gone to northern Norway in the 1860s because of the famine years in northern Finland. From there they left for America. It was through this route that Laestadianism first reached America.

Much correspondence took place between the emigrants and the Laestadian Elders. A collection of Erkki Antti's letters (121 in all) has been preserved and was published in a book edited by Pekka Raittila in 1979. Most of the letters had been sent to the Vadsø (Vesisaari) area (39 letters) and to the Laestadian leaders in America (22 letters). These two areas were his focus because dissensions had risen among the Laestadians in northern Norway and the USA, beginning in the 1870s, for which they consulted leading preachers and the "elders" seeking a solution.

Erkki Antti and the other elders were not familiar with the conditions in the new world, but they were drawn into the disputes and problems involved with the establishment of the immigrant church in

America. An excerpt from his letter to Olli Koskamo in 1889 reveals the strife going on in the American fellowship.

> ...Letters of accusation have arrived from America one after another all winter. They are accusing each other, those in Kittila and Vesisaari, as well as me and the Elder of Saivo [Juhani Raattamaa]. Should we also begin quarreling? God forbid: Since we have by the grace of God entered into that kingdom where sins are forgiven and we are freed from the accusations of the law.... We believe our sins forgiven in the Name and blood of Jesus and endeavor to preserve love and a forgiving heart toward those in Kittila and Vesisaari, be they Swedes, Finns or Lapps. We also continue to have a forgiving heart toward the Americans.

Erkki Antti's letters provide more insight on his personality than factual information. The letters do give information on the critical stage of American and Norwegian Laestadianism in about 1890. During the dissensions at the end of the 1880s, Erkki Antti, together with Raattamaa, strongly defended the authority of the Elders and the significance of the congregation of the Firstborn in unifying the Laestadian community. When the dissension among American Laestadians finally led to an open schism, Erkki Antti's attitude changed. After 1889, he wanted to stay aloof from the dissension, although he did state that his understanding of the American situation was not quite in agreement with Raattamaa's. Nevertheless, the letters these two sent to each other give evidence of mutual respect and confidence.

His attitude toward the American situation changed after the 1888 annual election to choose a minister in Calumet, Michigan. Takkinen lost and Juho Roanpää was voted in as minister. The supporters of Takkinen declared the election illegal. In the spring of 1889, the battle over church ownership went to court. Erkki Antti wrote a strong letter to Matti Pekkala in New York Mills, Minnesota, on July 15, 1889. This letter was widely circulated in America. He writes in part:

> ...Most of the letters I receive from America are about the sins of others. What good would it do if I repented of the sins of others? ...Each one should write about his own sins to Europe and America if they have reason to do so. Is it a fruit of faith that a Christian goes to court against a Christian before the judges of this world, over the minister and the church? ...In America, you

established a church separate from the dead state church, based on the Apostles, and now the state is qualified to determine matters of your minister and church!

Dear brothers, you ought to know that this is not according to the Gospel. In this matter, the law and human nature have taken over.

He concludes the letter by saying:

It would be wonderful to hear that in Calumet and everywhere sinners would throw their arms around each other and beg for forgiveness of their own sins... Greetings from all the Christians to the Lord's flock there...Your brother in the Lord and companion on the way to the beautiful shore of our heavenly home.

RELATIONSHIP TO OTHER MOVEMENTS

What was Erkki Antti's attitude toward other revival movements? Oskar Lindstedt (Lantto) from Pajala wrote in a letter dated February 21, 1893, which was published in *Sanomia Siionista* [*Messages from Zion*, a Laestadian publication], as follows:

Erkki Antti Anderson and I have written to D.L. Moody and briefly told him about the influence etc. of the so-called Laestadian Christianity. I believe it was a letter that brought joy to Brother Moody to hear that he has brothers and sisters this far north. (SS 1893, p.168)

In Swedish Övertorneå it was remembered that the Wales Revival especially captivated Erkki Antti. However, direct quotes about his relationship to other religious groups are limited to a couple of negative comments on the Baptists in Haparanda, Sweden.

FUNERAL

Erkki Antti passed away on November 2, 1900, and his funeral service was held on Sunday, November 25. The attendance at his funeral was estimated at one thousand people. A local newspaper reports that such a large crowd had not been seen at the Pajala cemetery except perhaps at the funeral of Pastor Laestadius. Pastor Pehr Olof Grape conducted the funeral service. He portrayed Erkki Antti as follows:

Erkki Antti understood the gospel and the gospel made him more evangelical but not in a way that would indicate that he loved or defended sin. He could, with sharp words, zealously rebuke sin, but he was ready to preach forgiveness of sins in the Blood of Jesus. He did not treat the sin-sick harshly but comforted them and encouraged them to believe.

Information from *Erkki Antti Juhonpieti: Kirjeet ja Kirjoitukset* edited by Pekka Raittila (Suomen Kirkkohistoriallinen Seura Tornedalica 1979) Excerpts from Erkki Antti Juhonpieti's autobiography, pp. 80-89. Translation and writing by Miriam Yliniemi

13

Aatu Laitinen
(1853-1923)

Uuras Saarnivaara

The fires of the Laestadian revival soon spread from northern Sweden to the neighboring countries of Norway and Finland. The languages spoken in the northernmost region of Scandinavia were the same: Finnish and Sami (Lappish). Finnish Lapland was less than two hundred yards from the Karesuando church and parsonage across the Muonio River. In its initial phases the revival was spread by lay preachers and through the testimony of believers, but somewhat later this congregation had a Church of Finland pastor belonging to the Laestadian revival movement, Aatu Laitinen.

CHILDHOOD AND YOUTH

Laitinen was born in Suonenjoki, central Finland, in 1853, the same year that Raattamaa used personal absolution for the first time with such blessed results. When Aatu was seven years old, his father died leaving his wife and seven children in poverty. Nevertheless, seeing how gifted Aatu was, his mother sent him away to school in Kuopio, there being no secondary school nearby. In his early school years, he often suffered want even going without food for several days during the famine period 1866-68. Although his family at home was subsisting on bread made of flour mixed with straw, his mother did manage to send Aatu a little bit  of money. Once some money arrived when he had been without food for three days, and he bought fish with it. His situation improved when Councilman K.V. Malmberg, who belonged to the pietistic Awakened movement, took him into his home.

Laitinen's mother was a God-fearing woman, and she taught her children to trust in God and pray, usually on their knees at their bedsides. Through his mother's prayers, teachings and songs the first spark of faith was kindled in Aatu's heart. However, his childhood faith was extinguished when was seven years old because he told a deliberate lie and did not confess it. His unrepented sin separated him from God. After his loss of a good conscience and faith the world soon took over his heart. While in school, his conscience was again awakened, but this did not lead to conversion. Conversations with Malmberg and contacts with others of the Awakened movement who often visited the Malmberg home kept his conscience awake. God's voice was never totally stifled in his heart even when he traveled the paths of sin, and he was never able to sin with a good conscience.

In 1874 Laitinen began his theological studies at the University of Helsinki. His choice of career was probably influenced by his restless conscience. He was concerned about his salvation, though he had not yet found the way. Two of his teachers, A.V. Ingman and C.G. von Essen, had belonged to the Awakened movement but were now followers of the "Biblicism" of Johann Tobias Beck of Tübingen, as was the young professor Gustaf Johansson, who became bishop of Kuopio and later archbishop of Turku. They emphasized faith in the authority of the Bible as God's Word. While teaching it as God's unerring revelation, they also emphasized the importance of new birth followed by a holy life. An older professor A.F. Granfelt favored the "Mediation Theology" of the Danish professor H.L. Martensen and was friendly toward the Finnish revivals, dedicating much of his theological work to them.

While listening to the lectures of these professors, Laitinen sensed that he did not have the living scriptural faith of which they spoke, although he had a yearning for it in his soul. He was ordained into the ministry in 1877 and was assigned to assist F. M. Relander, senior pastor of Kiihtelysvaara parish. He continued to be burdened by sin, and his uneasy conscience led him to make repeated resolutions to amend his life, particularly when he attended the Lord's Supper. He was never able to keep these resolutions, however. His heart longed for assurance of the forgiveness of sins and power to live a new life, but he was not yet ready to humble himself to repent. In fact, he did not even understand how to go about it.

In Kiihtelysvaara, Laitinen married Pastor Relander's daughter in 1877. She was a blessing to him as a good, faithful wife. However, neither one of them had yet experienced living faith and peace with God.

HIS CONVERSION AND INFILLING WITH THE HOLY SPIRIT

After a brief period in the Eno parish in eastern Finland, Laitinen moved to Enontekiö in Lapland. This broad-ranging parish on the Swedish border by Karesuando included the entire "arm of Finland" and its "shoulder" area. Having heard about the Laestadian revival movement before he went there, he was determined to root out this "wild doctrine" from the congregation and lead the parishioners to "sound Lutheranism."

At this time there was a powerful Laestadian revival in progress in Enontekiö. All over the parish, people were being awakened from the slumber of sin. One after another they repented and rejoiced in the peace and joy of the Holy Spirit which they enjoyed in the kingdom of God. Former enemies were reconciled and became friends in the Lord. People confessed their sins and crimes and made restitution to those who had been harmed. On the other hand, there were many, particularly among the "better class" of people, who bitterly hated and opposed the revival.

Although Laitinen himself still yearned for the peace of God, his prejudice against the Laestadian movement led him to frequent clashes with its representatives. He had a hot temper, and he was usually unable to control himself when conflicts occurred. Even though he continued to fight against it, he could not fail to realize that the Spirit of God was present in the revival. The uncompromising dedication to truth—as they understood it—that was manifest in the lives of the Laestadians touched his heart and made his conscience more restless than before. In spite of a growing feeling that he was wrong and these Christians right, his pride held his soul hostage to such an extent that he did not want to admit it.

One Sunday in the middle of the morning worship service, a Sami woman began to praise the Lord in a loud voice. Laitinen was annoyed by the interruption, and he lost his temper. He told the sexton to remove the woman. When the service was over, a short Sami man known as Ies-Pieti (Per Vasara) followed him out and said, "That was a strange thing you did! You drove out the Virgin Mary and left in impenitent whores." Laitinen felt the blood rush to his face, and he picked up his pace. Ies-Pieti did not give up but followed him to the parsonage. Regardless of the pastor's anger, he continued his gentle and loving admonitions. Laitinen began to feel that God was speaking to him through the little Sami man, and no excuses or rationalizations brought peace to his conscience.

A lay preacher, Ies-Pieti occasionally held home services in Enontekiö. On one occasion when Laitinen attended such services, he felt that the hand of God was on him so powerfully that he could not resist any longer. He humbled himself to repent and confessed the sins that had troubled his conscience for a long time. Above all, he repented of his ungodly opposition and hatred toward the Laestadian movement. Ies-Pieti lovingly laid his hands on him and blessed him with the Gospel of forgiveness in Jesus' name and blood. Divine peace descended upon Laitinen's soul. He was born as a child of God and also "born" into the Laestadian revival. The Laestadian Christians of the parish were overjoyed and praised God for the conversion of their pastor.

Laitinen's conscience was now at peace. He enjoyed the fellowship of the Laestadian Christians, for they had become his brothers and sisters in faith. He was not ashamed to identify with the movement, and he often participated services with lay preachers. Nevertheless, he felt that there was still something missing. He had the peace of a good conscience, but he did not have the power from above that he observed in so many Laestadian Christians and especially preachers. He felt that his experience of the power of Christ's blood and resurrection was rather shallow. In his heart he thirsted for a more living knowledge of Christ and for infilling with the Holy Spirit. We will let him tell it in his own words:

> I had been confessing faith all summer, but the Holy Spirit was not poured into my heart until the fall of 1881. It took place as follows: On my way home from Kittilä, I spent the night in a Kurkiovaara farmhouse. Brita, an elderly farmwife who was experienced in matters of faith, spoke to me of our Lord Jesus' atoning death for us; she did it with a broken and fervent heart. During my journey home the following day, I had a feeling of heavenly bliss in my heart. The mountains, trees, sun, earth, sky— all seemed to join with me in praising the good and mighty God for the salvation that we have in Jesus Christ our Savior, the precious bridegroom of our souls, who has redeemed us with His precious blood and washed us white as snow through His grace.

According to Laitinen it was through this experience that he truly came to know Christ as his Savior and comprehend Christianity. Even in his old age he recalled it with joy and gratitude. "Here among the Lapland elders," he said, "God again opened the door of His grace to me and poured the peace of His Spirit into my soul."

Even after this experience, Laitinen had periods of doubt, darkness and anguish in his life; whenever this happened, the Lord let the light of his countenance shine again into his heart, restoring to him the joy and assurance of salvation. At times he was granted visions which comforted his heart and strengthened him in faith. He describes them as follows:

> On one occasion I saw Jesus nearby. He was wearing a crown of thorns, and His face was bleeding. When he looked at me with compassion, I wept and rejoiced. Another time I heard from heaven the wonderful singing of the saints and angels; when this happened, I promised God that I would never again harbor doubts of His precious grace again. But alas, I have broken this promise thousands of times. A third vision came to me while I was meditating upon the resurrection of the saints that have gone before. When I looked in the direction of the graveyard, I saw a bright light rising upward, and an indescribable brightness shone over a wide expanse of sky. As I was gazing at it, my soul was filled with heavenly bliss. I received the assurance that in heaven the redeemed have no opportunity to remember their sufferings on earth.

Laitinen understood that he had tempted God with his doubts and lack of faith, but God in His mercy had consoled him by means of visions. Nevertheless, he understood that he should place his trust in God's unshakable word and not so much in visions.

Even in old age Laitinen's eyes filled with tears when he thought about these tokens of God's favor. In his study he had a picture of Christ on the cross and under it a picture of Ies-Pieti, whom he gratefully remembered as the man through whom the Lord had led him to repentance and faith.

BLESSINGS AND DIFFICULTIES IN THE MINISTRY

After he received the light and power of the Holy Spirit into his heart, Laitinen was bold in his witness and proclamation regarding sin and the salvation offered in Christ. He surpassed even Laestadius in lashing out against sin and empty ritualism. In addition to preaching and teaching, he was diligent in the use of his pen in the service of the Gospel. Some pamphlets issued time and again from his study as well as a collection of sermons. From 1888, on he edited the religious monthly *Sanomia Siionista* [*Tidings from Zion*]. It was read in Finland, Sweden, Norway and America. His sermon collection *Evankeliumisaarnoja* [*Gospel Sermons*] was first published in 1885 and reissued in 1950 by his son, Pastor E. V. Laitinen, and the industrialist-preacher Janne Marttiini. It was published in the English language in the United States under the title *Gospel Sermons* in 1968.

The Laestadian revival in Enontekiö, as well as Finnish Lapland in general, received fresh impetus after Laitinen came to faith and was filled with the Holy Spirit. He made preaching tours not only to the neighboring parishes in Finland but also to Sweden and Norway. There were conversions nearly every day, and often numerous people repented at his services. The leading preachers of the revival, Juhani Raattamaa, Olli Puljula, Antin-Pieti (Petter Nutti), and Erkki Antti Juhonpieti were close friends of Laitinen, and they often held home services together. They also received counsel, consolation and encouragement from each other in their good fight of faith and in their work in the Lord's vineyard.

One day soon after his conversion, Laitinen was participating in a meeting with Antin-Pieti. The room was full of people who had come to hear the newly converted young pastor. Antin-Pieti spoke first. After he had been speaking for a long time, Laitinen nudged him, saying, "Let me speak too." The preacher went on speaking as if nothing had happened. When renewed reminders failed to stop Antin-Pieti, Laitinen lost patience and left the room in exasperation.

When night came, Laitinen's anger turned to remorse. Sleep eluded him, and he was unable to soothe his conscience with any rationalizations. Finally he got out of bed and went to the room where Antin-Pieti was sleeping. From behind the door he could hear the preacher praying, "Dear Father in heaven. Thou hast begun Thy work in this young pastor; bend his heart according to Thy will." Laitinen could not restrain himself any longer. He burst into the room in tears and asked for forgiveness. Antin-Pieti assured him of forgiveness in Jesus' name and blood and said, "Well, I figured you would come."

Even before Laitinen's arrival in Enontekiö, there had been those who opposed the Laestadian revival, and these people were happy to receive this ally in their struggle against the "wild doctrine." When

Laitinen, following his conversion, began preaching against the sinful life and hypocritical nominal Christianity of these people, they became enraged and turned against him.

In the first issue of *Sanomia Siionista* (1888), Laitinen states that as many as ten charges had been brought against him in courts of justice. An Enontekiö official once took him to court for saying in a sermon he [the official] was making advances to other men's wives. Laitinen arrived in the courtroom dressed in a Sami fur coat. Because of this he was accused of contempt of court, but the charge was dropped. "The coat was saved," Laitinen said, "but soon we'll see what happens to the man." The witnesses tried to help him out by saying that they did not know whom he had meant when he spoke of a man who did not leave other men's wives alone. Laitinen interrupted them saying, "The accusation is true. This is exactly the man I was referring to, for he has a habit of carrying on with other men's wives." Laitinen would have been able to prove his allegation, but he preferred not to and paid the fine imposed on him.

After several complaints were made against Laitinen to the Kuopio Church Consistory, he was called before it in 1884. In his written defense, he demonstrated that the charges concerning false doctrine were unfounded. At the same time, he expressed his astonishment at the bias of the Consistory which had done nothing with regard to pastors who were guilty of drunkenness and adultery even though those things took place right under their noses. Instead it called to judgment a man who undertook a battle against all wickedness and evildoing in his parish and elsewhere.

The Consistory delivered a heavy sentence in 1889: suspension from the ministry for one year plus heavy fines and expenses. Laitinen spent that year on preaching tours which took him as far as southern Finland. The Lord blessed him richly during this time so that with the help of Christian friends in the homeland and in America he was able to support his family as well as pay his fine and debts. Thus, his sentence turned out to be a blessing even from a financial standpoint.

The chastening that Laitinen received made him realize that in his youthful fervor he had often made rash statements, and he tried to be more moderate and cautious in his words and actions. However, his zeal for the salvation of souls did not diminish, but he was careful not to offend people unnecessarily.

LITERARY STRUGGLES

In his day Laitinen was the foremost literary spokesman for the
Laestadian revival. When accusations and abuse were directed against
it from many directions, he refuted them with power and acumen. At
the same time, he helped the Laestadian movement to clarify its
position on various issues.

One of the chief issues of controversy between Laestadians and
their opponents was the use of personal confession and absolution.
Despite the fact that the section on confession and absolution in
Luther's Small Catechism was taught in both camps, the critics of the
movement held the opinion that God alone had the authority to forgive
sins, and man had no right to assume the prerogative of God. Laitinen
demonstrated from the Scriptures, Luther's writings, and the Lutheran
Confessions that the teaching and practice of the movement was in
conformity with Scripture and Lutheran doctrine. He expressed his
amazement over the fact that the opponents accepted the Lutheran
doctrine in theory but opposed it in practice. The Laestadians were
only putting the official teaching of the Lutheran church into practice.

Another accusation made against the Laestadians was that their
preachers used "indecent" language in their sermons. Laitinen
answered that their language was "indecent" only in the sense that they
exposed people's sins and called them to repentance. Actually the
Scriptures were just as "indecent" in this respect, for they too spoke of
sins by name. People wanted to hear of sin only in general terms and
indirectly, so they could continue their sinful lives undisturbed. They
were offended and enraged when their deeds of darkness were brought
to light.

A third charge against the movement regarded the outbursts of
distress and joy, "rejoicings," from people during the Laestadian
services and even in church. Laitinen called attention to the disciples
of Jesus who at Pentecost were accused of being drunk when they
were under the powerful influence of the Holy Spirit. He wrote to the
Laestadian Christians, "Children of God, you have not yet rejoiced as
much as the King, God Himself, commands you to do in His Word."
The Laestadians also pointed to the fact that people of this world
shouted and jumped up and down at athletic events without anybody
being offended. But when Christians wept over their sins and praised
the Lord for His grace, this was considered improper and offensive.
There was more reason to feel sorrow over sins than over losing an

athletic contest and much more cause to rejoice over the forgiveness of sins and salvation than over victories in athletics.

Laitinen's writings dealt with all the various issues and problems that resulted from the expansion of the Laestadian movement. His articles dealing with doctrinal issues brought increased clarity to the teachings of the movement and corrected misleading tendencies that appeared in various places. To some degree, these writings were also read by people who were outside the movement and were thus a blessing to many.

The main theological attack against the Laestadian movement was that made by Bishop Gustaf Johansson in his book *Laestadiolaisuus* (Laestadianism, 1892). Johansson criticized the movement from the Beckian viewpoint and asserted that its doctrinal foundation was erroneous. In his view this movement was a kind of spiritual mania, and he predicted that it would soon fade away.

Two Laestadian Church of Finland pastors, Aatu Laitinen and K. A. Heikel, responded to Johansson in a spirit of meekness but with keen insight. They pointed out that the bishop had badly misunderstood this movement, and they deplored the fact that he had written his book in a spirit of anger and judgment rather than in a spirit of love. Such a position would not increase love among the Laestadians for the pastors [of the national Lutheran church], which would be desirable and necessary, they said.

Bishop Jaakko Gummerus, formerly a professor of church history, is reported to have said that Johansson's book on Laestadianism was "a sin of church history." Johansson is said to have regretted it and even apologized for it in his old age, admitting that he had misunderstood the movement and had not recognized God's work in it.

LAST PHASE OF HIS MINISTRY

In the spring of 1897, Laitinen moved to Rovaniemi, the capital of Finnish Lapland, where he first served as assistant pastor and later senior pastor. In his farewell sermon in Enontekiö, he delivered his final warnings to the unbelievers and words of admonition and encouragement to the Christians. He said, "I have preached God's Word to you diligently in season and out of season according to the understanding that God has given me. It would certainly have saved your souls. I am now innocent of the blood of all of you on the day of judgment."

At about the time when Laitinen moved to Rovaniemi, the tension between different trends in the movement became apparent, soon leading to a split into three divisions, the Conservatives, Firstborn and New Awakened. By then Juhani Raattamaa was 88 years old and blind and, consequently, could do nothing to prevent the split. A couple of years later (1899), he passed on from time to eternity.

In Rovaniemi there was tension particularly between the Conservatives and the New Awakened. Laitinen tried to be impartial and understanding of both sides. He realized that Christians continually need a new awakening as St. Paul writes in Rom. 13:11. Nevertheless, he could not approve of certain characteristics of the New Awakened movement. He exhorted both sides to moderation and mutual love. "Let us stop our quarreling and jealousy," he wrote. "Let us not draw boundary lines on the basis of fruitless genealogies related to the old and new awakenings. Let all those who fight the good fight of faith be diligent in striving for a more intimate knowledge of our Lord Jesus Christ, a better acquaintance with the Word of God, a deeper understanding of ourselves, and a more steadfast, cordial and sincere love among ourselves."

Laitinen had been a strong fighter in his youth, and in old age he continued to be strong in his battle against sin and the temptations of the world. But he wanted to be a peacemaker among the children of God. He reminded Christians that they should follow truth in love rather than permitting their "Old Adam" to determine their relationships with each other.

Laitinen was unable to prevent the Conservatives and the New Awakened from splitting into two contentious groups. To his sorrow he encountered criticism from both camps because of his attempts at conciliation, and many of his old friends deserted him. These and other sorrows served to purify him. In the crossfire of human opinions and condemnation, he learned to depend ever more on the Word of God. His work in the extremely extensive parish of Rovaniemi continued to bear good fruit. He attempted to treat everyone with equal Christian love and gentleness.

On Christmas Day of 1923 Laitinen preached his final sermon. On the last day of the year, he had a heart attack which ended his earthly pilgrimage. His numerous friends in Lapland and other areas sorely missed this faithful servant of the Lord who had been instrumental in leading them to a saving knowledge of Christ. Shortly before his death, he wrote a hymn which has become a favorite among

Laestadians. In it he expressed his yearning for the heavenly wedding feast of his Lord, whose blood had cleansed him from sin.

From Uuras Saarnivaara. *He elivät Jumalan voimassa [They Lived in the Power of God]*. Suolahti, Finland: Ev. lut. Herätysseura, 1975. Translated by Rodger and Aila Foltz.

14

Absolution Introduced
"In Jesus' Name and Blood"

Seppo Leivo

The following is a translation of excerpts from an article by Seppo Leivo in the journal *Iustitia 14, 2001: Lestadiolaisuuden Monet Kasvot* [*The Many Facets of Laestadianism*]. Seppo Leivo is a Laestadian noted for his research on Laestadius and his sermons. The publication is edited by Jouko Talonen and Ilpo Harjutsalo and published by the Finnish Theological Institute. The portions of the article selected deal specifically with the Keys. Refer to the words of Jesus in Matthew 16:19: "And I will give unto thee the keys of the kingdom of heaven: and whatsoever thou shalt bind on earth shall be bound in heaven: and whatsoever thou shalt loose on earth shall be loosed in heaven."

PREFACE

Confession is often said to be the basic identifying characteristic of Laestadianism. However, it would be more to the point to say it is absolution (the forgiveness of sins). Many are of the opinion that Raattamaa discovered the Keys alone and the discovery came as a surprise. Naturally the matter has its own background and stages of development. Laestadius also played a part in this development which has not been well understood.

The introduction of oral absolution into the movement has been studied, but it does not lend itself easily to the researcher. The main problem is the lack of original source materials. When there are no descriptions dating to that time, the researchers have had to build upon secondary sources from that day, as well as later recollections and oral traditions. The sermons and writings of Laestadius have been studied, but there has been an element of uncertainty due to inaccuracies in the dating of his sermons. The situation regarding the dating has now improved with the publication in the year 2000 of a volume of Laestadius's sermons in the Finnish language entitled *Saarnat I-III*

[*Sermons I-III*]. In connection with the publication, the editors were able to date the sermons more accurately.

WORK METHODS STUDIED

In the early 1850s, it appeared that the initial phase of the revival was coming to a halt and even declining. This is evident from the sermons of Laestadius in which he laments that the revival dying out. Many of the awakened had become weary, quit testifying to the unawakened, and some had even fallen back into indifference. The events of Kautokeino in 1852 had a negative effect on the movement. Perhaps an important cause for the decline was the fact that, although many of the awakened received help when they were encouraged to believe, others never got beyond a consciousness of sin and did not experience reconciliation with God in their hearts. In the words of Laestadius, they were "in the valley of the shadow of death," captives to unbelief. Laestadius and Raattamaa were concerned about the situation. They were searching for methods and tools by which the walls of unbelief could be broken down and the spiritual revival could be reignited.

ABSOLUTION INTRODUCED

The solution to this quandary was the introduction of the loosing Key. There are several different accounts regarding this. The most detailed written account is one given by Erik Johnsen of Lyngen, Norway, to Martti E. Miettinen. Erik Johnsen had heard this from Juhani Raattamaa in 1894. According to him, the event took place in Gellivaara.

Raattamaa was conducting a mission school. He was just leaving to go home. The reindeer was harnessed and standing before the door. Many people had gathered at the house. Some were already in living faith. But one girl was moaning due to a troubled conscience.

Raattamaa and others preached to her about faith and the gospel, but she could not appropriate faith and was not comforted. Raattamaa put his coat on, bade farewell to the people, and went out the door; but then he turned, went back into the house, and asked the girl, "Do you believe that we are God's people?" The girl answered boldly, "I believe with all my heart that you are God's people." Again Raattamaa said, "Then you believe what we say to you in behalf of God." She responded, "I believe." Then Raattamaa went to her and placed his hand on her. When he had declared the forgiveness of sins to her, the girl was so overcome with joy that she began praising God. Then Raattamaa rode off, wondering the whole way whether he had done the right thing. According to Raattamaa, "When I arrived home and took my coat off, I took my New Testament and opened it. It opened to the Gospel of John chapter 20, which tells about how Jesus blew on his disciples and said, "Receive ye the Holy Ghost: Whose soever sins ye remit, they are remitted unto them; and whose soever sins ye retain, they are retained." Then I finally realized that this is indeed the command of Jesus."

DIFFERENT INTERPRETATIONS OF THE EVENT

Researchers have tried to explain the progression and background of this event because it has had such far-reaching effects. The lack of original source material has posed a problem, as has the fact that the available sources are from a later time period. This has given rise to various oral traditions regarding the event.

One of the earliest written descriptions is found in Aatu Laitinen's book *Muistoja Lapin Kristillisyydestä* (1918) [Published in English as *Memoirs of Early Christianity in Northern Lapland*]. It did not contain much detail. The time and the place are left open. The content ties in with the above account by Johnsen.

A better known work was written by Hjalmar Westeson: *Lapin Profeetan Oppilaita (1922)* [*Followers of the Lapland Prophet*]. The book is based mainly on stories told to Pastor Westeson by people in his parish. Westeson places the event at a mission school in the village of Lainio (Jukkasjärvi) in the beginning of 1848. According to this story, Raattamaa was disturbed by the distress of the awakened. With these thoughts in mind, he read from Luther's Church Postil the sermon for the First Sunday after Easter, in which he talks about absolution. Encouraged by this, Raattamaa declared the forgiveness of sins to the awakened. This created great joy in those individuals.

When Laestadius arrived in Lainio, Raattamaa discussed the event with him late into the night. At the conclusion of their conversation, Laestadius approved his action. The story related by Westeson became the authoritative description of the introduction of absolution into the movement, and for a long time was the generally accepted truth. Because Westeson's work treated the Laestadian revival in a respectful way (or appreciatively), the book received wide acceptance, therefore, it became oral tradition which spread far and wide.

Westeson also relates that Antin Pieti had received absolution at Balsfjord, Norway, as early as the spring of 1847, but it was without a lasting effect.

The first actual scientific research was done by Martti E. Miettinen, who published his findings in *Laestadiolainen heräysliike I* [*The Laestadian Revival Movement I*] which was based on extensive data and thorough consideration. Essentially it has retained its reliability. Miettinen concludes that absolution was first introduced at the Markettavaara mission school in Gellivaara in 1853.

A document by O.H. Jussila should also be mentioned here. The data used were detailed recollections which he recorded between 1910 and 1920 in the Tornio River Valley. He describes the development of the use of absolution in the 1850s. It fits seamlessly with Miettinen's conclusions and thus confirms his position.

There are two alternatives for the time when the loosing Key, or absolution, was introduced into the movement: Lainio 1848 or Markettavaara 1853.

According to Westeson, the event was tied to the study of Luther's Church Postil, the discussion of Raattamaa and Laestadius, and Laestadius's approval. In Miettinen's version, Luther's Postil and an immediate discussion with Laestadius are not tied to the event.

Only Raattamaa has given a first-hand account of the event, and he does not give much detail. From the writings of Laestadius and Raattamaa as well as oral tradition and the general history of the period, we can gain indirect evidence and insight. The question can be approached from different perspectives, but we can no longer verify facts with certainty.

LAESTADIUS'S VIEW

Laestadius has written nothing of the event itself. He does speak of absolution but rather little. The traditional view of the Lutheran church has been that the Christian congregation has the power to forgive sins, and this power is vested especially in the clergy. It is evident also from the Swebelius catechism used by Laestadius. This view appears now and then in the writings of Laestadius until the end. But when personal absolution was applied in the spirit of church discipline, mainly only to the most serious offences, it did not have many points of contact with the basic emphases of Laestadius...

Concerning the question of the power of individual Christians to forgive sins, there is mention of it here and there in Laestadius's sermons. Since he had the habit of speaking allegorically, it is difficult to tell whether he is speaking about Bible characters or the awakened and believers in his own day. Thus, it is not always clear who truly forgives sins.

Olaus Brännström supports the earlier date based on the sermon of Laestadius from 1849, which has a clear indication of the word form used in absolution. However, this particular portion of the sermon is not in Laestadius's own handwriting. It is an addition by the person copying the sermon.[7]

Then in 1856 there are more or less clear expressions of the power to forgive sins in several sermons which would indicate that the position of Laestadius had become clear. In his sermon for the Second Day of Prayer, Laestadius said, "In behalf of God Nathan forgave David his sins" (*Saarnat III*, 1652). In his St John's Day sermon he asks, "Who forgives the sins of the awakened...If the Son of Man on earth assures the penitent, sorrowful and doubting of the forgiveness of sins and if he says to the man with palsy, 'Thy sins be forgiven thee,' the priests, scribes, and Pharisees say, 'He blasphemes God'" (*Saarnat II*, 1443). In his sermon for the Third Day of Prayer Laestadius says,

---

[7] The sermon referred to is the 4th Sunday after Trinity sermon in 1849. The original sermon is missing the last page. It is also missing from the Postil. Koller's collection of copied sermons has the last part from which Brännström quotes on the declaration of the forgiveness of sins. The last portion of the copy is way too long to fit on the missing page. In where the last page should end, the nature of the writing changes and many words and phrases are foreign to the style of Laestadius. The copy is heavily edited with many additions even in the beginning sections. It was not rare that the copier, in the process of copying, received a "revelation of the Spirit" and supplemented and added to Laestadius's sermons. Later a copy book of Laestadius's sermons by Iisakki Poromaa has been found which has the sermon ending before the portion on the forgiveness of sins just as the Postil. Brännströms information has become a historical fact and it is referred to continuously, for example in Seppo Lohi's Laestadius biography. Lohi has himself concluded that it is in error.

"True Christians have received the power to forgive sins" (*Saarnat III,* 1751). In his sermon for the 27th Sunday after Trinity, he further discusses the role of man in coming to faith as follows: "If we look in the Bible to find out in what manner true and saving faith first came into the world, we see that even the first Christians received faith by means of other people or the apostles. When they died, the other Christians spread the faith. Nevertheless, it is not a faith given by people—God's Spirit has spoken through the mouths of Christians. God is the one who gives faith." (*Saarnat II,* 1390-1391) We must first state that Laestadius rarely speaks of the assistance of another person in coming to faith. Yet in the sermon for the Third Sunday in Advent 1858 he says very clearly, "God has given Christians the great power to forgive and bind sins" (*Saarnat I,* 105). And on the Fourth Day of Prayer 1860: "According to the teachings of the Pharisees, sins could not be forgiven by any man but only by God. Even today, the Pharisees have the same belief." (*Saarnat III,* 1906)

The sermon on the Keys mentioned earlier contains a comprehensive discourse on Laestadius's views of confession. To whom do the keys belong? Laestadius says that the Savior gave Peter (and the other disciples) the Keys of the kingdom of heaven, even though Peter was only a sinful man. The power to forgive sins is based not only on the words of Jesus but also on the fact that the believers know to whom forgiveness of sins can be preached, that is, to the penitent. Of the traditional view he says that the congregation has had the "outward faith" that the keys of the kingdom of heaven have been given only to the clergy, whom God authorizes to declare the forgiveness of sins to the communion guests or to those sentenced to church punishment. He expresses the opinion that the spiritual priest carries the keys with him at all times but the "indifferent" priest only when he is officiating. In the sermon there is strong criticism of the "papist" practice of confession that does not call for contrition, requiring only confession. Nevertheless, Laestadius does not approve of the conditional absolution in the Swedish church handbook at that time stating, "If your confession is sincere," etc. It leaves the person tortured by unbelief into uncertainty.

He argues for absolution as follows: "And when a repentant person cannot make himself believe, the church must assure the repentant of God's grace and the forgiveness of sins...through the pastor or another Christian...not only through the pastoral office but through every person who has himself experienced the grace of forgiveness." Referring to Article 12 of the Augsburg Confession he said, "The church of God imparts absolution to the repentant. True repentance is recognized from the contrition and terror smiting the conscience with a knowledge of sin."

Of the effect of the assurance of grace, Laestadius said, "You had your sins forgiven at the moment you heard from the mouth of Jesus the sweet words of grace: your sins are forgiven you…at the moment you believe, you will receive the power to rise and walk the way of Christianity."

Briefly said, only the repentant can receive the forgiveness of sins; every Christian has the power to forgive sins; and the Holy Spirit generates faith.

RAATTAMAA'S ACCOUNT

The report of the key person is always important. Juhani Raattamaa himself writes in the *Kristillinen Kuukauslehti [Christian Monthly]* 1881, page 180, about the discussion related to the use of the absolution. He writes:

> The spiritual movement had spread for six years before I experienced true freedom. From that time forward we, along with some brothers and sisters, started using the Keys of the Kingdom of Heaven. People under conviction [of sin] began to experience freedom, and prisoners of unbelief were loosed from their bonds.

We know that the revival actually started in Karesuando in 1846 and began to spread outside the congregation in 1847 and especially 1848. This fact would more likely favor the year 1853. We also note here that Laestadius was not mentioned in the decision-making process. Thus, Raattamaa's own words speak against the Lainio 1848 alternative.

Luther's Church Postil is often alluded to in establishing the date when the Keys were first used. The printing of the first Finnish language edition was begun as separate small booklets in 1846. Part I, which includes the sermon for the First Sunday after Easter mentioned by Westeson, was completed in 1848 after the Lainio mission school session. Part II was printed in 1851. The Palm Sunday sermon in the Church Postil (1847) and Luther's House Postil (1846) both speak of the power of the Keys. Even though the use of Luther's postils was theoretically possible in 1848, it is not very likely. There is no real evidence that Luther's postils were used that early in the area affected by the Laestadian revival.

AFTER MARKETTAVAARA

Based on all these facts, it seems probable that Raattamaa used the absolution for the first time as he was leaving the Markettavaara village mission school early in the year 1853. At the Kitkiöjoki School in the winter of 1853-1854, there was discussion not only about personal absolution but also about the use of general absolution, which meant that sins were declared forgiven by the speaker to the whole audience "wall to wall," as it is called. Their conclusion was in favor of the practice. There is plenty of oral tradition corroborating this discussion. Raattamaa refers to this when he says, "From that time on, along with some brothers and sisters, we began to use the Keys of the kingdom of heaven." Erkki Antti and many other early preachers soon approved of this decision.

It was natural that Laestadius would be informed of this new development. The guarded attitude of Laestadius is generally known. It is believed that his hesitation was directed at "wall to wall" absolution. Pronouncing absolution to the repentant would fit well with the basic view of Laestadius, but preaching the gospel to all listeners without examination or discrimination was a more foreign concept. This is supported by the following recollection: Laestadius had complained that Parka-Heikki preaches the gospel to every Greta and Pleta.[8]   Nevertheless, Laestadius did not challenge this, saying only that they could try it since it has been revealed to you. Laestadius was convinced of the value of absolution and used it himself. The intention of Raattamaa and his companions was not to dispense the gospel to the unrepentant, but even a slight restriction could be a hindrance to those hearers who had difficulty believing. For their benefit, more effective tools were needed.

The data collected by Miettunen and Jussila are mutually exclusive recorded oral traditions from a widespread area with notable similarities, which form a logically complete picture and confirm that they are genuine, even though the oral traditions in themselves have inaccuracies.

ABSOLUTION ACCEPTED GRADUALLY

Soon after the above-mentioned events of February 1854, Raattamaa writes to his Christian brothers and sisters:

---

[8] Meaning "every Tom, Dick, and Harry"

I still say to all pillars of Christianity: If the loosing Key is not used with the same power as the binding Key, the devil of unbelief and self-righteousness gets to be lord and finally brings even the repentant down to hell. No one can fight against sin without faith.

This exhortation was necessary, for the discovery did not take hold easily. Many well-known revival preachers such as Pekka Raattamaa resisted the use of absolution and broad preaching of faith. Letters by Erkki-Antti and Raattamaa indicate persistent and prolonged opposition. It took ten years before a general consensus was reached. This is not really surprising, since the movement had already spread to a wide area in a form characteristic of the early revival that has been described as zealous and even legalistic. After gaining a deeper understanding of the gospel and a clearer understanding of absolution of sins, the movement began to spread with new power in all directions, especially in Finland...

THE HISTORY IS RELATED TO THEOLOGY

Why have Laestadian circles placed so much emphasis on the time frame in which absolution was introduced? This question has a theological dimension. Absolution is priceless to the conscience burdened by the law, but the high value placed on it has also led to unbalanced interpretations. There is the notion that faith is born only through absolution. God's manner of working in the human heart to bring about faith has not always been recognized. The question arose: If absolution was not practiced from the beginning of the revival, how then did the first Laestadians come to faith? For that reason there is a tendency to place the first use of absolution at the very beginning of the revival.

A question closely related to this is: What part do other believers play in a person's coming to faith? When people become aware of the authority that Jesus gave to his disciples, it can lead to an excessive emphasis on the believer as well as the congregation. Laestadius himself did not point the movement in that direction. He consistently emphasized that Christ and God's work are primary—believers are only assistants.

Raattamaa and other older preachers were aware of these problems and endeavored to correct the distortions. Policy within the movement was clarified, especially in the 1870s. At the Alkkula meeting in 1875 "the three-cubit-god doctrine," according to which the Holy Spirit only works among believers, was rejected. The importance of the written word along with the spoken word was also emphasized. The meeting rejected a rigid formula for conversion and dropped the requirement of public confession. Many of these tendencies have been difficult to overcome and continue to exist on the fringes of Laestadianism.

THE GOSPEL USED FROM THE BEGINNING

Laestadius was not just a revivalist; he made use of the gospel word from the very beginning. But the way in which it was conveyed to others was greatly affected by his followers. This was not difficult for Laestadius to accept. From the beginning, he drew his followers into the work of the gospel and sincerely esteemed the opinions of the believers in his congregation. Laestadius took the priesthood of all believers for granted. Now believers were vested with the power to forgive sins, so they were no longer limited to assuring people of God's grace and encouraging them to believe. Actually this step was not as great as one might think. In the background, there was a clear understanding that faith comes when the gospel is heard and believed. Then God in his time, immediately or a little later, creates faith.

Translated by Miriam Yliniemi

15

The Power of the Keys
Uuras Saarnivaara

The teaching about the Power of the Keys is central to all of the Laestadian groups. In fact, Laestadians have maintained from the early days that they rediscovered the fundamentally important Power of the Keys, which have been neglected by the Lutheran Church..

Luther's teaching on the Keys is presented in the following excerpts from Uuras Saarnivaara's booklet *The Power of the Keys,* 1960 edition. The title page reads as follows: *The Power of the Keys: the Original Faith of the Lutheran Church Presented in Quotations from Luther and the Lutheran Confessions.*

FOREWORD

Luther wrote: "The Keys are the real sanctuary and the noblest and holiest treasure of God, Christ, and the Church, since they are sanctified by Christ's blood and still every day administer the blood of Christ." "Both of these Keys (the binding and the loosing Key) are necessary to such an extent in Christendom that one can never thank God enough for them. For no man can comfort a terrified, sin-troubled conscience; even the loosing Key has all it can do herein; so great is the affliction of the timid, weak conscience that preachers, ministers, and other Christians should most emphatically inculcate faith in the judgment of the Keys" (*On the Keys*, 1530, Weimar Ed. 30, II, 501, 504).

The *Augsburg Confession* describes the attitude of the Lutherans of that time toward the power of the Keys as follows: "And the people are most carefully taught concerning faith in the absolution.... Our people are taught that they should highly prize the absolution as being the voice of God, and pronounced by God's command. The power of the Keys is set forth in its beauty, and they are reminded what great consolation it brings to anxious consciences; also that God requires faith to believe such absolution as a voice sounding from heaven, and that such faith in Christ truly obtains and receives the forgiveness of sins" (Art. XXV).

I. WHAT IS THE CHRISTIAN CHURCH?

"The Church is the congregation of saints, in which the Gospel is rightly taught and the sacraments are rightly administered" (*Augsburg Confession*, Art. VIII).

"The Church on earth...is a gathering of such as hear, believe, and confess the right teaching of the Gospel of Christ, and have with them the Holy Spirit who sanctifies them and works in them by the Word and the sacraments. Yet among these some are false Christians and hypocrites, who, nevertheless, are at one with them in the same doctrine and also hold communion in the sacraments and other outward offices of the Church. Aye, such people the Christians must suffer in their congregation and cannot, as men are, avoid it or prevent them from being amongst them, nor can they remove them or turn them out of their congregation." (Luther, *Church Postil*, 20th Sunday after Trinity, Gospel sermon, Weimar Ed. 22, 344, 12).

"The Church is not only the fellowship of outward objects and rites, ...but it is originally a fellowship of faith and of the Holy Ghost in hearts.... And this Church alone is called the body of Christ, which Christ renews, sanctifies, and governs by His Spirit.... Wherefore, those in whom Christ does not act (through His Spirit) are not the members of Christ...the wicked are dead members of the Church.... For the wicked are ruled by the devil, and are captives of the devil; they are not ruled by the Spirit of Christ" (*The Apology of the Augsburg Confession*, Chapter IV, Art. VII and VIII).

II. WHERE SHALL WE FIND CHRIST AND HIS GRACE?

"Therefore *he who would find Christ must first find the Church.* How should we know where Christ and His faith were, if we did not know where His believers are? And he who would know anything of Christ must not trust himself nor build a bridge to heaven by his own reason; but he must go to the Church, attend and ask her.

"Now the Church is not wood and stone, but the company of believing people; one must hold to them, and see how they believe, live and teach; they surely have Christ in their midst. For outside of the Christian Church there is no truth, no Christ, no salvation" (Luther, *Church Postil*, Christmas Day Gospel Sermon, Weimar Ed. 10, I, 1, 140; Lenker Ed. 10, 169f).

"Accordingly we are directed to seek forgiveness of sins in the Word which is put in the mouths of men, and in the sacraments administered by men, and nowhere else, for nowhere else can it be found.

"Therefore, mark well these teachings what forgiveness of sins is, how you can be assured of it, and where you are to seek and find it; namely, that you are to seek it nowhere but in the Christian Church, which has the Word and the sacraments. In these means you shall surely find it, and not in heaven, as the Pharisees think... God has enclosed forgiveness of sins in holy baptism, in the Lord's Supper, and in the Gospel; yea, He has laid it in the mouth of every Christian, when he comforts you and assures you of the grace of God in Christ Jesus, and you should accept and believe all this as if you had heard these assurances from the mouth of Jesus himself" (Luther, *House Postil*, 19th Sunday after Trinity, Weimar Ed. 52, 501).

III. WHAT IS TRUE REPENTANCE?

When we rise from sins, or repent, we do but return to the power and the faith of baptism from whence we fell, and find our way back to the promise made to us, from which we departed when we sinned. For the truth of the promise once made remains steadfast, ever ready to receive us back with open arms when we return....

"How harmful an error it is to believe that the power of baptism is broken, and the ship is foundered, because we have sinned! Nay; that one, solid and unsinkable ship remains, and is never broken up into floating timbers; it carries all those who are brought to the harbor of salvation; it is the truth of God giving us its promise in the sacraments. Many, indeed, rashly leap overboard and perish in the waves; these are they who depart from faith in the promise and plunge into sin. But the ship herself remains intact and holds her steady course; and if one be able somehow to return to the ship, it is not on any plank (as Jerome and the Catholics taught) but in the good ship herself that he is born into life. Such a one is he who through faith returns to the sure promise of God that abideth forever" (Luther, *On the Babylonian Captivity of the Church*, 1521, Weimar Ed. 6, 528f).

"Touching repentance, they teach that such as have fallen (sinned) after baptism, may find remission of sins any time they come to repentance, and that the Church should give absolution unto such as return to repentance.

"Now, repentance consists properly of these two parts: One is *contrition*, that is, terrors smiting the conscience through the knowledge of sin; the other is *faith*, which is *born of the Gospel, or of absolution*, and believes that, for Christ's sake, sins are forgiven, comforts the conscience, and delivers it from terrors. Then good works are bound to follow, which are the fruits of repentance" (*Augsburg Confession*, Art. XII).

IV. TO WHOM SHOULD WE CONFESS OUR SINS?

"In the presence of *God* we should acknowledge ourselves guilty of all manner of sins, even those which we do not ourselves perceive; as we do in the Lord's Prayer. But in the presence of the confessor we should confess those sins alone of which we have knowledge and which we feel in our hearts" (Luther, *Small Catechism*).

"We know that the Scriptures speak of *three kinds of confession*. The first is that which is made *to God*, of which David speaks in Ps. 32:5: 'I acknowledged my sin unto thee, and my iniquity I did not hide: I said, I will confess my transgressions unto the Lord; and thou forgavest the iniquity of my sin." …Therefore, this kind of confession must be made, that you may condemn yourself as worthy of death and the fire of hell; thus you will anticipate God so that He will not be able to judge and condemn you, but must show you mercy.

"The second kind of confession is that made *to our neighbor*, and is called the confession springing from love, as the other is called the confession springing from faith…. In this confession, whenever we have wronged our neighbor, we are to acknowledge our fault to him, as Christ declares in Matt. 5:23-25: '…First be reconciled to thy brother, and then come and offer thy gift. Agree with thine adversary quickly, while thou art with him in the way etc.' God here requires both parties, that he who has offended the other ask forgiveness, and that he who is asked grant it; for God will be merciful to no one, nor forgive his sins, unless he also forgive his neighbor. In like manner, faith cannot be true unless it produce this fruit, that you forgive your neighbor, and that you ask for forgiveness; otherwise a man dare not appear before God. If this fruit is absent, faith and the first kind of confession are not honest."

"The third kind of confession is that which is privately made *to a minister* [or some other Christian]. Concerning this, we will say that God does not force you to confess in faith to Him, or in love to your neighbor, when you have no desire to be saved and to receive His grace. Neither does He want you to make (the private) confession against your will and desire; on the contrary, He wants you to confess of your own accord, heartily, with love and pleasure. In like manner,

He does not compel you to make a private confession to the minister when you have no desire of your own to do so, and do not long for absolution" (Luther, *Church Postil*, Palm Sunday Gospel sermon— "Confession etc."—Weimar Ed. 15, 482ff. Lenker Ed. 11, 195ff.).

V. WHAT SINS SHOULD WE CONFESS IN PRIVATE CONFESSION?

"It should be that you first of all feel that which weighs you down, and the sins that pain you most and burden your conscience you ought to delcare and confess to your brother. Then you need not search long nor seek all kinds of sins; just take the ones that come to your mind, and say, This is how frail I am and how I have fallen; this is where I crave consolation and counsel. For confession ought to be brief."

"If you recall something that you have forgotten, it is not to trouble you; for you confessed not in order to do a good work, or because you were compelled, but in order to be comforted by the word of absolution. Moreover, you can easily confess to God in secret what was forgotten, or you can hear the absolution for it during the communion service."

"We are therefore not to worry even if sins have been forgotten; though forgotten they are still forgiven; for God looks, not to the excellence or completeness of your confession, but to His Word and how you believe it. So also the absolution does not state that some sins are forgiven and others not; on the contrary, it is a free proclamation declaring that God is merciful to you. But if God is merciful to you all your sins must be blotted out."

"Therefore, *hold fast to the absolution alone and not to your confession*; whether or not you have forgotten anything makes no difference; as much as you believe so much are you forgiven" (Luther, *Church Postil*, Palm Sunday Gospel sermon,—"Confession, etc."— Weimar Ed. 15, 489; Lenker Ed. 11, 201f.).

"In the presence of the confessor we should confess those sins alone of which we have knowledge and which we feel in our hearts" (Luther, *Small Catechism*).

VI. WHAT IS THE VALUE AND BENEFIT OF PRIVATE CONFESSION?

"I will let no man take private confession from me, and would not give it up for all the treasures in the world, since I know what comfort and strength it has given me. No one knows what private confession can do for him except he who has struggled much with the devil. Yea, the devil would have slain me long ago, if the confession had not sustained me. For there are many doubts which a man cannot solve and understand by himself. When he now is in such doubt and does not know how to get out of it, he takes a brother aside and tells him his trouble, complains of his shortcomings, his unbelief and his sins, and asks for comfort and counsel. For what does it matter if he humbles himself a little before a neighbor and takes shame on himself?"

"When then you receive comfort from your brother, accept it and believe him as though God Himself had told it, as Christ says in Matt. 18:20, 'For where two or three are gathered together in my name, there am I in the midst of them.'"

"We must have much absolution in order that our fearing consciences and discouraged hearts may be confirmed and comforted before God" (Luther, Sermons in Lent, 1522, eighth sermon, Weimar Ed. 10, III, 61 f.).

"Therefore let every Christian, when the devil attacks him and suggests that he is a great sinner and he must be lost and condemned etc., not long contend with him or remain alone, but go or call his pastor, or any other good friend, lay his difficulty before him, and seek counsel and comfort from him, and remain firm in that which Christ here declares: 'Whose soever sins ye remit they are remitted unto them,' and as He says in another place: 'Where two or more are gathered together in my name, there am I in the midst of them,' and whatever this person says to him in the name of Christ from the Scriptures, let him believe it, and according to his faith it shall be done unto him" (Luther, *Church Postil*, first Sunday after Easter, third Gospel sermon, Weimar Ed. 49, 147; Lenker Ed. 11, 394).

VII. WHAT IS THE POWER OF THE KEYS?

"The keys are the office, power or command, given by God through Christ to Christendom to forgive men their sins."

"Note that [in the words, 'Whatsoever ye shall bind on earth shall be bound in heaven: and whatsoever ye shall loose on earth shall be loosed in heaven'] He promises positively that what we bind and loose on earth shall be bound and loosed. He does not say, 'Whatsoever I shall bind and loose in heaven, you also shall bind and loose on earth,' as the teachers of erring keys [papists] teach and imagine. When, then, could we know what God binds and looses in heaven? Never, and thus the Keys would be in vain and of no avail.

"Neither does He say: You must know what I bind and loose in heaven; who could and would be able to know that?

"But He says thus: When you bind and loose on earth, I will at the same time bind and loose in heaven. When you execute the work of the Keys, I also will do the same; when you do it, it is done, and I do not need to do it again. Whatsoever you bind and loose (I say), that will I no more bind and loose, but it shall be bound and loosed without my binding and loosing. *My work and your work shall be the same work*, and not two different works. My Keys and your Keys are the one and the same set of Keys, and not two different sets of Keys; when you have done your work, my work also is done; when you bind and loose, I also have done the binding and loosing.

"*He obliges and binds Himself to our work, so that He entrusts to us the execution of His own work.* Why, then, should we make the thing uncertain or pervert it by saying that He should first bind and loose in heaven?" (Luther, *On the Keys*, 1530, Weimar Ed. 30, II, 497f.).

Consider also the following statement from the Apology of the Augsburg Confession:

"The power of the keys administers and presents the Gospel through absolution, which [proclaims peace to me and] is the true voice of the Gospel. Thus we also comprise absolution when we speak of faith, because 'faith cometh by hearing' as Paul says in Rom. 10:17. For when the Gospel is heard, and the absolution (i.e., the promise of divine grace) is heard, the conscience is encouraged and receives consolation. And because God truly quickens through the Word, the keys truly remit sins before God [here on earth sins are truly canceled in such a manner that they are canceled also before God in heaven] according to Luke 10:16: 'He that heareth you heareth me.' Wherefore the voice of the one absolving must be believed not otherwise than we would believe a voice from heaven. And absolution [that blessed word of comfort] properly can be called a sacrament of repentance" (Art. XII, Of Repentance).

VIII. WHAT IS THE SPIRITUAL PRIESTHOOD OF CHRISTIANS?

*"Baptism, the Gospel, and faith alone make us spiritual and Christian people...*as the Book of Revelation says, 'Through thy blood thou hast made us unto our God kings and priests.' For if there were not in us any higher ordination than that which is given by the Pope or a bishop, then no one would become a priest through the ordination of the Pope or a bishop and could not administer holy communion,

preach, and proclaim absolution (Luther, *To the Christian Nobility*, 1520, Weimar Ed. 6, 407).

"We are also priests forever, which is far more excellent than being kings, because as priests we are worthy to appear before God to pray for others and to teach one another the things of God. For these are the functions of priests, and cannot be granted to any unbeliever.

"Thus Christ has obtained for us, if we believe in Him, that we are not only His brethren, co-heirs and fellow-kings with Him, but also fellow-priests with Him, who may boldly come into the presence of God in the Spirit of faith, and cry, 'Abba, Father,' pray for one another and do all things which we see done and prefigured in the outward and visible works of priests.

"But he who does not believe is not served by anything…. And so he is no priest but a profane man, whose prayer becomes sin and never comes into the presence of God, because God does not hear sinners.

"Who then can comprehend the lofty dignity of the Christian? Through his kingly power he rules over all things, death, life sin, and through his priestly glory is all powerful with God, because God does the things which he asks and desires, as it is written, 'He will fulfill the desire of them that fear him; He also will hear their cry, and will save them.' To this glory man attains, surely not by any works of his, but by faith alone" (Luther, *Treatise on the Freedom of a Christian Man*, 1520, Weimar Ed. 7, 28).

"Christ has established upon the earth a comforting and blessed kingdom, when He says: 'As my Father hath sent me, so send I you.' He has consecrated (ordained) us all to be priests, in order that one may proclaim to the other the forgiveness of sins" (Luther, *Church Postil*, 1st Sunday after Easter, 3rd Gospel sermon, Weimar Ed. 49, 150; Lenker Ed. 11, 398).

"This same power belongs to every Christian, since Christ has made us all partakers of His power and dominion. This power (to remit and retain sins) is here (John 20:23) given to all Christians, although some have appropriated it to themselves alone, like the pope, the bishops, priests and monks have done: they declare publicly and arrogantly that this power was given to them alone and not to the laity. But Christ here speaks neither of priests nor of monks, but says: 'Receive ye the Holy Spirit.' Whoever has the Holy Spirit, the power is given to him, that is, to every one who is a Christian. But who is a Christian? He who believes. Whoever believes has the Holy Spirit.

Therefore every Christian has the power...to forgive sins and to retain them...

"True, we all have this power; but no one shall presume to exercise it publicly, except the one who has been elected by the congregation to do so. But in private I may freely exercise it. For instance, if my neighbor comes and says: 'Friend, I am burdened in my conscience; speak the absolution to me'—then I am free to do so, but I say, it must be done privately... And thereby we serve our neighbor. For in all services the greatest is to release from sin, to deliver from the devil and hell. But how is this done? Through the Gospel, when I preach it to a person and tell him to appropriate the words of Christ and to believe firmly that Christ's righteousness is his own, and his sins are Christ's. This, I say, is the greatest service I can render to my neighbor" (Luther, *Church Postil*, 1st Sunday after Easter, 1st and 2nd gospel sermon, Erlangen Ed. 11, 330, 346; Lenker Ed. 11, 360, 375f.).

IX. HOW DO WE RECEIVE THE FORGIVENESS OF SINS?

"The Lord our God made forgiveness of sins contingent on no work that we might perform, but on the great work which Christ accomplished when He died for the world, and for our benefit arose from the dead. The application of this, His work, He makes through the Word which He entrusted to the apostles, to the ministers of the Gospel, yea, to every Christian, authorizing them to declare unto all who seek it the remission of sins."

"Thus we have pointed out to us the only way in which we can surely find remission of sins, and in the Word we are sure to find this remission. If we seek it not there, our sins will be retained, do what we may; for...there is no remission except in the Word of Christ. This Word, however, has been entrusted to the apostles and all Christians, and they are to apply it; he who seeks any other remedy for the ills of sin, shall not find it, no matter what he may do to accomplish that end."

"Whoever now desires remission of sins, let him go to his minister or to some other fellow Christian who has God's Word, and he will surely find consolation there." (Luther, *House Postil*, first Sunday after Easter, Weimar Ed. 52, 273).

X. HOW CAN WE APPROPRIATE THE RIGHTEOUSNESS OF CHRIST?

"How and by what means may we appropriate such righteousness, so that we may receive the treasure acquired by Christ?

"God has ordained that no one shall come to the knowledge of Christ, nor obtain the forgiveness acquired by Him, nor receive the Holy Ghost, without the use of external and public means; but *God has embraced this treasure in the oral word or public ministry, and will not perform His work in a corner or mysteriously in the heart,* but will have it heralded and distributed openly among the people.... Therefore this part also, namely the *external word or preaching*, belongs to Christianity as a *channel or means* (Rohre und Mittel) through which we attain unto the forgiveness of sins, or the righteousness of Christ, with which Christ reveals and offers us His grace or lays it into our bosom, and without which no one would ever come to a knowledge of this treasure.... Therefore I have always taught that the oral word must precede everything else, must be comprehended with the ear, if the Holy Ghost is to enter the heart, who through the Word enlightens it and works faith. Consequently faith does not come except through the hearing and oral preaching of the Gospel, in which it has its beginning, growth and strength" (Luther, *Church Postil*, 19th Sunday after Trinity, Gospel sermon, Weimar Ed. 29, 578ff.; Lenker Ed. 14, 224f.).

Consider carefully also the following counsels of Luther:

"Thank God for His grace and learn that God will forgive sins. But how? In no other way than we here read, 'that he has given such power unto men.' ... Thus everyone should seek forgiveness of sins among men, and nowhere else. Here alone it can be found; for the Lord Jesus promises, Matt. 18: 'Verily I say unto you, whatsoever ye shall loose on earth shall be loosed in heaven.' And again, John 20, 'Whose soever sins ye remit, they are remitted unto them.' God will not permit every one to build a flight of steps or a ladder of his own into heaven; that He will attend to Himself" (Luther, *House Postil*, 19th Sunday after Trinity, Weimar Ed. 52, 500).

"By means of this office (of forgiveness) the apostles and their successors [Christian ministers, and even all Christians] are exalted also as lords unto the end of the world, and there is given unto them such great authority and power as Christ, the Son of God, himself possessed...and everything that lives and is called human upon the earth, shall be in subjection to their rule, whether it be emperor or king, great or small, no one is excluded."

"Therefore he says: 'whose soever sins ye remit.' This 'whose soever' means nothing else than that all are included, Jews, Gentiles, great and small, wise and ignorant, holy or unholy; that *no one shall enter heaven and come to eternal life, except he receive it from you, that is, through the office which you have received.*"

"For they all are also subject and concluded under sin through these words...and one of two things must take place: either their sins are forgiven, if they confess and desire forgiveness, or they must remain eternally bound in sin unto death and condemnation" (Luther, *Church Postil*, 1st Sunday after Easter, 3rd Gospel sermon, Weimar Ed. 21, 295).

XI. WHAT IS THE MEANING OF THE LAYING ON OF HANDS?

"According to the ordinance of God, sins are forgiven through the laying on of hands."

"God himself wills to work through them [i.e. the means of grace]...they are His Word, His hands, His bread and wine through which He will sanctify you in Christ and save you in Christ who has merited this all for us through His death and given the Holy Spirit from His Father for such works" (Luther, *On the Councils and the Church*, 1539, Weimar Ed. 50, 645, 648).

"Thou art, therefore, bound to believe him as though Christ were standing there himself and would lay His hand upon thee and pronounce the absolution" (Luther, *Church Postil*, first Sunday after Easter, third Gospel sermon, Weimar Ed. 49, 148; Lenker Ed. 11, 395).

XII. DOES ABSOLUTION DEPEND ON CONTRITION, AND SHOULD IT BE PRONOUNCED CONDITIONALLY?

"Uncertain absolution is the same as no absolution; yea, it is perfectly the same as lie and deceit.... But it must be uncertain [the Roman Catholics hold] since repentance whereon it depends is uncertain; for who is able to say that his repentance is sufficient before God? And what repentance can be sufficient before God? For our own repentance does not suffice in His sight, but Christ himself with His suffering must be our repentance and satisfaction before God..."

"Keep in mind that the Key or forgiveness of sins is not founded on our contrition or worthiness..., but to the contrary, we should base our contrition, work, heart, and everything, on the Key and rely on it with our whole conviction, as on God's Word.... It is true, you should repent and be contrite; but the assumption that forgiveness of sins would become sure and the operation of the Key confirmed by that, would mean giving up faith and denying Christ. He will not grant and impart to you the forgiveness of sins through the Key for your sake, but for His own sake, by sheer mercy." (Luther, *On the Keys*, 1530, Weimar Ed. 30, II, 480f. 496)

"If a man were required to say he is truly penitent, he would be driven to presumption and to the impossible task of knowing all his sins and evil. ... Christians ought to be instructed that every penitent [one who makes a confession and seeks absolution] may know that before God no contrition is worthy or sufficient, and may say, 'Behold, dear Lord, I know that I will not be found truly contrite before thy judgment, and that there is still much evil lust in me which hinders true contrition, yet, because Thou hast promised grace, I flee from Thy judgment, and...put my reliance and my hope upon Thy promise in this sacrament (= absolution).'"

"If the minister inquires about his contrition, he ought to say, 'Sir, in my own eyes I am contrite, but in God's sight it is but a poor contrition, with which I am not able to stand in His presence; yet I hope in his grace, which you are now, at His command, to promise me'" (Luther, *Grund und Ursach* [Argument in Defence], Art. 14, Weimar Ed. 7, 384).

"When a Christian hears and is made to believe that the Key can err and go amiss, he can then by no means rely and believe that which the Key promises him. For of that in which one believes one must be sure and absolutely convinced beyond any doubt that it is God's word and truth. Otherwise there can be born only uncertain assumption and wavering faith, and even unbelief..."

"We are not speaking now on the question who believes and who does not believe, for we do know very well that only few believe; but we speak of what the Keys accomplish and give. Many people do not believe the Gospel, but the Gospel, nevertheless, does not lie. A certain king gives you a castle: if you do not accept it, the king has yet not lied nor deceived, but you have deceived yourself, and the fault is yours; the king has surely given it" (Luther, *On the Keys*, 1530, Weimar Ed. 30, II, 480-483, 499).

XIII. HOW ARE WE TO BELIEVE IN THE FORGIVENESS OF SINS?

"It is true that *the minister truly remits sin and guilt, but he cannot give faith* to the sinner who receives and accepts the forgiveness; *God must give the faith.* But, nevertheless, the remission of sins is as positively true as if God pronounced it, whether it sticks to the heart of man through faith or not" (Luther, *Treatise on Confession*, 1519, Weimar Ed. 2, 722).

"One knows not at what hour God may touch and illuminate his or another's heart. It may be in a time when we least look for it, or in the individual of whom we have least expectation. For the Spirit, as Christ says, breathes where He will, and touches hearts when and where he knows them to be receptive" (Luther, *Church Postil*, 1st Sunday after Easter, epistle sermon, WA. 21, 284, 31; Lenker Ed. 8, 242).

"Although I cannot give you the Holy Ghost and faith, I can yet declare them unto you; if you believe, you have it" (Luther, *Church Postil*, 19th Sunday after Trinity, first Gospel sermon, Weimar Ed. 22, 224; Lenker Ed. 14, 210).

"By the Word and Sacraments, as by instruments, the Holy Spirit is given; who works faith, where and when it pleases God, in those who hear the Gospel, to wit, that God, not for our merit's sake, but for Christ's sake, justifies those who believe that they for Christ's sake are received into favor" (*Augsburg Confession*, Art. V).

XIV. WHAT IS TRUE FAITH?

"Faith, if it is true faith, is of such a nature that it does not rely upon itself nor upon the faith; but holds to Christ, and takes refuge under his righteousness; and he lets this righteousness be his shield and protection just like the little chicken never trusts in its own life and efforts, but takes refuge under the body and wings of the hen... Oh, we must remain in Christ, upon Christ and under Christ, never stray from our mother hen, or all is lost. St. Peter says in his first epistle 4:8: 'The righteous is scarcely saved;' so hard is it to abide under this hen. For many different temptations, temporal and spiritual, tear us from her."

"Paul says (Rom 3:25) of Christ, 'Whom God set forth to be a propitiation, through faith in his blood.' It is not just 'faith' but 'faith in his blood.' With His blood He has rendered full satisfaction and become for us a throne of grace. We receive absolution and grace at no cost or labor on our part, but not without cost and labor on the part of Christ."

"We must, then, shelter ourselves under His wings (Matt. 23:37) and not fly afar in the security of our own faith, else we will soon be devoured by the hawk. Our salvation must exist, not in our righteousness, but in Christ's righteousness, which is an outspread wing, or a tabernacle, to shelter us."

"Guard, then, against false teachers and also against false faith. Flee to Christ; keep under His wings; remain under His shelter. Let His righteousness and grace, not yours, be your refuge... In the wounds of Christ, the soul is preserved. Observe, true Christian faith does not take refuge in itself but flees to Christ and is preserved under Him and in Him" (Luther, *Church Postil*, 2nd Christmas Day gospel s. and epistle s., Weimar Ed. 10, I, 1,281f. 125f.).

XV. WHAT ARE THE FRUITS OF A LIVING FAITH?

"Faith is a divine work in us. It changes us and makes us to be born anew of God (John 1); it kills the old Adam and makes altogether different men, in heart and spirit and mind and powers, and it brings with it the Holy Ghost. O, it is a living, busy, active, mighty thing, this faith; and so it is impossible for it not to do good works incessantly. It does not ask whether there are good works to do, but before the question arises, it has already done them, and is always at the doing of them. He who does not these works is a faithless man..."

"Faith is a living, daring confidence in God's grace, so sure and certain that a man would stake his life on it a thousand times. This confidence in God's grace and knowledge of it makes men glad and bold and happy in dealing with God and with all His creatures; and this is the work of the Holy Spirit in faith. Hence a man is ready and glad, without compulsion, to do good to everyone, to serve everyone, to suffer everything, in love and praise of God, who has shown him this grace; and thus it is impossible to separate works from faith, quite as impossible to separate works from faith, quite as impossible as to separate heat and light from fire..."

"For through faith, a man becomes free from sin and gets pleasure in God's commandments; thus he gives to God the honor that is His and pays Him what he owes Him; but he also serves man willingly, in every manner he can, and thus pays his obligation to everyone. Nature and free will and all our powers cannot bring into existence such righteousness" (Luther, *Preface to the Romans*, 1522, WA. Deutsche Bibel, 7, 11f.; an English translation e.g. in the Philadelphia (Holman) edition of Luther's Works, Vol. VI, 447ff., and in M. Reu's book, *Luther's German Bible*, II, 205ff.).

"The new creature, whereby the image of God is renewed (in man),...is a work of the Holy Spirit who cleanses our heart through faith (Acts 15:9) and works the fear of God, love, chastity, and other Christian virtues, and gives power to bridle the flesh, and to reject the righteousness and wisdom of the world. Here is no coloring or new outward show but a thing done indeed. Here is created another sense and another judgment, that is to say, altogether spiritual, which abhors those things that it greatly esteemed before..."

"This is the renewing of the mind through the Holy Spirit; after this follows a change of the members and senses of the whole body. For when the heart has conceived a new light, a new judgment, and new emotions through the Gospel, it comes to pass that the inward senses are also renewed; for the ears desire to hear the word of God and not the traditions and dreams of men. The mouth and tongue do not vaunt of their own works, righteousness and rules; but they set forth the mercy of God only offered to us in Christ. These changes do not consist in words but are effectual and bring a new spirit, a new will, new senses, and new operations of the body, so that the eyes, ears, mouth, and tongue do not only see, hear, and speak otherwise than they did before, but the mind also approves, loves, and follows other things than it did before. For before, being blinded with...errors and darkness, it imagined God to be a merchant who would sell unto us His grace for our works and merits; but now, in the light of the Gospel, it assures us that we are counted righteous by faith in Christ. Therefore, it now rejects all self-designed works and does the works of charity and of our vocation, commanded by God. It praises and magnifies God; it rejoices and glories in the only trust and confidence in the mercy of God, through Jesus Christ. If it must suffer any trouble and affliction, it endures it cheerfully and gladly, although the flesh repine and grudge at it" (Luther, *Commentary on Galatians*, 1531-35, WA. 40, II, 178f., Gal. 6:15).

"These works are a sure sign of faith, which in Christ receives remission of sins and the victory over death. For it is impossible for him who believes in Christ as a righteous Savior, not to love and do good. If, however, he does not do good nor love, it is sure that faith is not present. Therefore, man knows by the fruits what kind of a tree he is, and is proved by love and deed whether Christ is in him and he believes in Christ. As St. Peter says in 2 Pet. 1:10: 'wherefore, brethren, give the more diligence to make your calling and election sure; for if ye do these things, ye shall never stumble,' that is, if you bravely practice good works you will be sure and cannot doubt that God has called and chosen you."

"Thus, faith blots out sin in a different manner than love. Faith blots it out of itself, while love or good works prove and demonstrate that faith has done so and is present, as St. Paul says, 1 Cor. 13:2: 'And if I have all faith, so as to remove mountains, but have not love, I

am nothing.' Why? Without doubt, because faith is not present where
there is no love, they are not separate the one from the other" (Luther,
Church Postil, 1ˢᵗ Sunday in Advent, Gospel sermon, WA. 10, I, 2,
44).

"In the members and the flesh there is sin which wars against the
spirit; but because the spirit wars against it, and he does not obey it, it
does not harm, and God judges a (Christian) man not according to the
sin which assails him in the flesh but according to the spirit which
wars against sin and is thereby like the will of God which hates and
fights against sin. It is one thing, then, to say that sins are forgiven,
and another thing to say that there is no sin present. After baptism and
repentance all sins are forgiven, but sin is still present until death,
although because of forgiveness it does not prevent salvation, provided
we strive against it and do not obey it."

"Sin remains but is not imputed; and that for two reasons…—
first, because we believe in Christ who through faith becomes our
representative and covers our sin with His innocence; second, because
we strive unceasingly against sin, to destroy it. Where these two
reasons are not present, sin is imputed, is not forgiven, and condemns
eternally."

"This is the joy, the comfort, the blessedness and salvation of the
New Testament…. This makes free, glad, brave Christians, whose love
causes them to fight against sin, and who take pleasure in repentance"
(Luther, *Grund und Ursach,* 1521, Art. 2, WA. 7, 375; in English in
the Philadelphia (Holman) ed., vol. III, 35).

XVI. SHOULD WE USE PRIVATE CONFESSION AND ABSOLUTION BEFORE GOING TO THE LORD'S SUPPER?

"Confession in the churches is not abolished among us; for it is not
usual to give the body of the Lord, except to them who have been
previously examined and absolved" (Augsburg Confession, Art.
XXV).

"You must regard the Word, or absolution, great and of a high
value, a wonderful and great treasure which should be received with
great reverence and gratitude… We give this advice: If you are poor
and wretched, make use of this healing remedy. Now, he who realizes
his misery and need is kindled into such desire to make use of
confession, so that he joyfully hastens there. To the contrary, those
who do not mind of it and do not come of their own accord, may go

their way. But let them know that we do not consider them as Christians."

"Thus, we teach of the sweetness, value and comfort of confession, and furthermore, we admonish that this precious blessing should not be despised, especially since our need is great. If you are Christian you do not need at all my coercing…, but you coerce yourself of your own accord, and ask me to let you to have it."

"But if you despise it and proudly live without making use of confession, we draw the conclusion that you are no Christian, and cannot be admitted to participate in the sacrament (of the altar). For you despise what no Christian should despise, and the result of your behavior is that you cannot possess at all the forgiveness of sins. This is, furthermore, a sure token of the fact that you despise also the Gospel" (Luther, Large Catechism, "A short admonition to confession," Weimar Ed. 31, I, 236f.).

XVII. How Should the Celebration of the Lord's Supper Be Arranged, and Who Should Be Admitted to It?

"We should plan and accomplish it (the celebration of the Lord's Supper), as I have earnestly wished, that we might gather into one place those who truly believe, and acknowledge our faith before others. I earnestly desired to have this done long ago, but circumstances did not permit; for this truth has not been preached and urged enough."

"That is the way Christ did; he delivered his sermons to the multitude for everybody, as the apostles later did, so that every person heard them, believers and unbelievers; whoever caught it, caught it."

"We must do the same. But we are not to cast the sacrament (of the altar) among the people in a crowd, as the pope has done. When I preach the Gospel I do not know to whom it applies; but here I should be sure that it applies to those who come to the sacrament. Here I must not act in doubt, but be sure that the one to whom I give the sacrament has laid hold of the Gospel and has true faith, …neither the one who receives the sacrament should doubt."

"And if your faith is only a human thought, that you have originated, then remain away from this sacrament. For it must be a faith that God makes, you must know and feel that God works in you" (Luther, *Church Postil*, "A beautiful sermon on the reception of the holy sacrament," 1523, Erlangen Ed. 11, 203; Lenker Ed. 11, 230).

XVIII. WHO RECEIVES THE LORD'S SUPPER WORTHILY?

"He is truly worthy and well prepared, who believes these words: 'Given, and shed for you, for the remission of sins.' But he who does not believe these words, or who doubts, is unworthy and unfit; for the words: 'FOR YOU,' require truly believing hearts" (Luther, *Small Catechism*).

"It is necessary that...you distinguish well between the outward reception and the inner and spiritual reception...which is a reception in faith... There must be faith to make one well prepared for the reception and acceptable before God, otherwise it is all sham and mere external show, which is not Christianity at all..."

"But faith (which we all must have, if we wish to go to the sacrament worthily) is a firm trust, that Christ, the Son of God, stands in our place and has taken all our sins upon His shoulders, and that He is the eternal satisfaction for our sin and reconciles us with God the Father..."

"He who has this faith belongs to this sacrament, and neither devil nor hell nor sin can harm him... He who has such faith is fit for the altar and receives the sacrament as an assurance, or seal, or sign to assure him of God's promises and grace..."

"But such faith we do not all have; would to God one-tenth of the Christians had it. See, such rich, immeasurable treasures, which God in His grace showers upon us, cannot be the possession of everyone, but only of those who suffer either spiritual adversity: the bodily through the persecution of man and the spiritual by despair of conscience; outwardly or inwardly, when the devil causes your heart to be weak, timid and discouraged, so that you know not how you stand with God, and when he reproaches you with your sins. And in such terrified and trembling hearts alone God desires to dwell, as the prophet Isaiah says [66:2]. For he who has not felt the battle within him, is not distressed by his sins nor has a daily quarrel with them, and wishes no protection, defender, and shield to stand before God, is not yet ready for this food. This food demands a hungering and longing man, for it delights to enter a hungry soul, one that is in constant battle with its sins and eager to be rid of them."

"He who is not thus prepared should abstain for awhile from this sacrament, for this food is not for a sated and full heart, and if it comes to such, it is harmful. Therefore, if we think upon, and feel within us, such distress of conscience and the fear of a timid heart, we shall come with all humbleness and reverence... For this bread is a comfort for the sorrowing, a healing for the sick, a life for the dying, a food for all the hungry, and a rich treasure for all the poor and needy" (Luther, *Sixth sermon in Lent*, 1522, Weimar Ed. 10, III, 48ff. Philadelphia Ed. II, 417ff.).

16

The Impact of Immigration History on Apostolic Lutheranism

Elmer Yliniemi

What were the conditions that started the wave of Finnish emigration to America in the 1860s? Understanding the prevailing conditions in the homeland and the new world during the second half of the nineteenth century gives insight into the challenges that faced immigrants establishing a church in their new homeland.

CONDITIONS LEADING TO EARLY EMIGRATION FROM NORRBOTTEN

The borders of the Arctic area of the three Nordic countries (Sweden, Norway and Finland) were not well defined. A large Finnish-speaking population emerged in Norrbotten, the region west of the Tornio River, during the long union which existed between Finland and Sweden until 1809. Therefore, a large portion of the area's population was of Finnish or Sami ancestry.

Finns had moved to Finnmark (the northernmost province of Norway) as early as the 1700s to seek a better livelihood during wars and famines. The Finnish-speaking people were called *Kvens* by the Norwegians. During the nineteenth century, these numbers increased. The 1860s were especially difficult years of famine in Finland due to weather conditions which culminated in the terrible famine of 1867. The death rate rose and people resorted to eating *pettuleipä* (bread made from pine bark).

Arctic fishing and copper mining in Kaafjord drew the poverty-stricken Finns northward. Deep-sea fishing in the Arctic was not easy. They generally had to work for Norwegian employers in a cold, harsh climate. Sudden storms often took the lives of fishermen. The Finns were a rural agricultural people rather than a sea-going people. One person describes how fish had taken over their lives in Arctic Norway as follows:

Live fish, dead fish, dried fish, cured fish, fishheads, fish-entrails, smell of fish, stink of fish, and vessels which fetch fish, people who buy fish, and people who sell fish, people who only live for fish, only speak, think, and dream of fish—nothing else![9]

The Finns brought new farming techniques to Finnmark, but because of the climate and small plots of land, they could not survive on farming alone. Also the mining activities were slowing down and being terminated at that time.

In the midst of these difficulties, word came that there was free land available in America. In America, the Homestead Act of 1862 had been passed which provided 160 acres of land on condition of five years residence and cultivation of the land. There was also a labor shortage caused by the Civil War in the United States which legalized recruitment of foreign workers. It was at that time that recruiters were sent to Norway from the Hancock-Calumet mines to enlist workers.

MIGRATION MAP

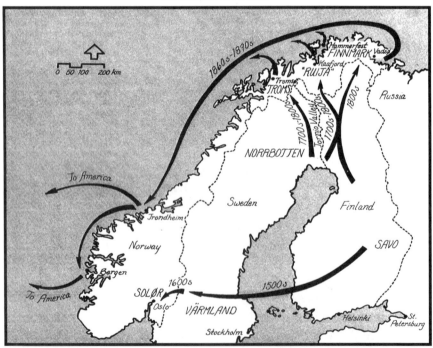

Major Settlement Areas for Finns in Norway and Sweden, 1500s -1800s.
(Arrows depict generalized migration flows only.) Map is from "The Norwegian Connection" by Arnold Alanen—used with permission.

---

[9] Kolehmainen, "Finnish Overseas Migration from Arctic Norway and Russia," **Agricultural History** 19 (October 1945) p. 226.

Since the Finns had already made a move and were unhappy with their circumstances, it was not as traumatic for them to leave for America as it was for those who had never lived outside of Finland.

During this time, the Laestadian revival was rapidly spreading among the Finns in the North. The famine put the Finns on the move, and the revival spread with them. Socio-economic conditions and natural disasters have moved people from one place to another throughout the ages.

Research on the first Finns who immigrated to America in the 1860s has been complicated by the fact that it involved three countries. It is difficult to tell how many Finns actually immigrated to the United States from official immigration and census records because most of the Finns in the 1860s and 1870s migrated via Arctic Norway. Many of the people who left for America from Norway considered themselves Finns and spoke the Finnish language although they may have been born on the Swedish side of the Tornio River which separates Finland and Sweden. For example, records indicate that between 1867-1873, 837 people left Vadsø, Norway (Finnmark) for America. Based on names, 556, or two out of three, were Finnish.

The numbers in those early years were not significant compared to the great mass migration of the 1880s. However, those who left in the earlier years were the true pioneers who knew little about the conditions they would face in the new world. From the perspective of Finnish-American traditions, this group of Kven pioneers, who came from very harsh, impoverished conditions, left a particular legacy during that phase of history. They were the ones who organized the first Finnish communities, established the first churches, and introduced the future immigrants to a new way of life.

There have been many misconceptions about the first immigrants who came via Norway. They were not all Laestadians by any means, and there is no evidence that they left due to persecution. However, since that was a time when the revival was rapidly spreading, there were a number of people who had been converted in the revival and brought the revival fires with them. Some were known to have preached in the Tornio Valley before moving to Norway. They had been in personal contact with the revival leaders and communicated regularly by letters. That is why it has been said that the revival leaders knew more about Cokato and Calumet than they did about Oulu and Helsinki in the 1870s. Actually the revival reached America before it reached southern Finland.

FIRST IMMIGRANT SETTLEMENTS AND THE CHURCH

Some of the early pioneers came to the Upper Peninsula of Michigan as a result of the mine recruiters sent to Norway, and some came directly to Minnesota. The Upper Peninsula was soon the largest Finnish settlement in America. Many came to the mines to earn money with the goal of moving on to purchase land for a farm.

In 1865-1866 three small Finnish farming settlements had been established in Minnesota: Cokato, Franklin and Holmes City. New York Mills, Minnesota, was settled in the mid 1870s and Savo, South Dakota, a couple years later.

Although the number of early immigrants from northern Scandinavia (1865-1875) was relatively small, they had a very special short-term role, which would impact the future. They faced overwhelming challenges in organizing the Laestadian communities and in their inner development which created traditions for future generations.

The most notable difficulty for the Laestadian Christians was the absence of a state church. Even though L.L. Laestadius had been very critical of the state church, he did not advocate separation from it, and state-church membership was a strong tradition in all the Scandinavian countries. The Laestadian movement in Finland had become increasingly independent, but the state church with its sacraments and educational system provided a framework in which they could operate. The pastors were responsible for keeping official records of births, marriages, and deaths, as well as supplying necessary certificates for employment, passports, inheritance, etc. The Laestadians were all members of the state church and paid taxes to support the church. The church had been instrumental in developing literacy through mission schools, confirmation classes, and reading examinations. According to U.S. immigration records at the turn of the century, 98 percent of the Finnish immigrants to America over 14 years of age were literate. During the same period, 74 percent of immigrant groups in general were literate.

The Finns were used to the dual system in Finland, so the American system seemed strange to them. In Finland they went to the local village church, which was usually located visibly in the center of the village to have their children baptized, to be confirmed, to receive communion, to be married and buried. Due to long distances in the large northern parishes, the mission schools and village prayer meetings provided gathering opportunities for the Laestadians.

As the revival spread, they had their own services in homes or prayer houses. The prayer houses were extremely modest buildings with a table and chairs for the preachers and a very simple order of service often including the reading of a sermon by Laestadius, songs led by a song leader due to lack of song books, and lay speakers testifying of their faith or explaining a portion of scripture extemporaneously. The prayer houses did not have altars. The Finnish village churches usually had a bell tower, organ, ornate pulpit, altar, altar painting and a liturgical service.

At first it seemed natural for the Laestadian immigrants in the Upper Peninsula of Michigan to be members of the Scandinavian Evangelical Lutheran congregation in Hancock-Quincy. However, it was not long until disputes developed, and they were forbidden the sacraments by Norwegian Pastor Roernaes. The Laestadian Christians were forced to seek their own fellowship.

Salomon Kortetniemi, a former sexton (church caretaker) in Ylitornio, who knew the Finnish state church order of worship, emerged as a leader in establishing the Finnish congregation in Calumet. He was trying to create a transitional church form between the village prayer house tradition and the necessary church organization in their new circumstances. The first organization of Laestadians took place on December 21, 1872, under the name "Solomon Kortetniemi Lutheran Society," with 119 men signing the Articles of Association. Many of the men had families, so there were many more members than the number implies. The certificate of incorporation was notarized on January 11, 1873.

This aroused criticism from the beginning. The disputes related to the official organization of the church and order of worship as well as the position of the pastor. The criticism increased in 1873 with the arrival of a group of Laestadians that included several young preachers who had been in direct contact with the current revival tradition and leaders in Finland.

Juho Takkinen (1838-1892) was sent to America by the Lapland elders in 1877 to settle disputes. He was instrumental in getting the name changed from Solomon Kortetniemi Lutheran Society to Finnish Apostolic Lutheran Church in 1879.

The Laestadians in Cokato, Minnesota, met as early as the late 1860s under the leadership of Barberg who left with his family from Swedish Ylitornio (Övertorneå) in 1866. The church in Cokato was organized in 1872 but was not officially registered. The first church in

Cokato was built in 1876. "The church building stood on a high knoll—that idea the founders had surely brought from Finland—where the first graves of the community had been dug. The builders were too poor to imitate the beautiful old churches at home, but copied the plain four-square meeting houses of pietists in the Old Country."[10] Even though it was less officially organized, the same conflicts emerged as in the Upper Peninsula.

Savo Church-1884 (A typical early Apostolic Lutheran Chuch building)

Under Takkinen's leadership the services, which had been a source of conflict during the Kortetniemi era, were simplified. The most important change was discontinuing the liturgy found in the Finnish church handbook. Standing for the Apostles' Creed and kneeling during the general confession of sins [by the congregation in unison] were dropped. Organs were not used. Taking oaths and making the sign of the cross in the Sacrament of Baptism were eliminated. The worship service adopted the "old country" village prayer meeting and mission school format with hymns, prayer, and sermon. However, the state church concept of open communion recommended by the Lapland elders was followed so that the Laestadian community could

---

[10] Lehtola, John. Finnishness as a Religious and Cultural Experience. (Master's Thesis) Helsinki 1992. p. 79. "The Annandale Advocate," July 9, 1986.

serve all Finnish immigrants in the area, since that was often the only church in the community. The Apostolic Lutheran church buildings differed from the prayer houses in that they added an altar rail for communion. The following is a description of the Riverside Church built in French Lake, Minnesota, in 1886:

> It was a spare and unadorned building, reflecting the spare and unadorned piety of its congregation. There was no cross, no stained-glass windows, none of the decoration that characterizes many churches. The pews were hand-made of local Norway pine, the altar was a simple structure of the same material. Its walls were covered in tin. Its ministers wore no vestments. The service—nearly always two hours long—consisted mainly of preaching...A long sermon and the singing of traditional Finnish Apostolic hymns: the service, like the building, was simple and unadorned.[11]

The Savo Church interior built in 1884, Dakota Territory

---

[11] Lehtola, John. *Finnishness as a Religious and Cultural Experience.* (Master's Thesis) Helsinki 1992. p. 81. "The Annandale Advocate," July 9, 1986.

Apparently Takkinen had help and support from Juhani Raattamaa in changing and cleansing the congregation from outward ritual. Raattamaa writes to Takkinen in a letter on June 10, 1878, as follows:

> I have already written that in my view the church in Minnesota is organized correctly in that both of the Sacraments belong to the congregation and not only to ordained pastors...Even the new church law in Finland allows the Lord's Supper to be served by any Christian, even if he is not an ordained pastor, in emergencies. Biblical explanations and oral declarations directed at the heart are appropriate for communion sermons and other sermons among the fellowship of saints. You have Luther's and Laestadius's sermons as we do, so that Solomon Kortetniemi or other lay preachers do not need to chant [the liturgy] or outline their sermons but use mission letters, as did the apostles. The reading of Laestadius's sermons is most suited to the people of our day especially on Sundays and holidays when the indifferent and the curious come to hear the Word. ...We here in Europe receive the sacraments from ordained pastors as the law requires. You can be free, if you wish, to tie yourselves to the apron strings of the state church which considers all of Europe Christian through infant baptism; that is the belief of the Greeks, papists and even Lutherans. You know, dear brothers, that the church of Christ is comprised of contrite and broken hearts. Therefore, let us build God's temple with sermons of the bloody gospel working on hearts to remain cleansed by the blood of the Lamb from sin which always clings to us...[12]

Takkinen was a gifted preacher who took his job seriously. He ministered in Calumet, Michigan, and the surrounding areas. He traveled throughout the congregations in Minnesota, the Dakotas, and even to Washington and Oregon to help organize their churches and set up a system for record keeping. He also conducted catechetical meetings, preached, and set up classes for children using the *Aapinen* [*ABC Book*] that he published in 1880. This book created a stir in America and in Finland when he added the word Gethsemane to the Apostles' Creed so the middle part of the second article read as follows:

---

[12] Raittila, Pekka. *Juhani Raatamaa: Kirjeet ja Kirjoitukset.* Helsinki, Finland 1976. pp.200-201.

...born of the Virgin Mary; descended into hell in Gethsemane, suffered under Pontius Pilate, was crucified, died and was buried: the third day He rose from the dead, ascended into heaven and sitteth on the right hand of God...

The content of the sentence concerning Jesus's descent to hell was not an arbitrary whim among Laestadians. Powerfully moving descriptions of the passion of Jesus and the mystique attached to it formed the core of the movement's milieu. In addition, this thought was expressed clearly in certain sermons of Laestadius: "When He [in the garden of Gethsemane] sweat blood for your sakes, he descended into hell and there suffered all its pangs" (Laestadius's Postil 1964 pp. 1417 and 672).[13]

The Lapland elders approved this change in the *Aapinen* and Raattamaa writes to Takkinen as follows:

What you asked concerning the opinion of the people on the changes to the *Aapinen*; all enlightened Christians are of the same mind as I when they read the American *Aapinen*. The old Christians of Lapland whose hearts have been touched by the suffering of Jesus in Gethsemane have said that their heartfelt belief is that Jesus suffered the pains of hell in Gethsemane and unto His death on the cross...But since Luther did not leave out the words "descended into hell" from the Apostles's Creed, let us laymen leave them where they are in Europe.[14]

However, the pastors in Finland who had been converted to the movement wrote against it in their publications. The dispute began when Heikel criticized and rejected the *Aapinen* which was published in the November 1880 issue of the *Kristillinen Kuukauslehti* [*Chritstian Monthly*].

Heikel and the people of Ylitornio who agreed with him held it highly questionable that the editors of the *Aapinen* had changed the mutual confession of faith held by all Christiandom, to which "hundreds of millions have held and died blessedly, and for which hundreds of thousands, even millions, of martyrs have given their

---

[13] Raittila, Pekka. "The Relationshhip of the First Generation Laestadians to Luther and the Church Confessions." Helsinki 1971. Translated by Don Kilpela.
[14] Raittila, Pekka. *Juhani Raattamaa: Kirjeet ja Kirjoitukset*. Letter written to Takkinen on April 12, 1981. p. 236.

lives" (*Kristillinen Kuukauslehti* [*Christian Monthly*], 1880, p 164).

The *Aapinen* still occupied people's minds even after the public dispute had abated. Aatu Laitinen, the new editor of the *Kristillinen Kuukauslehti* wrote a sympathetic letter to the "American brothers" entitled "Descended into Hell" which concluded with the recommendation: "Let us leave the Apostles's Creed as it is, when even beloved Luther, with his spiritual insight, has not seen it necessary to alter it (*Kristillinen Kuukauslehti*, 1883 pp. 24-27).

Laitinen's advice did not bear fruit immediately. When Takkinen had *Luther's Small Catechism* printed in 1885, it contained the Apostles's Creed in its 1880 altered form. Takkinen's removal in the late 1880s was, perhaps, in part, due to the fact that in editing the *New American Finnish Aapinen* he abandoned his earlier alterations and followed the arrangement of Aatu Laitinen's 1885 *Aapinen.* Takkinen's last *Aapinen* was published after his death in 1892. The Old Apostolic Lutheran Church in America still uses the altered wording today (their counterpart in Finland does not use it). However, no other Laestadian group uses the altered version in Finland or America.

THE MASS WAVE OF IMMIGRATION BEGINNING IN THE 1880S

The economic depression in America during the Ulysses Grant administration almost ended the arrival of new immigrants from 1873 to near the end of the decade. However, by the 1880s, the emigration movement was moving further south in Finland, as was the Laestadian revival movement. Before 1880, there are few reliable statistics on the number of Finns that immigrated to America. American officials recorded 1,942 arrivals from Finland, July 1871 through June 1883. From 1883-1920, the arrival of 257,382 persons were recorded. This doesn't mean that everyone who arrived became a resident. Many returned to Finland. Most of those who left were landless, rural people seeking employment and a better living in the new world. By this time, many had heard from the earlier immigrants in America about the employment opportunities, and a large number received tickets purchased by relatives and friends in America. The security of the close Laestadian immigrant community also drew Laestadian converts to America.

The earlier immigrants who left via Norway moved as families, since they had already moved as families to Norway. The later immigrants presented a different picture. Many of them were young and single. Studies starting at the turn of century indicate that about 75 percent of the passport applications were submitted by young single men and women.

A brief look at nineteenth century (1809-1917) Finland gives some clues to this. Finland was a grand duchy of Russia, ruled by a governor appointed by the Tsar. Finland had gradually begun to urbanize. There was a decrease in landowners and a great increase in landless workers. In 1874, the order of the Russian Tsar on general conscription, or the draft, went into effect. Hundreds of Finns left to escape military conscription or political pressures. Between 1882 and 1902, over 103,000, or 60 percent, of all those who emigrated were from the Vaasa and Oulu provinces. It was not until 1917 that Finland gained its independence.

It was in these two provinces that the Laestadian revival was spreading rapidly in that period, and there were many Laestadians among the new immigrants to the United States. By 1888, sixteen Apostolic Lutheran Church buildings had been erected in the United States which were located in the following places: the Upper Peninsula of Michigan, 3; Minnesota, 6; South Dakota, 4; and the West coast, 3.

During World War I, travel became uncertain and at times impossible, and immigration laws passed after the war made it difficult for new immigrants to enter the United States. The travel situation for a number of years during the war had prevented travel between the two countries. The immigrants had become settled in their communities and employment. Most of those who returned to Finland did so in the first five years; thus the immigrant population had become stable and there were very few new arrivals after 1920. By this time, Finland had become an independent country and socio-economic conditions were rapidly improving and emigration had virtually ceased.

CHALLENGES OF THE IMMIGRANT COMMUNITIES AND CHURCHES

How to reconcile disagreements within the immigrant groups as they became more heterogeneous was a challenge. Those arriving later from further south in Finland were bringing unfamiliar influences and reinforcing the position of those distancing themselves from the Lapland elders and leaders. A.L. Heideman was the only Laestadian pastor to immigrate to the United States (1890) who had a theological education and experience as a pastor in Finland. Upon his arrival, many heard his powerful message and revivals took place. The Laestadian community grew rapidly which created strife and criticism from the earlier leaders.

The uniqueness of the Finnish language made it difficult for the immigrants to learn English and to assimilate with the other nationalities among whom the immigrants lived. The Finns gathered where there were other Finns. The Finnish communities became very independent and retained their language longer than other nationalities. In many of the Finnish villages, the immigrants could conduct their business in Finnish and found little need for learning English. Most of them were literate in their native language, and through the immigration process they had been exposed to many cultures and languages. This broader perspective they were unable to convey to their children who were born during the hardships of pioneer life in the New World.

A great number of the first generation of children born in America never learned to properly communicate in English, but they did not receive much instruction in the Finnish language either. Without the educational resources that had been available to the immigrants in their native land through the state church, the education of their children on the new frontiers became a challenge. As far as books and teachers were concerned, there was a lack of educational resources, since there were no immigrants who had more than a Lapp ambulatory school level of training. This became a challenge for the church which it was not able to meet adequately. American compulsory education soon made the future generations conversant in the English language, but the church and many other institutions of the Finnish Americans retained the language for a long period of time.

Due to their exclusive nature, the Laestadian communities retained the language much longer than other institutions. This is due in part to children being encouraged to marry within their own spiritual fellowship and the strong connections the churches still have to Finland.

The 1930s to the 1950s were years of serious language crises in the Apostolic Lutheran churches. Some communities faced it earlier than others. In 1982, Pekka Raittila said:

The use of the Finnish language will cause problems in many congregations in the next ten years. Many congregations retained the Finnish language in their worship service much too long, to their detriment. Whether the congregation is serving people of predominately Finnish Laestadian origin or of several cultural or language backgrounds, it is difficult, if not impossible, for those of Finnish Laestadian origin to ignore their powerful Laestadian heritage. In fact, they do not wish to do so because of the spiritual and even temporal blessings that this inheritance has showered on people of Finnish Laestadian background.[15]

The Finnish language was used exclusively during services for so long that one generation was nearly lost to the church because the youth no longer understood the language. Many of the older folks almost considered Finnish a sacred language and were not willing to let go even when many of the younger people were leaving the church due to the language barrier. Gradually, the need for a change to the English language was recognized. Some churches had sermons in both languages—one following the other. In others the sermons were translated simultaneously in another room or side by side. There has been criticism over the years on the merits and methods of translation. By the 1970s and 1980s, most of the churches had dropped the Finnish except when guest speakers from Finland were invited. Some very strong rural Finnish communities still have some Finnish services. For example, as of 2005, the Spruce Grove Apostolic Lutheran Church, Wolf Lake, MN still has 40 out of 250 members that can fully communicate in Finnish although all are second or third generation Finns in America. One member, who is a more recent immigrant, does not understand English so Finnish sermons are still preached each month in addition to the regular English service. Also, a weekly Finnish radio sermon is broadcast from a local radio station.

Another challenge was to maintain unity with the Finnish communities scattered far from each other in the vast New World. There was no common training for ministers, and most of the pioneer preachers worked hard and long hours on their farms or in other jobs to provide a living for their family and also ministered on Sundays. They came from varied backgrounds. Some were more recent converts while others were more established in the Word. Many of the disagreements were related to organization and personal relationships, but these were also conditions, which led to doctrinal confusion and disagreements.

---

[15] Raittila, Pekka. "The Roots and Development of the Laestadian Movement." Unpublished manuscript prepared from lectures presented October 18-19, 1982 at the Inter-Lutheran Seminary.

Baptism has been a divisive issue from the beginning. This is perhaps due to the dual heritage where the Evangelical Lutheran Church of Finland retained the administration of the Sacraments, but the Laestadian congregation held the spiritual authority. They had to go outside of "the Kingdom of God," so to speak, to receive the sacraments from "dead faith" clergy. What could they do? As a priesthood of believers, they could proclaim the forgiveness of sins. The absolution was emphasized and the sacraments minimized. It did not mean that the Laestadians wanted to depreciate the sacraments. Without question, children were baptized and attendance at communion was considered important, but little was written or preached about the importance of the sacraments. If they were talked about, it was usually presented as what they were not.

Should the crucified or the resurrected Christ be preached? This is a question that surfaced in Cokato as early as the 1870s. Isak Barberg had been ministering in Cokato in the late 1860s. Jaakko Rovainen who arrived five years later had gained the respect of the Lapland elders and had been preaching actively before leaving for America. A conflict arose between the two. He had written a strong letter of instruction to Vadsø, Norway, in the fall of 1869, stating that the suffering and resurrection of Christ belong inseparably together: "He whose heart does not consider these two of equal value scatters the truth and becomes one-sided in doctrine and life." It is believed that these views had a connection to the Cokato conflict but definite conclusions are not possible.[16]

The attitudes and outlook of the pioneer immigrants were shaped by the heritage and conditions they left behind. To keep unity among immigrants, they sought answers from those they left behind who were not familiar with their new circumstances. Combining these two traditions in their new situation resulted in disputes on church discipline.

In spite of the challenges, Laestadianism was the most widespread Finnish community in America until the mid 1880s. For this reason, they played a key role in the Finnish-American scene. This included the first educational pursuits which were an unfamiliar role for the early Laestadians. Participation in founding the first newspapers and publications as well as schooling for immigrant children created conflicts in the immigrant Laestadian communities. When the great

---

[16] Raittila, Pekka. "Ylitorniolta Cokatoon" Tornionlaakson Vuosikirja 1981. p. 94.

migration in the mid 1880s became a mass movement, it overshadowed the special role of the northern Laestadian immigrants. Their internal disagreements limited their influence, although they left a permanent imprint on Apostolic Lutheranism in America.

TRADITIONS AND CUSTOMS

Some of the practices of the early revival grew out of a culture of poverty and necessity, which later were given spiritual significance. For example, some groups still have another preacher read the text for the one that is speaking. This practice originated when Juhani Raattamaa in his last years was almost blind and had to have someone else read his text. It was considered an honor to be able to read for the respected elder.

Whether the preacher should sit or stand while preaching has caused dissension in various groups over the years. Laestadius and other pastors in the movement preached standing in the church pulpit but during informal home services and in prayer houses they usually sat for practical reasons. The people in the early days did not all have Bibles. The Bibles they had were large family Bibles and the Postils were also large. Therefore, they could not be held while reading or preaching, which made it necessary for the readers and preachers to sit at a table where the books could be placed perhaps next to a candle or lamp.

Other traditions have been emphasized or rejected during church disputes and divisions. When the people met together for services, they kneeled to pray during the early period of the revival. At the turn of the century when the first major divisions came, the New Awakenists emphasized praying on their knees, therefore the other groups discontinued it and later all the groups gave it up.

Laestadius prepared and wrote all his sermons. That is how we have his Postils today. He sent out laymen to read his sermons. At the prayer meetings they read a sermon of Laestadius, which was followed by discussion and singing. When the revival began to spread, the new converts started testifying of their faith. Extemporaneous preaching was not practiced until the latter 1860s. Many did not have the skills and knowledge to prepare sermons, but they were moved by the Holy Spirit to speak of what God had done in their lives and the revival spread rapidly and lives were changed. However, the preachers often spoke on their favorite texts and the congregation did not get a broad Scriptural teaching.

Since the early leaders were critical of the state church and its "dead faith" pastors, there was a tendency on the part of the immigrants to reject all practices of the state church as "dead faith" practices in their new circumstances. Therefore, in Apostolic Lutheranism, prepared sermons were generally not acceptable, and in some groups those in full-time ministry were talked about as "bread and butter" pastors.

In recent years, one well known lay preacher in Finland, who has traveled on preaching tours in America, expressed himself as follows:

> In the church of Christ, laymen and clergy go hand in hand. They are one in Christ. Cooperation and interaction assure that mission work remains alive and effective. If these two look down on each other scornfully, it will result in distortion of doctrine and activity. If the clergy aspire to have an upper hand, Christianity withers into scholarly hairsplitting; however, lay leadership lacking theologians leads to factionalism.[17]

Studies have found that immigrants often become fixated in a mode they had at the time they left their former homeland. In the process of revival, the emphasis is on repentance, faith and a new life in Christ, with the focus on a personal relationship with Christ. Unfortunately, when the initial revival fires begin to die, the emphasis shifts to methods and the nature of the church as the leaders try to preserve spiritual traditions. This brings about divisions and dissension within groups.

---

[17] Korteniemi, Paavo. *Arno Korhonen--Jumalan Sissi. 2004. p 198,199.* Translated by Miriam Yliniemi

The following three pages contain text copied from legal documents taken from the Calumet Apostolic Lutheran Congregation Bylaws printed in 1929. These first two documents are on the organization of the first Laestadian congregation in America (1872-1873), and the third marks the name change to "Apostolic Lutheran" in 1879.

ARTICLES of ASSOCIATION
OF THE
Salomon Kortetniemi
LUTHERAN SOCIETY

TO WHOM IT MAY CONCERN:

It is hereby certified, that the subscribers being persons of full age and residents of theTownship of Calumet, County of Houghton and State of Michigan, and being Lutherans in religious belief, are desirous of forming themselves into a religious Society, under the Statutes of said State, in such case made and provided, that the place of meeting of such Society shall be in some suitable building in said Township of Calumet and that the name of such Society shall be **THE SALOMON KORTETNIEMI LUTHERAN SOCIETY:** That the temporal affairs of such Society shall be placed in charge of Trustees, who shall hold offices for one year, or until their successors shall be elected. That the further necessary steps for the formation and incorporation of such Society be taken in the manner required by Law. In witness whereof we have hereunto set our hands at the Township aforesaid, the 21st day of December, A. D., 1872.

August Tapio and 118 others.

Certificate of Incorporation of
SALOMON KORTETNIEMI
LUTHERAN SOCIETY

We undersigned, being two of the persons who signed the Articles of Association of The Salomon Kortetniemi Lutheran Society, of Township of Calumet, County of Houghton, and being legal voters of the election herein after named, do certify to all whom it may concern as follows: That of the 5th day of January A.D., 1873, pursuant to public notice duly given, more than fifteen days previous thereto on these Sabbaths immediately previous said last mentioned day, at the place of stated meeting of such Society for public worship at a meeting of said Society at the School-house in said Township held on said day at 11 o'clock in the forenoon, called for the purpose of perfecting the organization of such Society by the election of Trustees to control and manage the temporal affairs thereof, pursuant to the Statutes of the State of Michigan in such case made and provided, we were nominated by majority of the voters present, as inspectors of such election and to receive the votes cast and determine the qualification of voters at such election, Salomon Kortetniemi was chosen as president of the Corporation herein after named and of the meetings thereof: That by a plurality vote of the legal voters present the following named persons were chosen Trustees of said Society, to wit: John H. Johnson, John O. Lindstrom, John Isaacson, John Aronson, John T. Helso, Abram Michael, Isaac Isaacson, Petter Johnson, and Jacob Wuollet. That said Trustees and their successors in office shall hereafter for ever be known as and called, "The Trustees of the Salomon Kortetniemi Lutheran Society."

In witness whereof we have pursuant to law, subscribed our names to this Certificate, this 11th day of January A.D., 1873, at the Township aforesaid.

> John H. Johnson
> John Aronson

State of Michigan   )
County of Houghton)   On this 11th day of January A.D., 1873 before me, a Notary Public in and for said County personally came John H. Johnson and John Aronson, known to me to be the persons who subscribed the foregoing Certificate and acknowledged that he executed the same freely and for the uses and purposes therein mentioned.

> Thomas L. Chadbourne
> Notary Public of and for said County,

Received for Record January 11th A.D., 1873

Certificate for Change of Title from
SALOMON KORTETNIEMI
LUTHERAN SOCIETY
to
FINNISH APOSTOLIC
LUTHERAN CONGREGATION

This is to certify to whom it may concern, that a regular meeting of the members of the Religious Society, incorporated under the laws of this State and be thereto known and designated under the name of the Salomon Kortetniemi Lutheran Society, of the Township of Calumet, County of Houghton, held at their House of public worship, in the Township of Calumet, Houghton County, Michigan of the 22th day of April A.D., 1879, of which meeting notice, stating the object thereof, was duly given more than twenty days previous to the last named day, called for the purpose of changing the corporated name of said Society from the Salomon Kortetniemi Lutheran Society to the Finnish Apostolic Lutheran congregation, more than two thirds of members of said Society, to wit: One hundred and sixteen members (116) thereof present and voting to change the name of said Society from Salomon Kortetniemi Lutheran Society to the Finnish Apostolic Lutheran Congregation, and I, David Castren, the Secretary of the said meeting, do hereby, pursuant to the Statutes in such case made and provided, certify the foregoing facts accordingly and declare that the corporate name of the said Society is the Finnish Apostolic Lutheran Congregation. Witness my hand at said Calumet this 22th day of April A.D., 1879.

David Castren.

I, Ole Simonson, the presiding officer of the meeting above mentioned in testimony of the facts above set forth have countersigned the foregoings at said Calumet, this 22th day of April A.D. 1879.

State of Michigan)

County of Houghton)   On this 22th day of April, A.D., 1879, before me, a Notary Public in and for said County of Houghton, personally came David Castren and Ole Simonson, known to me to be the persons who certified and countersigned the foregoing Certificate and severally acknowledged that they executed, certified, and countersigned the same freely and for the uses and purposes therein mentioned.

SEAL   D. T. Macdonald
                         Notary Public, Houghton County

Received for Record the 6th
May A.D., 1879 at 2 o'clock P.M.   Thos. Mead, Register.

The following tables include lists of preachers and important leaders in the Laestadian movement who immigrated to America mainly before 1900. This gives some clues as to the spread and development of the Apostolic Lutheran movement in America as well as early immigration patterns. These individuals were already lay speakers or leaders before moving to America. The following data, related to America, is charted by Elmer and Miriam Yliniemi from *Laestadiolaisuuden Matrikkeli ja Bibliografia [Register and Bibliography of Laestadianism]* compiled by Pekka Raittila (Suomen Kirkkohistoriallinen Seura, Helsinki, Finland 1967).

Laestadian lay-preachers who immigrated to America from Finland 1865-1904

Name	Birthplace	Date	Left Finland from or via	Date	Location in America	Death
Ahola, Matti	Kuusamo	1826	Rovaniemi→Tervola	1873	UP[18]→Klickitat, WA 1877	?
Alajoki, Juho Vilhelmi	Kalajoki	1865	Kalajoki	1887	Menahga, MN (1891)	1932
Autiovaara, Juho	Kuusamo	?	Kuusamo?	1977	Astoria, OR 1877	?
Blomberg, Johan	Helsinki	1853	Russia→Helsinki	1890s	Worchester and Boston 1904-1920	1920
Erkkilä, Jaakko	Kemijärvi	1848	Kemijärvi	1971	UP→New York Mills, MN 1880	1918
Erkkilä, Matti	Kemijärvi	1862	Kemijärvi	1880	Black Hills, SD→New York Mills, MN	1953
Esko, Pekka Olli	Alatornio	1836	Oulu-via Norway	1870s	UP→Thomson, MN 1877	1883
Färdig, Bernhard G.	Uusikaupunki	1850	Uusikaupunki	1883	SanFrancisco,CA→Berkley, CA (1890)	1934
Hedtneimi, Sakarias	Pyhäjärvi	1856	Haapajärvi	1893	Lanesville, Mass.	1932
Hernesaho, Elias[19]	Evijärvi	1852	Evijärvi	1894	?	?
Hietanen, Aapo	Muonio	1833	Sodankylä	1888	?→Died in Boston Hotel from gas light	1896
Hurula, Sakarias	Karunki	1866	Karunki	1895	Ely,MN→Ironwood,MI→Kingston, MI	1945
Jänkälä, Heikki	Alatornio	?	Alatornio?	1880s	Ironwood, MI	?

[18]   UP refers to Upper Peninsula in MI
[19]   Also known as Ranta-Aho

Name	Birthplace	Date	Left Finland from or via	Date	Location in America	Death
Junkkonen, Juho	Lumijoki	1835	Lumijoki	1872	Thomson, MN 1872	1918
Juola, Eeli	Nivala	1840	Sievi→Haapavesi	1888	Michigan→Thomson, MN	1928
Juuma (Virkkula) Juhani	Kuusamo	1854	Kuusamo	1881	Alllouez, MI	1888
Kankkonen,Franz	Kaarlela	1864	Kokkola	1893	Astoria, OR	1919
Karjalainen, Hermanni	Kuusamo	1843	Kuusamo	1872	NY Mills→Holmes City, MN 1872	1905
Karjalainen, Matti[20]	Kuusamo	1830	Torp (Alakitka)	1882	New York Mills, MN	1921
Kela, Aatu	Taivalkoski	1858	Pudasjärvi	1889	New York Mills, MN	1934
Kemppainen, Aatami	Puolanka	1859	Kajaani	1885?	Salo, MN	?
Kiilunen, Juho	Lappajärvi	1867	Lappajärvi (trip)	1880s	Moved to America in 1902	1950?
Koistinen, Juho	Oulujokiq	1838	Kalajoki (1881)	1887	Lake Norden, SD	1922
Kopra, Pietari	Terijoki	1865	Terijoki	1893?	Brush Prairie, WA	1914
Korteniemi, Salomo	Turtola	1819	Ylitornio→Hammerfest	1871	Calumet,MI 1871	1904
Laitila, Matti	Laihia	?	?	1903	Fitchburg, MA	?
Lukkonen, Juho	Utajärvi	1841	Utajärvi	1873	Franklin→New York Mills 1873	?
Lumijärvi, Juho	Tervola	1854	Muonio1871→Hammerfest	1882	Calumet, MI→Astoria, OR in 1884	1923
Mällinen, Aapo	Tyrnävä	1852	Oulu	1873	UP→Thomson, MN 1883	1911
Mariapori, Juha Erkki	Alajärvi	1845	Kittilä→Alajärvi	1873	Ohio→UP→Kingston, MN 1890	?
Marttala, Juho	Haapavesi	1838	Via Norway	1865	Cokato, MN→Franklin, MN 1875	1910
Marttiini, Martin	Sodankylä	1840	Sodankylä	1880	New York Mills, MN	1900?
Mursu, Juho	Ii (Oijärvi)	1847	Ii	1880	New York Mills, MN	1911

[20] Also known as Karjala

Name	Birthplace	Date	Left Finland from or via	Date	Location in America	Death
Mustola, Jooseppi	Lohtaja	1850	Kalajoki	1880	Mpls.→SD→Astoria →Clatskanie, OR	1937
Nikkila, Heikki	Simo	1843	Via Norway	1873	UP→Savo, SD 1883	1914
Nikula, Hermanni	Kemijärvi	1862	Kemijärvi	1882	Republic, MI	1924
Nurmi, Juho Heikki	Alajärvi	1849	Utsjoki→Russia	1871-73	UP→Cokato1878→Kingston 1888	1933
Oberg, Taavetti	Rautalampi	1862	Karttula→Lapeenranta	1892	Cromwell→Cokato, MN→Laurium, MI	1946
Ojala, Kalle	Alavieska	1858	Alavieska	1878	Calumet→Oregon 1917-1928→Mpls.	1941
Ojala, Taneli	Kuusamo	1842	Kuusamo	1882	Michigan	?
Onkka, Juho Kustaa	Muonio	1857	Muonio?	1881	Calumet,MI→Cokato,MN→Astoria, OR	1932
Pekkala, Matti	Muonio	1849	Muonio	1883	New York Mills, MN	1922
Pelto, Aapo	Tervola	1836	Vadsø, Norway	1873	Calumet→Cokato→Frederick, SD 1883	1903
Peltoniemi, Matti	Kemijärvi	1855	Vadsø Norway	1881	Brush Prairie, WA	?
Pietilä, Niilo	Alatornio	1847	Tornio	1881	Calumet, MI→Black Hills, SD 1885	1927
Pikkarainen, Heikki	Oulu	1845	Rantsila	1873	Calumet, MI 1973	1940?
Planting, Kustaa Vilh.	Kemijärvi	1845	Kemijärvi	1871	UP→Pendleton, OR 1877	1911
Pohjonen, Heikki	Alatornio?	?	Alatornio?	1880s	Poinsett, SD	?
Pollari, Juho	Veteli	1865	Toholampi	1893	Maple, WI	1945
Puotinen, Aleksanteri	Evijärvi	1855	Himanka	1886	Thomson, MN	1940
Puumala, Erkki	Lappajärvi	1846	Alajärvi	1880s	?	?
Räisänen, Olli	Kemijärvi	1847	Vuostimo	1904	Annandale, MN	1923
Rajaniemi, Antti	Alavieska	1853	Nivala→Toholampi	1892	Calumet, MI	1897
Rauhala, Antti	Ylivieska	1843	Ylivieska	1871	UP→Pendleton, OR 1877	1916
Reiman, Erkki	Loviisa?	1853	Loviisa	1893	Minneapolis, MN	?

Name	Date	Birthplace	Left Finland from or via	Date	Location in America	Death
Riikonen, Kaarle	1852	Halikko	Hämeenlinna	1883	?	?
Rivinoja, Matti	1850	Piippola	Iisalmi	1897?	Lead, SD	1932
Ronkainen, Matti	1835	Kuusamo	Turtola→Vadsø, Norway	1873	UP→New York Mills, MN 1876	1926
Ruonavaara, Juho	186_	Kemi	Norway 1860	1873	Hancock, MI→Jacobsville, MI	1879
Ruuhijärvi, Juhani	1854	Turtola	Ylitornio	1879	Tower, MN→Duluth, MN	?
Saarela, Aukusti	1865	Haapajärvi	Haapajärvi	1891	Laurium, MI	1948
Savela, Sefanias	1840	Haapavesi	Haapavesi	1890	Michigan	1908
Stark, Nils Petteri	1838	Norway	Alatornio	1870s	UP→Frederick, SD→Ludden, ND	1931
Takkinen, Juho	1838	Kuusamo	Kuusamo	1877	Calumet, MI 1877-1892→died-Finland	1892
Tauriainen, Matti	1858	Suomussalmi	Taivalkoski	1891	UP→Sebeka, MN	1933
Törmälä, Sakari	1840	Siikajoki	Siikajoki	1871	Calumet, MI→Franklin, MN 1875	1915
Uskoski, Akseli	1886	Perho	Perho	1887	Son of Matti	1955
Uskoski, Matti	1862	Perho	Perho	1887	Michigan→Gackle, ND	1919
Vanttaja, Heikki	1837	Kuusamo	Tornio	1880's	Dakota (Frederick?)	1890
Viinamaki, Leander	1861	Lappajärvi?	Lappajärvi?	1886	Michigan	1945
Vuollet, Jaakko	1844	Lohtaja	Vadsø, Norway	1871	UP→Cokato 1873→Mpls, MN 1912	1923
Vuollet, Kaaleppi	1847	Lohtaja	Vadsø, Norway	1873	UP→Cokato, MN	1904
Wilén, Kaarle	1845	Perniö	Helsinki→Turku→Uusikau.	1890	?	?
Wilen, Kustaa	1845	Pernio	Helsinki	1894	?	1904
Ylen, Juho	1857	Janukkala	Helsinki'	1892?	Minnesota?	1930

A Godly Heritage

Laestadian lay-preachers who immigrated to America from Sweden 1865-1900

Name	Birthplace	Date	Left Sweden from or via	Date	Location in America	Death
Barberg, Iisakki	Hietaniemi	1840	Pajala→Swedish Ylitornio	1866	Cokato, MN 1867	1883
Daniels, Kalle Jaakko[21]	Sw Alatornio	1850	Vadsø, Norway 1868	1873	Calumet→Savo, SD	1917
Fjelborg, Nils	Jukkasjärvi	1833	Karesuando	1891	(*Married to Raattamaa's daughter ?*)	?
Hagel, Israel	Sw Alatornio	1846	Norway 1860's	1873	UP→New York Mills, MN 1877	1934
Kangas, Iisakki	Pajala	1833	Pajala	1891	Hancock, MI	?
Perä, Juhani	Sw Ylitornio	1839	Sw. Ylitornio	1898	Calumet, MI	1904
Raattamaa, Iisakki	Karesuando	1841	Norway 1868	1873	UP→Thomson, MN 1877	1936
Raattamaa, Petteri	Karesuando	1849	Karesuando	1883	New York Mills, MN	1921
Rovainen, Jaakko	Sw Ylitonrio	1828	Norway 1868-69	1871	Cokato, MN	1898
Sikainen, Juhani	Hietaniemi	1840	Norway 1864	1870	UP→Cokato, MN→Savo, SD 1883	1885
Vittikkohuhta, Antti[22]	Sw Alatornio	1816	Hammerfest, Norway 1866	1869	UP→Holmes City, MN→Cokato	1890

Laestadian lay-preachers who immigrated to America from Norway 1865-1900

Name	Birthplace	Date	Left Norway from or via	Date	Location in America	Death
Estensen, Torsten	Alta	1852	Alta, Norway	1868	UP→Lake Norden, SD 1878	1919
Fogman, Iisakki	Sw Ylitornio	1858	Norway 1868	1880's	?	?
Johanson, Alexnder[23]	Alta	1856	Alta	1873	Calumet, MI→Kingston, MN	?
Koller, Iisakki	Skjervøy	1851	Skjervøy	1880	New York Mills→Ironwood→Astoria	1925

21 Also known as Tiinan Kalle
22 Also known as Witikko or Brännäri
23 Also known as Paulson

Name	Birthplace	Date	Left Norway from or via	Date	Location in America	Death
Koller, Matti	Skjervøy	1849	Skjervøy	1870?	New York Mills, MN	1913
Lindström, Johan	Alta	1846	Alta	1870	Calumet, MI	?
Maaherra, Heikki	Sw Alatornio	1822	Hammerfest, Norway 1847	1875	UP→Pendleton, OR 1877	1887
Matoniemi, Olli	Vadsø	1848	Vadsø, Norway	1873	UP→LakeNorden, SD→BlackHills, SD	1925
Peltoniemi, Matti	Kemijärvi	1855	Vadsø, Norway 1864	1881	Brush Prairie, WA	?
Pokan, Kusto	Alta	?	Alta	1880	?	?
Roanpää, Juho	Alta	1849	Alta	1870	Calumet, MI (died in Boston Hotel)	1896
Strolberg, Petteri	Sw Alatornio	1847	Norway 1852	1870	Calumet→Hancock, MI	1918

Laestadian Ordained Pastor who immigrated to America in 1890

Name	Birthplace	Date	Left Finland from or via	Date	Location in America	Death
Heideman, Arthur L.	Oulu	1862	Kivijärvi	1890	Calumet, MI	1928

Important Laestadian Individuals (not preachers) who immigrated to America

Name	Birthplace	Date	Left Finland from or via	Date	Location in America	Death
Berg, Henrick	Muhos?	1843	Oulu	1879	Calumet, MI→Cokato, MN	1920's
Berg, Nils Petteri	Råneå	1852	Pudasjärvi (1854)	1882	Calumet, MI→Astoria, OR	1930's
Ylivieska		1840	Oulainen→Tervola	1873	UP→NYMills1890→Virginia, MN 1910	1920
Jokela, Mikko[24]	Kittilä	1849	Kittilä	1881	Franklin, MI	?
Kieri, Johannes	Ylitornio	1852	Alatornio 1877	1888	Calumet, MI	?
Koller, Henrik[25]	Skjervøy	1859	Skjervøy	1870	Calumet, MI	1935

[24] Married Charlotta (Lotta) daughter of Lars Levi Laestadius born 1842 and died 1900

Name	Birthplace	Date	Left Finland from or via	Date	Location in America	Death
Kynsijärvi, Olli	Pudasjärvi	1840	Pudasjärvi	1876	UP→Astoria→Quincy, OR	1922
Lahti, Petteri	Kittilä	1859	Kittilä	1888	Calumet, MI→Lake Linden, MI	1936
Mullo, Juho	Kalajoki	?	Kalajoki	1880	Calumet, MI	1913
Ojanperä, Jaakko	Kalajoki	1838	Kalajoki→Norway 1870		Cokato→UP 1871→Cokato 1883	1919

Laestadian lay-preachers who made preaching trips to America 1865-1900

Name	Birthplace	Date	Dates in America	Comments and Explanations	Death
Branström, Iisakki	Sw.Ylitornio	1833	6/14/1866-4/28/1867	Traveled with his family-later drowned in Finland	1873
Ervasti, Paavali	Pudasjärvi	1840	1890-91 & 12/1895-10/1896	Speaker - Song writer- Died in Oulu on return	1896
Halonen, Kaaperi	Utajärvi	1851	1911-1912 with Rantala	Spoke against new awakenism	1936
Hannila, Jakob	Kaarlela	1857	1872-1874	Preached in Finnish and Swedish	1925
Hautajärvi, Juho	Kuolajärvi	1847	1903-1904	Traveled with Rantala	1940
Jakola, Mikko	Sievi	1850	1881,1887,1900	3 travel dates found in Finland-no record in Am.	1938
Jussila, Heikki	Haukipudas	1863	1924 & 1930-1931	Leader in SRK[26]	1955
Juuso, (Ojala) Iisakki	Ylitornio	1825	7/15/1891-10/3/1892		1897
Kangas, Fredrik	Perho	1850	1880's		1918
Karvala, Jaakko	Lappajärvi	1850	1884	Believed to have been to America	1906
Koskenranta, Mikko	Laihia	1867	?		1953
Lahti, Juho	Sievi	1850	1889		1935

[25] He was known for being a strong supporter of J. Takkinen and preserver of Laestadius' writings. He also published a paper, **Siionin Sanomat** (Zion's Tidings) 1891-1896.

[26] **SRK** is known as Laestadian Lutheran in America

Name	Birthplace	Date	Dates in America	Comments and Explanations	Death
Lakso, Juho	Karunki	1840	1892		1925
Lakso, Pekka	Karunki	1866	After 1886	Preached in 1890's in America ➜ Finland	1944
Mantyvaara, Juntti	Jellivaara	1845	1893	With Joonas Purnu	1920
Nikka, Frans Heikki	Oulu	1845	1877-1878	Went with Takkinen to America ? if he preached	1892
Niku, Iisakki	Jukkasjärvi	1866	1920-1926	Western Laestadianism[27]	1929
Nygard, Iisakki	Sievi	1851	1881		1910
Parakka, Frans	Jukkasjärvi	1873	1920 & 1926 &1930	Western Laestadian Elder	1935
Parkajoki, Heikki	Pajala	1813	1876	Sent by Raattamaa to America	1894
Posti, Juhani	Simo	1836	Summer 1882-fall 1883		1918
Purnu, Joonas	Jellivaara	1829	1893 (Sent by Raattamaa)	First leader of Western Laestadianism	1902
Pyörret, Juho	Kalajoki	1853	1893 &1910-11 & 1912-13	Leader in new awakenists-traveled with Saarenpää	1918
Raattamaa, Erkki	Karesuando	1817	1891-1894	Brother of Juhani Raattamaa	1901
Rantala, Mikkeli Paulus	Enontekiö	1862	1903-1904	Leading speaker at turn of century	1936
Rova, Iisakki	Sw. Karunki	1841	? Supposedly in America	Lived in Norway in 1860's	1921
Saarenpää, Mikko	Kurikka	1853	7/1910-1/11 & 9/1912-4/13	Leader in New Awakenist movement	1914
Sallinen, Juhani	SW.Karunki	1833	Early 1890's	Traveled in western States	1910
Solkela, Juho	Vähäkyrö	1844	1880's		1925
Talonen	Vähäkyrö	1844	1880's	Traveled with Solkela	1932
Tapani, Aapo	Ylimuonio	1834	1876 and 1888	First trip with Parkajoki-second with Hietanen	1910
Typpo, Leonard	Rautio	1868	1889-1895 Fitchburg, Mass	Author - song writer – Song book ed. -Statesman	1922

[27] Western Laestadians were known as the Old Apostolic Lutherans in America

17

Laestadianism in North America Until 1885

Pekka Raittila

INTRODUCTION: THE STARTING POINT OF THE RESEARCH

Laestadianism is a religious movement within Lutheranism which had its beginning in Swedish Lapland in the middle of the nineteenth century. The impetus behind the awakening was the powerful repentance preaching of Pastor Lars Levi Laestadius (1800-1861). During his lifetime the movement spread widely in the northern parts of Sweden, Finland and Norway. After Laestadius's death, lay preachers rose to leadership in the movement, the most important being Juhani Raattamaa (1811-1899). The great expansion of Laestadianism began in the 1860s. It spread rapidly as far as southern Finland and even St. Petersburg, Russia, where a considerable Finnish population formed a vigorous congregation. Among the Finnish settlers in northern Norway, it became the most important religious movement.

During the ensuing decades, the movement spread practically everyplace where Finnish was spoken. Although Laestadianism originated in a parish with a Lapp majority, it became mainly a Finnish movement. Nowadays its support base is primarily confined to Finland, especially to Finland's northern province of Oulu. However the tradition of connections extending over national borders is still strong, especially within the Arctic Circle.

From the beginning the main characteristics of Laestadianism were powerful repentance sermons, oral confession of sins and absolution, and the so-called "liikutukset" (emotional outbursts). One of the themes in the repentance sermons was opposition to the use of alcohol, and many sermons were also preached advocating simplicity of dress and lifestyle. In order to become part of the fellowship, it was necessary for the individual to make confession of sins and receive absolution. Confession was also a regular routine in dealing with matters of conscience. The "liikutukset" were semi-ecstatic phenomena; in the early phase of the movement feelings of anguish over sin and the joy of salvation led to strong outbursts among the people at religious services.

Rather early on, the Laestadian community became exclusive in its character. The distinction between Christians (= Laestadian believers) and outsiders was made clear. A Laestadian fellowship was self-sufficient in all of its activities and spiritual care. Although the movement was widespread and there was no official organization, its internal unity remained very strong. This did not, however, mean separation from the state church. The sacraments were still received in church in accordance with ecclesiastical practice. From the 1870s onward, Laestadiansim has had many members of the state church clergy among its supporters. Juhani Raattamaa and the other lay leaders rejected suggestions, though infrequent, to separate from the state church.

It is commonly known that Laestadianism played an important role among the early Finnish immigrants in America. The history of Laestadianism in America was researched extensively by Uuras Saarnivaara. Mention of Laestadianism in America has also been included in works dealing with Finnish church history in the U.S.A., particularly in those dealing with the Suomi Synod (e.g., V. Rautanen and Douglas Ollila). These studies, however, fail to give a clear and objective picture of the early years. A natural explanation for this is that in the early days there were certain elements which disappeared or changed in the course of later developments; at the same time others were forgotten or were given a new interpretation in the commonly accepted Finnish-American tradition. Historical research concentrates mainly on the end of the nineteenth century or on the twentieth century. For this reason also the pioneer phase relating to the earliest generation of settlers has not been thoroughly investigated.

The present research primarily utilizes written sources dating back to the period being studied, i.e., the time before 1885. This is the only way to correct the misconceptions about the early period held by the various Laestadian groups on the basis of oral tradition. The number of available sources has increased considerably since the earlier studies were completed. A great number of letters shedding more light on the first big crisis of American Laestadianism have been found in the past few years both in northern Sweden and in the U.S.A. There are, as yet, unresearched sources in the United States dealing with the early stages of the Finnish Evangelical Lutheran church. The most important of these are the first Finnish-American newspapers and the publications of the Norwegian-Danish Conference. Also the archives of the oldest Finnish settlements in the U.S.A. would most likely add even more details to the information now available. The archives of congregations and other communities date from the late 1880s. This research is based on Scandinavian and American sources that are available in Finland.

The starting point in this research is the fact that the earliest Finnish immigrants came mainly from those regions of Finland, Sweden and Norway which were above the Arctic Circle. Later, in the 1880s, emigration became a mass movement in Finland, and the most important centers of emigration shifted to the province of Vaasa and neighboring areas. Prior to that the northernmost parts of Finland, Sweden and Norway had been the most significant source of Finnish-speaking immigrants. Hence, it must be noted that the Finnish language united immigrants from three different countries. In the oldest Finnish settlements, these people from the north were in the majority until the beginning of the 1880s. This was the case in the 1870s in the entire Copper Country by Lake Superior, especially in the mining town of Calumet, Michigan, as well as in the farming villages of Minnesota, of which Cokato was the most notable. The northern immigrants also dominated some Finnish settlements in the states of Washington and Oregon. Since Laestadianism was vigorously spreading in northern Scandinavia in the 1860s and 1870s—a time of lively emigration to America from this region—Laestadianism was to play a crucial role in the formation of the immigrant communities.

THE RELIGIOUS ORGANIZATION OF THE FINNISH IMMIGRANTS AND THE BEGINNING OF LAESTADIANISM

The Copper Country of Michigan became the center of Finnish religious organization. The Scandinavian settlements were primarily confined to the Midwest. The Copper Country was at the fringe of the Scandinavian congregational network and synods. Since people coming from northern Norway had played a central role among Scandinavians in the copper mining boom of the 1860s, it was natural that Norwegians became the leaders of the Scandinavian religious activities in this area. The Scandinavian Evangelical Lutheran parish of Hancock-Quincy was founded in 1867. When the Norwegians withdrew from the Augustana Synod, this congregation joined a new one, the Norwegian-Danish Conference, probably in 1871.

Finns who had migrated from or by way of northern Norway made up the majority in the Scandinavian Evangelical Lutheran parish in the

Copper Country. This majority steadily increased during the early 1870s. In the leadership of the conference at that time there were pastors (J. Olsen and A. Weenaas) who had become familiar with Finns while in northern Norway and thus were able to pay special attention to their needs. The second pastor of this Copper Country parish, Hans Christian Roernaes, was born in Lyngen, Norway, where he worked as a teacher among the Lapps. Undoubtedly he had come in contact with Laestadians there. He also knew some Finnish. Roernaes served as a pastor in the Copper Country from 1871 to1873 and continued to visit during the years 1873-1876 from nearby Ishpeming, after which he moved away from the district. His successor, Nils E. Bøe, who served in the Copper Country from 1873 to 1879, knew only Norwegian. There is little information about his contacts with the Finns.

During Roernaes's time the congregation split in two. The main cause of the rift was the strong spread of Laestadianism primarily among the Finns. The first accounts of the beginnings of Laestadianism in the Copper Country are included in Roernaes's descriptions from the years 1872-1873 (the Conference periodical *Lutheraneren* and a private letter). According to these sources, the movement began in the beginning of the 1870s. Also the information gained from Laestadian tradition seems to support this assumption. According to the traditional sources, the first key figures of the movement were Antti Vitikkohuhta and Salomon Kortetniemi, who immigrated to the Copper Country in the late summers of 1869 and 1871 respectively. Hence the earlier notions—that the Finns from northern Norway who had started coming to the Copper Country in the mid-1860s were for the most part already Laestadians and that the movement had taken root at that time—are false.

A conflict developed between the Laestadians and Roernaes, which most likely started shortly after his arrival in the Copper Country. It was due to some features of early Laestadianism, such as the "rejoicings," emotional outbursts, which caused a disturbance in worship services. Apparently related to this conflict is the unusual fact—as stated in the annual report presented at the June 1872 Conference—that the Calumet congregation had expelled 39 and the Quincy congregation 14 of their members. It is not until the end of 1872, however, that the official organization of the Laestadians took place.

The organization, founded in 1873, and registered as the Salomon Kortetniemi Lutheran Society, included people of the entire Finnish settlement in the Copper Country. It had its center in Calumet where the first Finnish-American church was erected in 1873. Smaller Laestadian churches were built in Hancock-Quincy in 1875 and in the mining village of Allouez in 1876. Otherwise there is little information available on the religious activities led by Kortetniemi. As a result of the economic recession, which began in the fall of 1873 and lasted for several years, Finnish immigration to the Copper Country slowed. Many of those who had come earlier moved further west in subsequent years.

The founding of the Laestadian church meant a significant loss to the Evangelical Lutheran parish. The Conference, however, seemed to consider this disturbance to be a temporary setback. During the following years, the pastors of the Conference made several attempts to get a Finnish-speaking pastor for the Evangelical Lutheran parish. As a result A. E. Backman, a young pastor from northern Finland, arrived in Calumet in the autumn of 1876 and was appointed pastor of the Finnish Evangelical Lutheran parish of the Conference.

Contrary to the earlier studies, it must be emphasized that according to the sources the Norwegian pastors of the Conference played a decisive role in getting the Finnish pastor. Also the misconception that it was a group of Finns who wanted a pastor has to be corrected. In the middle of the 1870s the original members of the Evangelical Lutheran parish were still largely Finns from northern Norway; Laestadianism had by no means attracted all of them. And it was these Finns who had the least difficulty with the affiliation to the Norwegian Conference. On the other hand, the development of a Laestadian church was likely due—in addition to the religious factors—to the increasing self-confidence of the Finnish-speaking people coming from Sweden and Finland. The immigration originating in regions south of the Laestadian areas in Finland which finally tipped the scales in favor of the Evangelical Lutheran congregations, did not have an effect until the 1880s.

Religious activities in the Finnish settlements of Minnesota probably started in the 1860s. They seem to have followed the tradition of village devotional meetings common in northern Scandinavia. At least in Cokato the leader of the activities was a farmer who was already known to have been a Laestadian in the old country. A characteristic of congregational development in the Finnish farming villages of Minnesota was a greater community spirit and informality than in the Copper Country. Here the division into

Laestadian and Evangelical Lutheran congregations did not take place until the 1880s.

THE DISSENSION CAUSED BY THE CONGREGATIONAL ORGANIZATION (ABOUT 1875-1878)

In the early 1870s, there was already some dissension among the American Laestadians. However, there are only a few fragmentary sources dating back to the years before 1876 which relate to this. Later American Laestadian tradition has explained these conflicts in a way that has been repeatedly mentioned in historical studies but calls for clarification. When interpreting contemporary sources, it is important to bear in mind the overall conditions in which the first Finns—and Laestadians—lived in America. These conditions changed considerably later on.

The years during which the Salomon Kortetniemi Lutheran Society was established were also a time when large numbers of Finns who had been involved with the recent expansion of Laestadianism in the old country arrived in America. Many of them had already distinguished themselves as preachers in Europe. These people began to criticize the activities of the Laestadian leaders in America, and they sent letters to Finland seeking support from the most prominent leaders of the movement. On the basis of these sources, we know about a dissension in Cokato, Minnesota, between the first religious leader of the settlement and an immigrant who had gained a reputation as a preacher in the Tornio River Valley and moved to America in 1871. The most prominent centers of dissension, however, were Calumet and the Copper Country.

Two lay preachers, Heikki Parkajoki and Aapo Tapani, were sent to America in the summer of 1876 by Juhani Raattamaa and the representatives of the oldest Laestadian regions to take a closer look at the American situation and to act as consultants. Although Parkajoki was one of the most respected Laestadian leaders, this trip was not a success. After a short period of reconciliation, dissensions broke out again both in Cokato and in Calumet. As can be seen from the preachers' reports and letters written during the succeeding years, the central disagreements were about the official organization of the congregation, the conduct of the religious services, and Kortetniemi's ministerial authority.

In the light of later developments, it is only natural and inevitable that the Laestadians created an independent organization in America where a state church could not exist. For the first immigrants, the situation was different. Many of them did not yet know whether they would remain permanently or just work for some time and return to their homeland. Back home, especially in Finland where emigration was totally new, they were still regarded as members of their respective state church congregations. The validity of ministerial acts provided in America, especially marriage ceremonies, proved to be a serious issue for those who returned to Finland. In Scandinavia Laestadianism was generally regarded as a sect. Since the confession and ministerial acts of several Scandinavian synods in the United States tended to follow the practice of the European state churches, their congregants were considered members of their respective state churches. After the arrival of Pastor A. E. Backman in Calumet in 1876, the Finns there had an opportunity to participate in "state church" style services in their mother tongue. This increased the rivalry between the Laestadian and Evangelical Lutheran congregations and offered Finns a more realistic alternative to the Laestadian congregations.

Scandinavian Laestadianism could not serve as a model for the formation of an independent organization in the United States. Although in Scandinavia the movement was independent, it still remained within the state church. The Laestadian devotional meetings followed a very simple format: hymns, prayers, and a sermon. In practice lay preachers exercised great spiritual authority, but their position was totally unofficial. In this respect the leadership of Salomon Kortetniemi was an exception. As the Laestadian congregation assumed the responsibility of administering the sacraments, the religious services became more formal than the traditional meetings. As a condition for the right to perform wedding ceremonies, the marriage laws of the United States stated that in a religious community one of its members shall exercise ministerial authority. Criticism of the religious services and of the entire congregational organization focused on Kortetniemi, whose thirst for power was believed to be the cause of all the problems. Evidently similar views were also behind the accusations against the leader of the Cokato congregation. The letters sent to America from Lapland by Juhani Raattamaa and other Laestadian Elders in 1877 provide a good picture of the connections between the Laestadians of the Old and New Worlds. The concept of the congregation of the "Firstborn" came to the fore at that time. The "Firstborn" congregation had several characteristics. In practice it primarily signified unity with the oldest generation of Laestadians. It was a guarantee of the unity of the Laestadian community regardless of borders and distances. On the other hand, this unity also meant that the American immigrants still belonged to their original congregations in their homelands. They were known best there, and thus congregational discipline could be imposed on them. Hence, the information about Kortetniemi's earlier misconduct received from his home congregation in Ylitornio became a crucial weapon in the efforts to oust him.

In the fall of 1877, a new man was sent to America to try and clear up the situation. Although Juho Takkinen belonged to the younger generation and was from a region peripheral to the Laestadian areas in the homeland, he had gained a reputation as a powerful preacher during the 1870s. Especially Raattamaa had great confidence in him. Takkinen spent about six months in the Copper Country and Minnesota in 1877-1878. His goal was to destroy Kortetniemi's "papacy." At the beginning of his trip he had some success, but he did not gain the full support of the church until the beginning of March 1878. On behalf of the church, a letter was sent to Raattamaa requesting his permission for Takkinen to remain permanently in America.

The following summer the principles for organizing the Laestadian congregation were defined. While Takkinen was visiting Juhani Raattamaa, a letter was sent to America expressing contentment with Takkinen's work and giving approval to a model of congregational organization which in reality was very similar to that designed by Kortetniemi. Only the liturgical order was somewhat simplified. Also it was suggested that the minister of the congregation (a layman in this case) should have the right to conduct marriage ceremonies, although this was not Takkinen's original intention. This decision, made by the persons with the highest authority in the movement, encouraged Takkinen to accept the invitation of the American Laestadians. In the fall of 1878, he was appointed minister of the Calumet congregation.

The attitude of the Laestadian leaders in Europe toward the organization of the American movement had changed in the course of the year. Obviously in their opinion, the problem had to do with Kortetniemi and Takkinen as individuals. Also an increasing understanding of the American situation must have affected their decisions. In America the submission to Takkinen's leadership did not, however, eliminate all the problems.

THE APOSTOLIC LUTHERAN CHURCH IN JUHO TAKKINEN'S TIME

In the fall of 1878, Juho Takkinen started organizing the work of the congregation with firm determination. The following spring the name of the Laestadian Church in Calumet was changed to "The Finnish Apostolic Lutheran Church of Calumet." The reason for choosing this name was most likely the desire to emphasize the idea that the fellowship was Lutheran but held to the Bible as its highest authority. Thus Apostolic Lutheran gradually became the established name for Laestadians in America.

The fact that the Laestadian church had become active meant a threat to the Evangelical Lutheran Church led by Pastor Backman. The membership of his church diminished during the subsequent years. In 1880 Backman transferred the administrative center of the Evangelical Lutheran Church from Calumet to Hancock where it had always had greater support. In 1881 he made a trip to Finland and returned there permanently in the late summer of 1883.

The Laestadians distinguished themselves in the earliest Finnish-American cultural activities. The *Amerikan Suomalainen Lehti* [*Finnish-American newspaper*] (1879-) at first professed religious neutrality. But as early as the following winter, the paper started co-operating with the Laestadians, a relationship which lasted for several years. An organization for publishing religious literature, Amerikan Suomalaisen Kirjallisuuden Seura [Society of Finnish-American Literature], was founded as an instrument for the Laestadian cultural activities. Also the first efforts to establish Finnish schools were led by Laestadians.

The most prominent leader of the activities mentioned above was Juho Takkinen. It is obvious, however, that the initiator of the Laestadian publication and educational work was David Castrén, who for some years also served as secretary of the Apostolic Lutheran Church. Takkinen's involvement in these activities resulted in some criticism from the conservative branch of the Laestadian movement. In any case it is evident that the Laestadians had a role of decisive importance in the cultural aspirations of the Finnish pioneers. Takkinen's strong negative reaction to the musical interests of the teacher of the Finnish school in Calumet led to the demise of Laestadian dominance in the Finnish-American educational work.

Juho Takkinen's influence was felt not only in Calumet but everywhere among the American Laestadians. The parish of the Apostolic Lutheran Church of Calumet, which consisted of at least three minor congregations in addition to the one in Calumet, was a sort of mother congregation. Takkinen regularly visited the Finnish settlements in Minnesota and, from the year 1881 onwards, also in South Dakota. He conducted two-week confirmation schools and officiated at confirmation services in various congregations also endeavoring to organize and control their activities. In 1883 he made a trip to the Finnish settlements in Washington and Oregon. The Laestadian congregations on the West coast were led by Juho Lumijärvi, who had come to the Copper Country in 1882 to assist Takkinen and moved to Astoria, Oregon, in 1884. Although Finns have settled in many states since the 1880s, Laestadian mission activity seems to have been directed only toward those regions which already had Laestadians.

Takkinen's success did not last long. In fact as early as 1880, some Laestadians began to criticize him. The issues were much the same as in Kortetniemi's time: the development of the official organization of the congregations and the position of the minister, which was considered to be too prominent. Especially in Cokato and elsewhere in Minnesota there were aspirations for independence from Takkinen's leadership. In both Europe and America a major dispute took place over the *Amerikan suomalainen aapinen* [*Finnish-American Primer*] published by the Society of Finnish-American Literature in the summer of 1880. It included the Apostles' Creed in a slightly changed form. According to the book, Jesus descended into hell in Gethsemane, i.e., before his crucifixion. Takkinen's book and his other activities received the support of Raattamaa. Takkinen's critics, however, made repeated appeals to the Elders in the old country, petitioning for preachers from Europe to help settle the American situation. Takkinen traveled to Europe in the fall of 1882. In meetings held in December 1882 in northern Sweden, the organization of the Calumet congregation, "the lay congregation," was approved by the most prominent Laestadian leaders, thus establishing the independence of American Laestadianism. It did not, however, pacify Takkinen's critics, and at the end of the decade, a permanent schism developed in the Laestadian movement in America.

There are few sources dealing with the Apostolic Lutheran congregations that date back to the time under consideration. By 1876 four churches had been built, three in the Copper Country and one in Cokato. Apart from the Calumet church, they were probably rather humble meeting halls. No additional churches were built prior to 1884 and 1885, at which time churches were erected in New York Mills,

Franklin, and Holmes City, Minnesota; as well as Savo and Poinsett in South Dakota; Centerville, Washington; and Pendleton, Oregon.

Just as in the old country, the Laestadian congregations had preachers who preached not only in their home regions but in other areas as well. In addition there were elected ministers, songleaders and other functionaries. Takkinen was both the leading preacher and minister; until 1883 no other preachers were authorized to officiate at weddings. Other ceremonies such as religious services, baptisms and funerals were assigned to the local leaders in each congregation. It is necessary to note that the ministerial authority did not necessarily have to coincide with preacher status; in other words, it was possible that a "preacher" was not the "minister" of a congregation. The basic requirement for a minister was literacy. It was also possible to change ministers because the functionaries of the congregations were elected annually.

The religious services had a close resemblance to the traditional village devotional meetings which in northern Scandinavia were based on a simplified version of the church service. Most of the liturgical tradition of the Scandinavian state churches was rejected as being "papal."

The traditional state church practice was the model for Holy Communion, however. It was celebrated once a month. Confirmation school was a prerequisite for participation. When Pastor Aatu Laitinen, editor of the Laestadian monthly in Finland, put forward the idea of children taking part in Holy Communion, the proposal encountered opposition especially in America. Access to the Communion table was open in the same sense as in the old state church. In one of his letters, Raattamaa gave his consent to the practice that also non-Laestadians were permitted to receive Holy Communion. Undoubtedly, this was in conformity with the Laestadian understanding of the Sacraments. In America it was also frequently due to the position of the Laestadian congregation as the only Finnish religious community in some settlements.

Newspaper articles about American Laestadianism, especially around 1880, emphasized that all this was done in accordance with the old state church traditions. For the most part the claim is true, although the intention was to reinforce the legal validity of the Apostolic Lutheran church in the eyes of the authorities in Finland. As a matter of fact, the "papal" liturgical tradition of the Lutheran Church had been simplified by the lay-led congregations of the Laestadian church, and generally the Laestadians did not recognize any obligations (doctrinal, liturgical, etc.) except those to be found in the Bible, in the teachings of the Prophets, Jesus, and the Apostles. Not even the oldest Confessions of the Lutheran Church were considered binding. In reality, however, the Laestadian practice reflected state church traditions, especially with regard to the Sacraments.

Although the freedom of religion in America had facilitated entirely new solutions, the state church tradition was still imposed on Laestadians internally on the one hand and by external pressure on the other. The internal unity of the movement was also a major influence. Since the leading Elders were in Europe and Scandinavian Laestadianism was not separate from the state church, it was not possible to develop any independent nonconformist theology in America. Further, this would have been impossible due to a lack of intellectual resources.

Pastor J. K. Nikander came to the Copper Country from Finland in the beginning of 1885 and undertook the work of organizing a Finnish church body which after some years resulted in the establishment of the growing Suomi Synod. Laestadianism soon lost the predominance which it had had during the pioneer phase of Finnish immigration. Certain developments within the Laestadian movement finally led to a split. The reasons behind that are different from those of the crises dealt with in this research.

From Pekka Raittila, *Lestadiolaisuus Pohjois-Amerikassa vuoteen 1885 [Laestadianism in North America Until 1885].* Helsinki: Suomen kirkkohistioriallinen seura, 1982). pp. 235-343. English Summary from book— edited by Rodger and Aila Foltz.

18

Laestadianism/Apostolic Lutheranism in North America Today

Jouko Talonen

INTRODUCTION

This is a brief and concise description of North American Laestadianism/Apostolic Lutheranism at the present time. I will outline the movement's different groups including basic facts about each of the them. The information has been gleaned from literature, interviews, and the materials acquired over the years from various collections and archives. During my six visits to the United States between 1992 and 2003, I collected information and made observations about the various groups in different parts of the country. I consider my visit of February 1 to March 17, 1995 to be especially important. On that journey I had the opportunity to acquaint myself with North American Laestadianism in the western, eastern, as well as the central states. I interviewed several members in at least five of the groups.

I will endeavor to present all of the Laestadian/Apostolic Lutheran groups in North America in order of their size. The focus is on the current situation; consequently, the earlier periods will not be dealt with in detail. The purpose is to present the membership, preachers, distribution, activities and some special characteristics of each group. Unless noted, most of the ministers are not seminary trained. The membership and other statistics are from the years 1995-2005. There may be some inaccuracies in details, but the basic situation becomes clear. In this context there is reason to note that the membership figures for these groups are partially affected by large families. Revival preaching intended to reach outsiders has not ceased, but especially since World War II, Laestadianism/Apostolic Lutheranism has maintained its position largely through successful Christian education.

The groups in North America, with the exception of the latest division of 2004 and the "Pollarites" (The Apostolic Lutherans who aligned themselves with John Pollari), have sister organizations in the Scandinavian countries. The Pollarites (two main groups), are an American phenomenon, although it has its "roots" in Finland in that the preacher John Pollari immigrated from Finland. An attempt has been made to find a counterpart in Finland for the Pollarite Apostolic Lutheran movement, but historically it is a chapter unto itself.

The groups, presented in order of size, are as follows (the American name first, with the Finnish sister organization in parentheses):

1. **OLD APOSTOLIC LUTHERAN CHURCH**
   (Esikoislestadiolaisuus =Firstborn)

2. **APOSTOLIC LUTHERAN CHURCH OF AMERICA**, "Federation"
   (Rauhan Sana group also known as Pikkuesikoiset=Small Firstborn)

3. **LAESTADIAN LUTHERAN CHURCH**, LLC
   (Suomen Rauhanyhdistysten Keskusyhdistys, SRK)

4. **FIRST APOSTOLIC LUTHERAN CHURCH**, Apostolic Lutheran Mission, or so-called "Torola group,"
   (Vahoillislestadiolainen Rauhanyhdistys, VLR)

5. **THE POLLARITE GROUPS** (Leaders in brackets):
   ➤ Independent Apostolic Lutheran Church [Matt Reed]
   ➤ Apostolic Lutheran Church [Aunes Salmela]

6. **GRACE APOSTLES LUTHERAN CHURCH**
   (New group separating from First Apostolic Lutheran Church in 2004)

The different Laestadian/Apostolic Lutheran groups in both North America and Europe have certain common characteristics. Lay leadership and the priesthood of all believers have been part of the heritage of the movement from the beginning of the revival. The Lutheran state church conditions in the Arctic region of the Nordic Countries led to laymen having a central role in the revival movement from the start. The concept of the priesthood of all believers gave this development greater emphasis. The right to proclaim the forgiveness of sins belongs to all believers who have received the Holy Spirit (John 20:22-23). When many of the pastors expressed disapproval or downright opposition to the Laestadian revival, the movement became increasingly estranged from the Evangelical Lutheran Church and clergy. The pastoral office of the established church did not play a significant role in the doctrinal views of the movement. The most important thing for them was a living relationship with God as His children and the priesthood of all believers which follows from that.

The emphasis on the unity of one's own fellowship group has also led to an emphasis on the uniqueness of one's own particular religious group. After the 1800-1900 division, the view of the largest group in Finland [today called the SRK in Finland and the Laestadian Lutherans in America] was that no true Christians are found outside their own group. This exclusivist thinking has been a strong element in American Laestadianism. It is typical of the Apostolic Lutheran Mission or so-called Torola group and also found in the Old Apostolic Lutheran Church and the Pollarite groups. The exclusivism tradition and forms vary. For example, the traditional Laestadian greeting of "God's Peace" is still used by all groups, however, they view it from different perspectives. Most of the groups greet only members of their own fellowship with "God's Peace" and see it as accepting the person they greet as a brother or sister in faith. Some, especially in the Apostolic Lutheran Church of America, view it as confessing their own faith to another person regardless of what the other person may believe. Even in the Apostolic Lutheran Church of America exclusivistic characteristics have appeared at times, but increased international contacts have brought more openness to the group. On the whole, The Apostolic Lutheran Church of America and its sister organizations do not practice exclusivism as far as the doctrine of salvation is concerned.

Another characteristic feature of the Laestadian tradition is that the sacraments have not played a central role in the movement's proclamation and teaching. Most of the members of Laestadian groups do not accept the view held by confessional Lutheranism of baptism as new birth. New birth is connected to personal repentance and conversion. The majority of Laestadians emphasize that children are born believers. In addition, there is an observable emphasis on the doctrine of baptism, which appears to have been influenced by American baptistic and revival-evangelistic theology in general, for example the separation of "spirit baptism" and "water baptism." Alongside this, throughout the history of Laestadianism, there has been the doctrine of baptism, which is based on *Luther's Small Catechism* and traditional Lutheran teaching. Baptism has been a divisive issue in Laestadianism from its inception.

A source of tension emerging in all the groups throughout the years has been the proper distinction between the law and the gospel.

Most of the growth in all the groups is from within. Large families are common for all major Laestadian/Apostolic Lutheran groups since the general teaching is opposition to birth control. Another common group norm is total abstinence from alcohol which has been the teaching since the beginning of the revival.

THE OLD APOSTOLIC LUTHERAN CHURCH
(Esikoislestadiolaisuus)

MEMBERSHIP

There are approximately 10,000 members in this group. Congregations are located in the following states: Washington, Michigan, Minnesota, South Dakota, North Carolina, Delaware, Wyoming, Montana and Wisconsin. The most significant membership (3000) is in the Brush Prairie, Washington, area. Other large congregations are located in Hancock, Michigan (600), Minneapolis, Minnesota (600), and Detroit, Michigan (500). It is a growing movement. There are members also in Canada and in Alaska. There are seventeen church facilities in the United States and one in Canada.

MINISTERS AND ACTIVITIES

There are approximately thirty-eight preachers. Traditionally special Christmas and Midsummer services are held, as in Scandinavia. The Christmas services alternate between Detroit, Brush Prairie and Minneapolis. Mission services are also held in Alaska. The activites are traditional Laestadian. English has long been the prevalent language, although sermons are translated (Finnish/English) to some degree. They were the first group to have an English-speaking preacher, which was in 1899. A sermon of Laestadius is still read at their services. This is an independent group that has from the beginning had close ties with Finland and the other Scandinavian countries.

PUBLICATIONS

This group has no periodical of its own. *Rauhan Side* [*Bond of Peace*] published in Finland is read to some degree. However, they have seen to the translation and publication of several books of sermons by Laestadius as well as his *Ens ropandes röst I öknen* [*The Voice of One Crying in the Wilderness*].

APOSTOLIC LUTHERAN CHURCH OF AMERICA
(Rauhan Sana/pikkuesikoiset)

BACKGROUND

Following the Finnish model initiated in Oulu in 1906, the Conservative Laestadians in America held their first annual "Big Meetings" (national summer services) in Calumet, Michigan, in 1908. On that occasion a segment of the Old Laestadians returned to the Conservative fold. However, Pastor A. L. Heideman assumed a negative attitude toward this development, and gradually a division developed. The Heidemans, father Arthur Leopold and son Paul (both had received their theological education at the University of Helsinki and were ordained in the church of Finland), had close friends in the SRK in Finland and created close ties with that group. Therefore, the Heidemans became the trusted channel of communication from America for the SRK. As a consequence of this division, the "Apostolic Lutheran Church of America" (also called the Federation) was organized in 1928 by the supporters of the so-called "Big Meeting Group." It was not accepted by the followers of Heideman. A similar division occurred among the SRK Conservative Laestadians in Scandinavia in 1934. The sister organization of the Federation is called the Rauhan Sana group in Finland. Prior to 1928 the congregations had been fully independent with some cooperation in arranging the Big Meetings. After the Federation was organized, congregations could choose to join the Federation to work for common causes. If a new congregation wishes to join now, the congregation must make an application which must be approved by the central board and delegates.

Seminary training for pastors has been a source of tension in the Federation in more recent times. Opinion at one time regarding the Inter-Lutheran Seminary in Hancock, Michigan (originating in Plymouth, Minnesota in 1967 with Uuras Saarnivaara as one of the founders) was divided, but at the present time it has somewhat wider acceptance. The Seminary is currently under the leadership of Pastor James P. Weidner, who is a former pupil of Dr. Saarnivaara. Numerous Apostolic Lutheran pastors have studied in the seminary. Some of its graduates are serving in other denominations.

MEMBERSHIP

Originally the Federation was the largest Laestadian group in North America. Since the 1930s, however, the membership has steadily declined. The membership was 15,000-16,000 in 1946 but only about 7000 in 1985, which is also the present membership estimate. The estimated attendance at the national summer services ("the convention") was 6000 in 1930, and in recent years it has been around 2000.

According to the 2004 annual report, there are fifty-six congregations in fourteen states and four in Canada. The largest congregations are: Hockinson, Washington (1100); New Ipswich, New Hampshire (700); Esko, Minnesota (300); Hancock, Michigan; New York Mills, Minnesota; and Wolf Lake, Minnesota (250) (Spruce Grove). Many congregations are small, having 25-100 members. There are sixteen congregations in the Copper Country (in the Upper Peninsula of Michigan), traditional Laestadian territory. In recent years, as a result of mobility and new employment opportunities, congregations have sprung up in South and North Carolina. It is typical of the Apostolic Lutheran Church of America for local congregations to be very independent and have individual characteristics. Consequently this organization acts as an umbrella encompassing different elements.

MINISTERS AND ACTIVITIES

In 2004 there were seventy-nine ministers on the official roll of the Apostolic Lutheran Church of America. There are about eighteen Seminary trained pastors ministering in ALCA congregations, eight of whom are on the ministerial roll. Twenty-five of the total number of ministers are serving in full-time ministries, while the others have secular jobs along with their ministry positions. Some of the congregations are involved in annual Bible camp programs, and some sponsor youth events and mission trips for young people. The pastors in Michigan sponsor an annual confirmation camp in which youth from other states can also participate. Other congregations have confirmation programs for their own youth. The annual summer convention is hosted by congregations in different parts of the country. Regional fall services are also planned in various areas.

ORGANIZATION

The congregations are autonomous and the polity congregational. The Federation has a Central Board of nine men who are elected at the annual convention. The Central Board carries out decisions made at annual meetings. New congregations make an application to join which must be approved by the Central Board. Due to the nature of the organization, there are churches in fellowship with the Federation that are not official members, as well as pastors and speakers in congregations who are not on the official ministerial role of the Federation. Inner mission activity is directed by an Eastern and Western Mission Boards. A National Sunday School Board and Foreign Mission Board are also elected at the annual convention. Along with services at the summer convention there is a Pastors' Meeting, annual meeting of congregational delegates, national Sunday School meeting, and meetings of the various boards.

FOREIGN CONNECTIONS

Sister organizations include the Lähetysyhdistys Rauhan Sana in Finland, the Laestadianernas Fridsföreningars Förbund (LFF) in Norway, the so-called Alta movement, and the Tornio Valley movement in Sweden. Usually a speaker from Finland, Sweden or Norway is invited to tour the American congregations once a year by the Federation and some individual congregations may invite guest speakers from these countries as well.

PERIODICALS

The *Christian Monthly* is a publication of the Federation. *Where He Leads...Foreign Mission News of the Apostolic Lutheran Church* of America is published quarterly. In addition there is a publication describing inner mission work entitled *The Lord is My Shepherd (News of the Apostolic Lutheran Mission).* Many congregations have their own monthly newsletter which are widely distributed in the Federation. The Federation (www.apostolic-lutheran.org) and some congregations have web sites.

MISSIONS

Since the 1960s there has been a lively though scattered involvement in missions on the part of the Central Board and individual congregations. Mission work began in Nigeria in 1965, giving birth to the national Apostolic Lutheran Church of Nigeria. Connections with Guatemala opened up in 1968. Subsequently, mission trips have been made to South American countries, India, and Eastern Europe (Latvia as well as Ingria—the region surrounding St.

Petersburg, Russia). Many local congregations have their own mission involvement in various areas of the world.

In India Syam Kummar, M.D., has played an important role. He has visited the United States as well as Laestadian circles in Finland (2003). The work is rapidly increasing in India and Sri Lanka as a result of the tsunami disaster. Mission trips have also been made by Apostolic Lutherans to other countries where contacts have developed through personal relationships or correspondence.

Kingisepp and Yekaterinburg, Russia have been a very important focus for mission work in recent years. Dennis Hillman (who is fluent in the Russian language) and his wife Birgitta, as well as Vilma Vähäkangas, all from Finland, have served in Yekaterinburg for longer periods of time supported by Americans. Certain individuals within the Apostolic Lutheran Church have financially supported the mission efforts of Finnish and American believers.

LAESTADIAN LUTHERAN CHURCH, LLC
Formerly Association of American Laestadian congregation, AALC, (Suomen Rauhanyhdistysten Keskusyhdistys, SRK)

BACKGROUND
In the split that took place in the so-called Heideman group in 1972-1973, those who sided with Finland's SRK organized the AALC in 1973. From the beginning it has maintained close ties to Finland and the SRK. Headquarters of the church are in Minneapolis, Minnesota.

MEMBERSHIP
The membership of the Laestadian Lutheran Church is 5000 to 6000 including children. There are twenty-three congregations in the United States and seven in Canada. The largest congregations are located in Minneapolis, Rockford, Cokato, and northern Minnesota; Phoenix, Arizona; Seattle and Longview, Washington; and Saskatchewan, Canada.

PREACHERS/ACTIVITIES
The Laestadian Lutheran Church has seventy-seven preachers, including two full-time pastors educated at the Theological Department of the University of Helsinki. The central organization has eight full-time employees and six part-time employees.

They have two Bible Camps: Stony Lake Camp (Park Rapids, Minnesota) and Hasscib lake Camp (Champion, Michigan) which have very active programs. Other camp programs are held in rented facilities in Washington. They have a continuous camp program for adults and youth from April to October. Camp programs include: Confirmation, Pre-confirmation, Music, Seniors, Mothers, Couples, Mother-Daughter, Father-Son, Parenting, Ministers, Language, Bible Courses, Youth and International Couples Camp. A great deal of attention is devoted to work with children and youth.

They also have radio ministries and sermons available on their website (www.laestadianlutheran.org). Their national summer services are hosted by congregations in a different area of the country each year and are well attended.

PERIODICALS

Among their publications are *The Voice of Zion,* a children's paper called *The Shepherd's Voice,* and a special Christmas publication *Christmas in Zion.* In recent years they have been actively publishing books for adults and children.

FOREIGN CONNECTIONS/MISSIONS

They are in direct communication with the SRK in Finland. On a regular basis preachers from Finland make preaching tours, young people are sent to SRK folk high schools, and there are youth exchanges. There have been numerous international marriages among the young people. There is a keen interest in the SRK mission work in Russia.

In recent years the LLC has directed its energies toward foreign mission work in Ecuador and Togo (Africa). The folk school exchange programs and tourism have opened mission work opportunities which have been productive. The LLC follows the example of its Finnish sister organization in its mission efforts. Since the late 1980's the SRK has vigorously expanded its mission effort to Central Europe, England, Russia, the Baltic countries and Africa.

SPECIAL CHARACTERISTICS

The LLC has a strong organization and close ties to the SRK group in Finland. In fact, it dogmatically follows SRK's policies. The doctrine of the church is very exclusive. However, this group is dynamic in its operations and responds to today's challenges. There is a concern for addressing the needs of the younger generation. Theological training is not viewed negatively. In some ways it is the most modern of the Laestadian groups in North America (forms of activity, attitude toward theological training, etc.). They have well-designed websites for their churches.

FIRST APOSTOLIC LUTHERAN CHURCH
(Apostolic Lutheran Mission) (Vanhoillislestadiolainen rauhanyhdistys, VLR)

BACKGROUND

The so-called "Heideman group" of Laestadians (corresponding to the SRK Laestadians in Finland) split in the years 1972-1973. The controversies dated from the latter part of the 1960s and, to some degree, even earlier. The preacher Heikki Saari from Finland had a significant role in the disputes. In the United States, the old preacher Walter Torola opposed the direction taken by the SRK. Many of the people in the Heideman group followed Torola, while a significant segment remained in fellowship with the SRK. Paul Heideman, who died in 1973, is viewed by both parties as "their own." The Torola group maintained its hold primarily in the Upper Peninsula of Michigan, and it retained the organization and periodical of the original group. Those who maintained ties with the SRK had supporters especially in Minnesota and the west coast. They organized as the Association of American Laestadian Congregations and later changed their name to Laestadian Lutheran Church.

MEMBERSHIP

The membership is about 5000-5500 including the children. The most significant concentration is in the Copper Country of Upper Michigan, the traditional Finnish and Laestadian region (Calumet and Houghton, about 1500 members). Other large congregations: Detroit, MI (1000); Cokato, MN (650); Minneapolis, MN (500); Runeberg, MN (300); Zion, IL (250). There are twenty-three congregations. In Canada there are four small congregations without church facilities. In addition services are held in Alaska.

PREACHERS/ACTIVITIES

The group has about twenty-six preachers, with only two in full-time ministry. The leading figures have been the late Walter Torola and his son Peter Torola. They continue the traditional national St. John's services in Calumet, Michigan, each year and the national annual meeting is held at that time. Some of the congregations continue the tradition of spring and fall services with guest speakers.

PERIODICALS

The *Greetings of Peace* is published in Calumet, Michigan, and has 1300 subscribers. They have no other recent books or publications.

FOREIGN CONNECTIONS

They have ties to Finland with the organization formed by those who were separated from the SRK in the 1970s: Suomen Vanhoillislestadiolainen Rauhanyhdistys (SVR), The Finnish organization has in recent years taken over the publication of *Rauhan Tervehtys* under the name *Armon ja Rauhan Tervehdys* [*Greetings of Grace and Peace*], which has a few subscribers in the United States. In northern Sweden there is a small group of supporters with a prayer house in Morjärvi. In Finland and Sweden there are less than 200 supporters and two preachers.

SPECIAL CHARACTERISTICS

Their doctrine of the church is in principle very exclusive (they view their own group as exclusively the body of believers), although in practice not everyone agrees with this concept. They hold the traditional Laestadian view of the sacraments according to which the purpose of Holy Communion is "to strengthen the faith of believers," and children are believers before Baptism, which is a "covenant" and not a means of grace.

The group is very traditional in its modes of activity. They have no organized activities for the youth other than Sunday school. They have no mission outreach other than to visit their own members in isolated areas.

POLLARITE GROUP
(Matt Reed and Aunes Salmela)

BACKGROUND

In the late 1800s an extreme evangelical trend developed in the conservative Laestadian movement in North America, which shunned the preaching of counsel, admonition, and repentance to Laestadian believers. This way of thinking received reinforcement from John (Juho) Pollari (1865-1945), who came from Veteli, Finland, to Lanesville, Massachusetts, in 1893. His family belonged to Finland's Evangelical Movement, but he had joined the Laestadian movement in the early 1880s and become a lay preacher. As the trend began to gain an ever stronger foothold in the Heideman group, the supporters of Heideman and Pollari separated from each other in 1920-1921 while Pastor O.H. Jussila of Finland was on a preaching tour in the United States, becoming final by the mid 1920s.

The Pollarites have proven to be a very schismatic group, dividing into several subgroups. The first split took place in the mid 1930s when part of the group followed Pollari, Walter Isaacs and others, and part followed the preacher John Koskela who preached antinomianism (opposition to and rejection of the law). Nine preachers served the Koskela group until the mid 1980s. Services were held in several places in Wisconsin (including Van Buskirk), Minnesota, and California. This group has ceased to function.

The Pollarites split further in 1962-1963 into groups led by Matt Reed and Aunes Salmela. There was a new schism in the latter group at the end of the 1970s. In 1978 a faction broke off from the Aunes Salmela group which subsequently split into two parts. The larger group gathered around David Salmela and the smaller group around Melvin Hanka. These two small groups comprise a total of seventy members. They are extremely exclusive in nature. They will not be discussed here separately.

THE SUBGROUPS

1. The Independent Apostolic Lutheran Church (Matt Reed group) is the largest of the Pollarite groups. It has a membership of approximately 3000, with the largest congregation of several hundred members being in Minneapolis, Minnesota. There are other large congregations in Duluth, Minnesota; Kenosha, Wisconsin; and Ishpeming, Michigan. They have nineteen preachers with eleven church facilities (plus one jointly with the Aunes Salmela group). They have no periodicals but do publish a newsletter announcing the activities to their members.

2. The Apostolic Lutheran Church (Aunes Salmela group) has about 600 members. They have eleven preachers with five congregations. The largest congregations are in Minneapolis,

Minnesota (250 members) and Marengo, Wisconsin (125 members). They have no publications.

SPECIAL CHARACTERISTICS

The feature most characteristic of the Pollarites is the long-standing tension between law and gospel, which has given rise to repeated schisms. Confession has always been minimized among the Pollarites, and the emphasis has been on believing. This may have something to do with John Pollari's evangelical background and the "extreme evangelical" stream in the Finnish Evangelical Movement explains some of this. The "joyful christianity" of the Pollarites manifests itself as extreme emotional outbursts and a strong tradition of hymn singing. Singing often takes up the greater part of the service, but they do not use an organ or musical instruments. Their services are very simple and traditional. The speakers sit while speaking. The Pollarites have generally avoided all kinds of organization and organized activity.

FOREIGN CONNECTIONS

The Pollarites have no sister movement in European Laestadianism. However, there were trends in the SRK group in Finland during the 20th century which have displayed some characteristics of the same spiritual mentality. A few examples are given here. In the 1930's there was a movement characterized by ecstatic phenomena gathered around an individual name Juho Ansamaa. The last supporters of this group in the early 1970s were described by Hugo and Warren Hepokoski as "having been justified by faith." Maria Jantunen of Simpele, Finland, brought some Pollarite influences from the United States to the Conservative Laestadians in the region of Imatra. The influence of the preacher Erkki Simppala, which was felt among Laestadians in Tervola and elsewhere in southern Lapland from the 1930s onward, can scarcely be considered the counterpart of Pollarism in Finland, although Erkki Reinikainen has characterized it as "a schism tinged with Kosonism and Pollarism."

They do not have any organized mission outreach to those outside of their fellowship.

GRACE APOSTLES LUTHERAN CHURCH
(Group separated from the First Apostolic Lutheran Church in 2004).

BACKGROUND

The Grace Apostles Lutheran Church was formed in 2004 after a group from Cokato, Minnesota, seeking reform and discussion over doctrinal concerns was voted out at the annual meeting of the First Apostolic Lutheran Mission in Calumet, Michigan, in 2004. Some preachers, members, and congregations were excommunicated from fellowship with the First Apostolic Lutheran Church.

MEMBERSHIP

It is not known at this time how many members this separation will affect since it is so recent. The group was first organized in Cokato, Minnesota. Presently there are three congregations: Cokato, Minnesota; Lansing, Michigan; and Phoenix, Arizona. Currently, there are 200 plus members.

PREACHERS AND ACTIVITIES

The group has seven ministers. They have Sunday school and services every Sunday with Bible studies during the week as well as youth group meetings.

CHART SUMMARIZING THE ACTIVITY OF THE VARIOUS GROUPS IN NORTH AMERICA (1995-2005)
All figures are estimates

GROUP	MEMBERSHIP	CONGREGATIONS	CHURCH BUILDINGS	PREACHERS AND PASTORS	PUBLICATIONS
Old Apostolic Lutheran Church	10,000	15-20	18	38	None
Apostolic Lutheran Church of America	7,000	60	60	79	*Christian Monthly Where He Leads... The Lord is My Shepherd* Local Newsletters
Laestadian Luthern Church (LLC)	5,000-6,000	30	18	77	*The Voice of Zion The Shepherd's Voice Christmas in Zion*
First Apostolic Lutheran Church	5,000-5,500	27	14	26	*Greetings of Peace*
Independent Apostolic Lutheran Church (Reed group)	3,000	22	11	19	Newsletter
Apostolic Lutheran Church (Aunes Salmela group)	600	5	5	11	None
Grace Apostles Lutheran Church	200+	3	0	7	None
Estimated Totals	32,300	167	126	257	7 + Newsletters

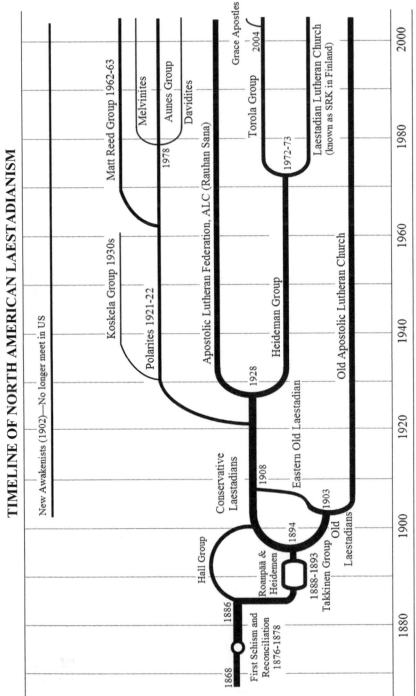

TIMELINE OF NORTH AMERICAN LAESTADIANISM

Adapted from diagram by Marko Sagulin, Tuomas Palola, and Jouko Talonen—used with permission.

19

Apostolic Lutheranism (Laestadianism) From an International Perspective

Jouko Talonen

THE EXPANSION OF LAESTADIANISM OUTSIDE OF SCANDINAVIA

In the early 1870s, the Laestadian movement gained a foothold in St. Petersburg as Laestadians joined the stream of Finns seeking employment in the metropolis. It later spread to the surrounding Finnish-speaking area known as Ingria. It is remarkable that Laestadiansim, about which nothing was known for some fifty years, survived the Soviet era and was rediscovered in the early 1990s. The history of Laestadian Christianity under Soviet repression has not been thoroughly researched as yet, but the preservation of this small group and its expansion under those difficult conditions is an indication of a definite religious identity. Since the 1990s the SRK (Laestadian Lutheran Church), Firstborn (Old Apostolic Lutheran Church) and Rauhan Sana (Apostolic Lutheran Church of America) groups have made it their mission to work in the former Soviet Union. In addition to people of Finnish background, the movement is reaching ethnic Russians.

The awakening reached Estonia early on in 1886. An Estonian hymnal was published by the SRK in 1999. All three Laestadian groups have had connections with Latvia. Through a Finnish-Hungarian theological exchange program in the 1930s, the Hungarian Lutheran Church was influenced by the SRK. After World War II Firstborn Laestadians labored in eastern and central Norway. There was some Laestadian activity also in Denmark.

In more recent times, the Laestadian groups have spread even further. A natural explanation for this development is that members of the groups have moved to foreign countries, and these believers have had a desire to hear the same preaching as in the homeland. Thus, SRK church members formed cells in England, Germany and Thailand in the 1990s. The old connections with Hungary have reopened. A

German collection of the Finnish hymnal *Siionin Laulut ja Virret [Hymns and Songs of Zion]* has been published. In recent years SRK activity reaches to Turkey and Africa as well.

Firstborn Laestadians have made mission trips to Central Europe for the past twenty years. In 1999 Mission Services were conducted in Reisfeld (Germany) and Arnheim (the Netherlands). Guests arrived from the United States, Germany, the Netherlands, England and Finland. At these services the sermons were translated into the Dutch language for the first time. Regular home services are held in London, and there are larger gatherings when preachers arrive from Norway.

In 1997 representatives of the Finnish Rauhan Sana group and the Apostolic Lutheran Book Concern initiated a joint venture to publish a book of Bible stories. This volume is available in the English, Finnish, Estonian, Russian, Latvian, Lithuanian, Swedish, Spanish and Telugu (India) languages.

The Laestadian movement spread to the United States as early as the 1870s with the stream of emigration from the northern regions of Scandinavia. American Laestadian churches have been passive with regard to foreign missions until recent times. Lately members of the Laestadian Lutheran Church have made mission trips to South America (Ecuador) and Africa (Togo and Ghana).

APOSTOLIC LUTHERAN CHURCH OF AMERICA FOREIGN MISSIONS

The Apostolic Lutheran Church of America began mission work in Africa in 1965. Andrew Mickelsen, president of the church federation, visited Nigeria upon receiving an invitation from a group of Nigerians and encountered interest in the Apostolic Lutheran (Laestadian) message. Philip and Naomi Johnson were sent to Nigeria in May 1966. A mission house was built, congregations were established, and preachers were taught during their stay. The family returned to the

Church near mission house in Ishiet Erong, Nigeria in 1977

United States in June 1967, after the death of Philip in an auto accident. At that time the Biafran war broke out in the region in which the churches were located. Consequently the doors to that area were closed for several years, and there was no contact between the American and Nigerian churches. Elmer and Miriam Yliniemi were sent in November 1976 and returned home a year later. There were 25 congregations with approximately 2500 members at the time. In 2005 the Apostolic Lutheran Church of Nigeria has five parishes comprised of 22 congregations, totaling over 2000 members. Four pastors oversee

The mission house in 1977 which is now used as a primary school

the work in the parishes, with evangelists and preachers in charge of individual congregations. The church has established a primary school with over 200 students in the mission house built in the 1960s, with plan for future expansion. Naomi (Mickelsen) Johnson played an important role in the publication of the Apostolic Lutheran Hymnal, which was published in the Efik language in 1969. A couple of men from Nigeria studied at the Inter-Lutheran Seminary in Minneapolis, Minnesota, supported by American Apostolic Lutherans. The Nigerian Apostolic Lutheran Church has functioned independently for several decades with brief mission trips annually in the last few years by men sent by the Foreign Mission Board of the Apostolic Lutheran Church of America. The Apostolic Lutheran Church of Ghana has begun association with the ALC of America, and missionaries have visited churches in South Africa.

In four major areas of **India** the Foreign Mission Board of the ALC is working with pastors and churches which have been drawn together from various denominations. They are established under their own name but receive support, instructional materials and visits from the ALC. Over a hundred pastors receive financial support, and about 400 attended seminars taught by ALC pastors. Dr. K. Syam Kumar heads the group of 106 churches with approximately 45,000 people in Andhra Pradesh State, of which 34 are in the area hit by the tsunami. A substantial amount of assistance has been provided by the Foreign Mission Board to aid tsunami victims. Dr. Kumar is also director of a free medical clinic and hospital for the poor and destitute, along with two satellite clinics. The churches operate two orphanages with close to 200 children, and the ALC provides them with support and Christian education materials. Two more orphanages are under construction. One of these is for children orphaned by the tsunami and is receiving funding from the Andhra Pradesh State government. Publications include a Telugu hymnal entitled *Spiritual Songs* and a bimonthly magazine called *Spiritual Food*.

The ALC has worked for two years with Pastor Lynton Silva who is responsible for ten house churches in **Sri Lanka**. He made contact after reading a "God's Peace" tract distributed by the ALC fifteen or twenty years ago.

Another mission field has been **Central and South America**. Guatemala is the most important, but preachers have visited other countries as well. Some Laestadian writings have been translated into Spanish, and at least two hymns popular among Laestadians are now sung in the Spanish language.

In **Guatemala** the way for Apostolic Lutheran mission work opened in 1966 when a conservative Methodist missionary named Orlando Wolfram received an English-language copy of a booklet entitled "The Awakening Cry and the Way of Salvation" written by the Finnish lay preacher Janne Marttiini. Two years later Andrew Mickelsen, accompanied by Willard Tervo, made the first mission visit to Guatemala. Today there are two Apostolic Lutheran churches in Guatemala—in Zacapa and Piedras Azulas. Jose Antonio Salguero, who formerly served in the Lutheran Church-Missouri Synod, was ordained into the Apostolic Lutheran ministry in 1975 and labored faithfully for many years. Since his retirement, the major burden has fallen on his son-in-law, Solomon Leon, assisted by Alberto Torres and Ernesto Pineda. The Apostolic Lutherans there have had firm ties with their Christian brethren in the United States who provide them with spiritual and material assistance. The Federation has regularly sent preachers as well as groups of young people on short-term missions.

Apostolic Lutherans have also been financially supporting the work in the former Soviet Union. Preachers have been sent to **Latvia** and **Ingria**, an area surrounding St. Petersburg which long ago was settled by people from Finland. In **Russia** the Apostolic Lutheran Church of America has focused mainly on the Kingisepp and Yekaterinburg congregations. The Finnish counterpart has sent missionaries to Kingisepp for a number of years for longer periods of time, and they now have Jukka and Kristina Paananen as resident missionaries. Dennis and Birgitta Hillman have been serving for several years as missionaries in Yekaterinburg (Siberia). Mikhail Krupinov of Kingisepp is in charge of the translation of articles, printing and distribution of a monthly paper called *News-Christian Journal* which has a circulation of 3000 copies. He works closely with the Mission Board of the Apostolic Lutheran Church which subsidizes the publication. There is also a website which includes the Journal and other information.

According to the Foreign Mission Board report of the Apostolic Lutheran Church of America 2004, Apostolic Lutheran **literature** was translated and distributed in the following countries: India—Telugu, Hindi, Kannada and several other more minor languages; Myanmar—Burmese language; Pakistan—Urdu language; Sri Lanka—Tamil and Sinhala languages; Guatemala, San Salvador, Peru and Colombia—Spanish language; Russia—Russian language. A total of 4,245,200 pieces of literature, including Sunday School materials, tracts, hymnals, etc., have been distributed. There are plans for much more to fill the requests received. An HIV/AIDS booklet written from a biblical perspective by Dr. Kumar has been in very great demand in several countries.

LAESTADIAN IDENTITY

In general all of the Laestadian connections have retained a strong identity which is based on the heritage from northern Scandinavia. The distinctive teachings of the movement and its simple congregational form have prevented it from melding with the religious identities of it surroundings. This is evident especially in regard to the SRK. In Russia the SRK has striven to retain its own identity, while the other Laestadian groups have been satisfied to work within the Ingrian Evangelical Lutheran Church. Since the revival movements in Finland

and Sweden are used to working under the umbrella of their state churches, they feel that they can reach more people with the Word of God and a revival message by working within the Ingrian Church. The small number of Firstborn Laestadians in western and central Europe also consider it important to retain their own religious identity. Another example of this is the Apostolic Lutheran Church in Guatemala, where Apostolic Lutheranism has its own identity differing from the Catholic Church, the Evangelical churches, and the Missouri Synod. Its church buildings have the character of Laestadian prayer houses, and the services follow the traditional prayer house format. A unique feature there is the use of guitars to accompany singing.

Translated by Aila Foltz with input from Miriam Yliniemi

20

What Can We Learn from History?

Elmer and Miriam Yliniemi

In ancient Israel, God persistently called His children back to Himself when they strayed by raising prophets who directed the people back to the Word of God. God has raised and continues to raise messengers, empowered by the Holy Spirit, throughout the world to awaken people and bring them to His Word through revivals. God often uses outward circumstances such as the political and moral climate of a nation, economic crisis, war, and natural disasters to awaken people to recognize His sovereignty.

Laestadius, an ordained pastor in the State Church of Sweden was one person God used mightily in northern Scandinavia and in many of our lives. Throughout this book, we have seen God working through sinful people and various circumstances to bring about a movement of God, empowered by the Holy Spirit, that has changed hundreds of thousands of lives in the past 160 years. As we look at the moral, economic and even the weather conditions in northern Scandinavia in the mid 1800s, we can see the people being prepared by God to receive His Word. The political and economic conditions in Finland as well as the Civil War in America, which created a labor shortage, all contributed to the mass migration to America in the 1880s. As we study history, we see the hand of God moving and guiding in bringing His will to pass not only in this movement but also throughout time.

Laestadianism is the most widespread revival movement originating in Scandinavia. Of the Finnish revival movements during the 1800s, it is also the most international because the larger factions have continued to reach new areas. On the other hand, this movement has experienced many divisions. The division phenomenon, which began 100 years ago, has by the year 2005 resulted in nineteen groups internationally that can be identified as having a common Laestadian heritage, each with their own emphasis.

It was also the most rapidly spreading Scandinavian revival movement because Laestadius trained and involved lay leaders to spread the Good News of salvation they had experienced. An emphasis on the priesthood of all believers became an important element in Laestadianism. A change in the lives of people was seen. For example, some of the northern parishes which were in danger of destroying themselves with alcohol became completely alcohol free.

What can we learn from the study of history? We can learn how God has worked through those who have gone before us. The Bible tells us to "remember the days of old, consider the years of many generations: ask thy father, and he will show thee; thy elders, and they will tell thee" (Deuteronomy 32:7). As we learn how God has brought about revivals in the past, may it help us recognize the work of God in the future.

History also teaches us that revival movements survive 100 to 150 years. By the third and fourth generation, they have become teaching movements steeped in tradition and are no longer revival movements in the true sense of the word. A revival starts with an awakening, then moves on to organize into a movement and finally builds on tradition. Revivals are not static; they evolve with the people.[28]

> Laestadius declared the law and repentance, warned of grace thieves and taught an emotionally experienced new birth that took place in conversion. Gradually the declaration of the forgiveness of sins became an emphasis. The Pietistic repentance sermon gradually gave way to a Moravian type of broad declaration of grace and a de-emphasis of strong emotional experience. An attempt to return to the repentance sermons created a division in the movement.[29]

Trying to bring together two opposing concepts—tradition and renewal—has recurrently created conflict, as a tidal wave, over the years. People begin to rely on the faith of their fathers without having a personal relationship with Christ. "Think not to say within yourselves, We have Abraham to our father: for I say unto you, that God is able of these stones to raise up children unto Abraham" (Matthew 3:9).

The Bible exhorts us to "Remember...them who have spoken unto you the word of God: whose faith follow, considering the end of their conversation" (Hebrews 13:7). It is good to honor the traditions of our heritage, but may the Lord give us wisdom by His Spirit to discern the

---

[28] Raittila, Pekka. Summarized and translated from lecture notes .

[29] Junkkaala, Timo. "Mita Meidan pitäisi oppia Lestadiolaisuudesta?" Perusta 1/2000.

difference between traditions and the Word of God in a changing world. "Forasmuch as ye know that ye were not redeemed with corruptible things, as silver and gold, from your vain conversation[30] received by tradition from your fathers; But with the precious blood of Christ, as of a lamb without blemish and without spot." (I Peter 1:18, 19). The emphasis is not to be on Laestadius and the traditions of the revival but the crucified and risen Christ.

History shows us that God is in ultimate control. He is directing the course of history even when things seem to be out of control. "For as the heavens are higher than the earth, so are my ways higher than your ways, and my thoughts than your thoughts. For as the rain cometh down, and the snow from heaven and returneth not thither, but watereth the earth, and maketh it bring forth and bud, that it may give seed to the sower, and bread to the eater: So shall my word be that goeth forth out of my mouth: it shall not return unto me void, but it shall accomplish that which I please, and it shall prosper in the thing whereto I sent it" (Isaiah 55:9-11).

We do not need to despair, we can trust in the hidden wisdom and power of God to lead His children even through dark times. He can bring order out of chaos. He has promised to never leave or forsake us (Heb. 13:5). May we continue to uphold the Word of God and follow the instructions of Jesus to His disciples: "Thus it is written, and thus it behooved Christ to suffer, and to rise from the dead the third day: And that repentance and remission of sins should be preached in his name among all nations, beginning at Jerusalem" (Luke 24: 46, 47).

"For I am not ashamed of the gospel of Christ: for it is the power of God unto salvation to every one that believeth" (Romans 1:16).

"For God so loved the world, that he gave his only begotten Son, that whosoever believeth in him should not perish, but have everlasting life" (John 3:16).

---

[30] NIV: your empty way of life.

21

Farewell Sermon of Laestadius

Farewell to all grace "pups." I entrust you to God's care!

Farewell to all young chickadees and swallows! May the gracious Lord Jesus preserve you from the claws of the hawks and feed you with mosquitoes.

Farewell to the lambs of Jesus, whom the chief shepherd has snatched from the teeth of the ravenous wolf. May the Lord Jesus bring you to the best pasture and feed you with choice field hay when winter comes.

Farewell to all young tender grains still growing in God's field! May the Lord of the seed provide suitable weather that you might be filled out before the frost comes and that you would become beautiful grain for the reapers to gather into their granary. May the Lord of life preserve this small field from blizzards and hailstorms so the frost would not destroy these small grains before the harvest.

Farewell, you newborn babies, whom the heavenly Parent has delivered with great pain and shedding of blood. Farewell to the newborn babies who lie on the cold floor of this world crying. May the heavenly Parent lift you up, wash you clean with the water of life and wrap you in a clean blanket and place you at His bosom. May the breast be placed in the mouth of the crying child until the crying ceases and they behold their Creator with joy.

Farewell to all the winter chickadees and summer swallows! May the heavenly Parent who gives food to the ravens in due season when they call upon Him, give you milk, butter and honey, when you are hungry. May He guard and protect all the small birds from the talons of the hawk.

Farewell to the snowbirds and nightingales who have chirped and sung to the lonely traveler from the precious tree. May God give me the grace to hear the snowbirds and nightingales twittering before God and the Lamb in the Kingdom of God and singing a new song in the Tree of Life.

I am like a lonely bird perched on a limb. Pray that the gracious Lord Jesus gives me strength and courage to cry out:

- To the straying travelers, so they would turn back to the road of life.

- To all the sorrowful and downcast that they would rise from the valley of sorrow to Mount Zion.

- To all the poor and infirm that they would beg for food before they starve.

- To all the hungering and thirsting that they would seek water.

- To all those who are distressed that they would cry with such a loud voice that they would be heard in heaven.

If I had a voice so loud that I could scare the wolves and the lions from the flock, I would cry so that all hills, rocks and mountains would echo: Amen, hallelujah! Praise, glory and honor to God and the Lamb who sit on the throne.

May the gracious Lord Jesus give us the grace to see one another in heaven and there sing: Amen, Hallelujah, forever!

Excerpts from the farewell sermon of Laestadius when he left the Karesuando parish in 1849, to take a pastorate at Pajala. *Katso Jumalan Karitsa.* Translated by Miriam Yliniemi.

Bibliography

Aho, G. A. & Nopola, J. E., *Evankelis-luterilainen kansalliskirkko.* Ironwood, MI, 1949.

Alanen, Arnold R. "The Norwegian Connection." *Finnish Americana* 6 (1983-1984). Editor Michael Karni. Parta Printers, Inc. New York Mills, MN.

Calumetin Apostolis-Lutherilaisen Seurakunnan Säännöt. Calumet, MI. 1929.

Castrren, Kaarlo. *Kiveliön suuri herättäjä Lars Levi Laestadius.* Helsinki: Otava 1932.

Esala, Philip J. "American Laestadianism Schismatic?" *Concordia Historical Institute Quarterly* 58.4 (Winter 1985).

Juhonpieti, Erkki Antti. *Kirjeet ja Kirjoitukset.* Edited by Pekka Raittila. Suomen Kirkkohistoriallinen Seura Tornedalica 1979.

Harjutsalo, Ilpo, and Talonen, Jouko. Editors. *Iustitia* 14: *Lestadiolaisuuden monet kasvot.* Helsinki, 2001.

Havas, Väinö. *Laestadiolaisuuden Historia.* Suomen Lähetysseuran Laestadiolainen Haaraosasto: Oulu, Finland 1927.

Hepokoski, Warren. *The Laestadian Movement: Disputes and Divisions* 1861-1997. Culpeper, VA, 1997. A copy.

Hepokoski, Warren. *Lars Levi Laestadius and the Revival in Lapland.* Culpepper, VA, 2000. A copy.

History of Living Christianity in America. Compiled and edited by the committee selected by the Old Apostolic Lutheran Church of America. Hancock, MI, 1974.

Hoglund, A. William. *Finnish Immigrants in America 1880-1920.* Madison: U of Wisconsin Press, 1960.

Holmio, Armas K. E. *History of the Finns in Michigan.* Detroit: Wayne State U Press, 2001.

Ilmonen, S. *Amerikan Suomalaisten Historia I.* Hancock, MI, 1919.

Ilmonen, S. *Amerikan Suomalaisten Historia II.* Hancock, MI, 1931.

Ilmonen, S. *Amerikan Suomalaisten Sivistyshistoria I.* Hancock, MI, 1930.

Juntunen, Wayne Roger. *Where is the Apostolic Lutheran Church Going?* Diss. Faith Evangelical Lutheran Seminary. Tacoma, WA, 1988.

Juva, Mikko. "Lestadiolaisuuden leviäminen läntiseen Afrikkaan." *Suomen kirkkohistoriallisen seuran vuosikirja.* 64-67 (1974-1977). Helsinki, 1977.

Kaups, Matti E., "The Finns in the copper and iron ore mines of the Western Great Lakes region, 1864-1905".— *Migration Studies* C 3, Institute of Migration, Turku, Finland, in cooperation with the Immigration History Research Center, University of Minnesota 1975.

Kolehmainen John I., "Finnish Overseas Migration from Arctic Norway and Russia." *Agricultural History* 19 (October 1945).

Kolehmainen, John Ilmari, *Suomalaisten siirtolaisuus Norjasta Amerikkaan.* Fitchburg, MA, 1946.

Kinnunen, Mauri. "Facts About Laestadianism in America." Kinnunen's Internet Home Page on "Laestadianism," 2003.

Kukkonen, Walter. "Process and Product: Problems Encountered By The Finnish Immigrants In The Tranmission of a Spiritual Heritage." *Migration Studies* C 3, Institute of Migration, Turku, Finland, in cooperation with the Immigration History Research Center, University of Minnesota 1975.

Kulla, Carl A. *The Journey of an Immigrant Awakening Movement In America.* Brush Prairie, WA 2004.

Kulla, Carl A. *The Streams of Life.* Brush Prairie, WA. 1985.

Kulla, Carl A. *The Continuing Streams of Life.* Brush Prairie, WA. 1993.

Kurtti, James. "Finnish and Sami Settlement in Michigan's Copper Country" Arran (Quarterly of Sami Siida of North America & Lappmark Lag) Fall 1998 #12.

Laestadius, Lars Levi. *Behold the Lamb of God.* English version edited by Carl A. Kulla, 1986.

Laestadius, Lars Levi. *Fragments of Lappish Mythology.* Edited by Juha Pentikäinen. Translated by Börje Vähämäki. Beaverton, Ontario: Aspasia Books, 2002.

Laestadius, Lars Levi. *New Postilla.* Hancock, MI. Old Apostolic Lutheran Church, 1960.

Laestadius, Lars Levi. *The Voice of One Crying in the Wilderness.* USA: Old Apostolic Lutheran Church, 1988.

Laitinen, Aatu. *Memoirs of Early Christianity in Northern Lapland.* Translated by Helmar Peterson. New York Mills, MN: Apostolic Lutheran Church Federation, 1973.

Lamppa, Marvin G. "Preservers of a Faith: American Influences on Laestadian Congregations in Northern Minnesota, 1870-1950." *Migration Studies* C 9: *Finns in North America,* Michael G. Karni, Olavi Koivukangas, Edward W. Laine, eds. Proceedings of Finn Forum III, 5-8 September 1984, Turku, Finland.

Lehtola, John. *Finnishness as a Religious and Cultural Experience.* (Master's Thesis) Helsinki, Finland 1992.

Lehtola, Jim, and Nevala, Peter. "Excerpts from the history of Living Christianity in America." Text on wall calender 1994. LLC, Minneapolis, MN.

Lohi, Seppo. *Sydämen Kristillisyys.* SRK, Oulu, 1989.

Lunde, May. *Assimilation of the Old Apostolic Lutheran Church of Calumet, Michigan.* M.A. Thesis, University of Oslo, Norway 1983.

Nikander, J. K., "Suomalaisten kirkollinen tila Amerikassa ennen Suomi-Synodin perustamista." *Kirkollinen kalenteri* (1903).

Ollila, Douglas John. *The Formative Period of the Finnish Evangelical Lutheran Church in America or Suomi Synod.* Diss. Boston U, 1963.

Pietilä, Antti J. *Helsingistä Astoriaan.* Porvoo: Werner Söderström, 1927.

Raattamaa, Juhani. *Kirjeet ja Kirjoitukset.* Edited by Pekka Raittila. Helsinki, Finland 1976.

Raittila, Pekka. *Lestadiolaisuuden matrikkeli ja bibliografia.* Suomen kirkkohistoriallisen seuran toimituksia (SKHST) 74. Helsinki, 1967.

Raittila, Pekka. *Lestadiolaisuus 1860-Luvulla.* Helsinki 1976.

Raittila, Pekka. *Lestadiolaisuus Pohjois-Amerikassa vuoteen* 1885. SKHST 121. Helsinki, Finland.

Raittila, Pekka. Personal notes of Elmer Yliniemi from Raittila's lectures in Helsinki, 1974.

Raittila, Pekka. "The Relationship of the First Generation Laestadians to Luther and the Church Confessions." 1971 (Translated by Don Kilpela).

Raittila, Pekka. "The Roots and Development of the Laestadian Movement." Unpublished manuscript prepared by Melvin Salo from lectures presented October 18-19, 1982 at the Inter-Lutheran Seminary. Translated by Elmer Yliniemi.

Raittila, Pekka. "Ylitorniolta Cokatoon." *Tornionlaakson Vuosikirja* 1981.

Rautanen, V. *Amerikan suomalainen kirkko.* Hancock, MI, 1911.

Saarisalo, Aapeli. *Laestadius, Pohjolan Pasuuna.* Porvo-Helsinki: Werner Söderström, 1970.

Saarnivaara, Uuras. *Amerikan lestadiolaisuuden eli Apostolis-luterilaisuuden historia.* Ironwood, MI 1947.

Saarnivaara, Uuras. *He elivät Jumalan voimassa [They Lived in the Power of God].* Suolahti, Finland: Ev. lut. Herätysseura, 1975.

Saarnivaara, Uuras. *The History of the Laestadian or Apostolic Lutheran Movement in America.* Abbreviated version of above Finnish-language history. Ironwood, MI 1947.

Saarnivaara, Uuras. *The Power of the Keys: the Original Faith of the Lutheran Church Presented in Quotations from Luther and the Lutheran Confessions.* 1960.

Salo, Melvin F. *Laestadian Roots of the Apostolic Lutherans.* Diss. Luther Northwestern Theological Seminary. St. Paul, MN 1987.

Selected Hymns and Altar Services by the Old Apostolic Lutheran Church of America. Reprinted 2/77.

Sentzke, Geert. *Finland Its Church and Its People.* Helsinki, 1963.

Skaates, Michael, J. "Historical Survey of the Finnish Lutheran Churches in America." Paper presented at the Lake Superior Pastor-Teacher Conference, Peshtigo, WI 1978.

Talonen, Jouko. "Guatemalan lestadiolaisuudesta" *Suomen kirkko-historiallisen seuran vuosikirja* 84-85 (1994-1995). Helsinki, 1995 (1996).

Talonen, Jouko. "Kansainvälistyvä lestadiolaisuus." *Turun Sanomat* 36/7 Feb. 1998.

Talonen, Jouko. "Kansainvälistä lestadiolaisuuden tutkimusta." *Rohkea, reima ja horjumaton [Samuli Onnelan 60-vuotisjuhlakirja}.* Scripta Historica XXVIII. Oulu, Finland, 1998.

Talonen, Jouko. "Laestadianism in an International Perspective." *Laestadius 200 år.* Høgskolen i Finnmark Rapport 2001:6. Alta 2001.

Talonen, Jouko. "Lestadiolaisuuden poliittis-yhteiskunnallinen profiili Skandinavian maissa ja Pohjois-Amerikassa 1900-1940." Faravid XV. Rovaniemi 1991.

Vähämäki, Börje, Editor. *Exploring Ostrobothnia.* Special Issue of Journal of Finnish Studies volume 2, Number 2, December 1998. University of Toronto, Canada.

"Who We Are." Main page of LLC official website. May, 2003.

Wasastjerna, Hans R., *History of the Finns in Minnesota.* Minnesota Finnish-American Historical Society, New York Mills, MN, 1957. <www.mfahs.org> or <www.historymuseumeot.org> (Accessed April 2004).

Zidbäck, Aulis. *Pohjolan suurin maalikkosaarnaaja Juhani Raattamaa.* Helsinki: Otava, 1941.

About the Authors and Editors

Dr. Rodger Foltz, Pastor of various congregations including the Plymouth Apostolic Lutheran Church, Plymouth, MN. He is a graduate of Suomi Seminary and studied theology and church history at various Universities and seminaries in the United States and Finland.

Aila Saarnivaara Foltz, studied at Suomi College and the University of Helsinki. She received a B.A. in English from Northern Illinois University and has experience as a translator with certification in Finland.

Seppo Leivo, Architect, a lay theologian who has devoted years to the study of Laestadian history. He is unbeaten in the study of the life and sermons of Laestadius

Dr. Pekka Raittila (1923-1990), Finnish Church historian. Professor of Church History at the University of Helsinki. He has sometimes been referred to as "the grand old man" of Laestadian research.

Dr. Uuras Saarnivaara (1908-1998), Finnish theologian, widely known Bible scholar, author and researcher of Luther's theology. He taught in several Bible schools and seminaries both in the United States and Finland.

Dr. Jouko Talonen, Professor of Church History at the University of Helsinki. He is an author and researcher of the history of European revival movements and Baltic church history. He has been involved with research on Laestadian history since the early 1970s.

Miriam Suomala Yliniemi, B.S. and graduate work at the University of Minnesota and a year of study at the University of Helsinki in church history and Finnish language.

Elmer Yliniemi, Pastor of Spruce Grove Apostolic Lutheran Church, Wolf Lake, MN. He received a B.S. from Bemidji State University, is a graduate of the Inter-Lutheran Seminary, and studied for a year at the University of Helsinki in church history under Dr. Pekka Raittila.